# KINGS OF FASHION

*For Claire and Isabelle*

# KINGS OF FASHION

by

ANNY LATOUR

Translated from the German by

MERVYN SAVILL

WEIDENFELD AND NICOLSON

7 CORK STREET LONDON W1

First published in Germany in 1956 under the title
*Magier der Mode*
First published in Great Britain 1958




PRINTED AND BOUND IN ENGLAND BY
HAZELL WATSON AND VINEY LTD
AYLESBURY AND SLOUGH

N. 6116

*CONTENTS*

## *ILLUSTRATIONS*

# *FOREWORD*

A SMALL girl who was recently asked to name the two most famous men of our time replied: 'Picasso and Christian Dior.'

An artist and a *couturier*!

Whence derives the aura that today surrounds the Grand Couturier? Why was the tailor who designed a beautiful dress never numbered among the artists? Since time immemorial there have been real masterpieces of costume—Crétan sculpture and Egyptian frescoes testify to this—and, what is more, the men were as superbly, elegantly and colourfully dressed as the women. When one examines more closely the miniatures or paintings of the Old Masters one is astounded at the impeccably fitting garments, the boldly arranged drapery and the artistically cut sleeves. All these were the results of a technically and artistically perfected tailor's art.

But who today knows the creators of those garments? Who were the men who designed those jewels of form and colour, the dresses that invested women like a melody and inspired great artists to their finest achievements? How is it that for centuries they remained anonymous? Why did fashion artists suddenly spring to fame and honour in the middle of the dying Rococo and then exclusively in France? And this, moreover, at a time when cavalier costume with its galloons and ruffles was giving place to simple bourgeois dress, while fashion and its whims gradually became concentrated solely on women's clothes.

The purpose of this book is to try to solve these questions. I was curious to know why an ever faster-living society produced the fashion house as its most individual creation; why dressmakers and milliners became the undisputed arbiters of Fashion; why, at the beginning of the Industrial Age, the ways of the milliners and tailors parted, until finally a new creative art was born: *Haute Couture.*

For centuries French modes and manners have set the tone for cultured European society. A feeling for proportion, harmony, a discreet balance of values and the curbing of imagination to its correct measure are French national characteristics. No one who has once crossed the Place de la Concorde or the Place des Vosges can fail to sense this.

Thus today, too, Haute Couture is deep-rooted in French tradition. It personifies the Frenchman's love of artistic craftsmanship, his dislike of mechanization and standardization, his joy in individual creation and also the importance he attributes to the fashion creation as an art.

Fashion in France was already considered as an art long before the Haute Couture was born. Michelet had already said: 'I would exchange three classical sculptors for a tailor who has a feeling for natural forms, who models and embellishes them.' Countless remarks of this kind can be found in French literature.

With the coming of Haute Couture, the profession of the couturier has far outstripped that of the tailor. He is an artist who signs his work like a painter or a sculptor; he is an industrialist who employs hundreds of workers and employees, and his artistic creations have become one of the most important items of the French export trade.

And yet the fame of a Grand Couturier is short-lived and he is all too soon forgotten. His creations are transitory and there is nothing more difficult than to assess the absolute value of a work of art that no longer exists.

I have presumed to restore to life the creators of these transitory works of art. I shall try to deport them as they built their creations, and show how they dealt with their customers, how they were linked up with the industry and trade, the fashion papers and publicity, the society and politics of their age.

Fashion is the outward and visible sign of a civilization, it is part of social history. But Haute Couture has an interest which goes beyond mere social history: it is a human activity which partakes of our needs and our tastes, which involves the labours and creative genius of the fashion artist, which has its own laws, its power and its mystery.

# I

# THE BIRTH OF THE FASHION ARTIST

## IN THE BEGINNING WAS THE MILLINER . . .

AMONG trifles of satin, lace, flounces, ribbons and bows, in the outwardly so serene and yet so contradictory world of the Rococo, where a new philosophy of life announced the right to personal freedom and yet woman was bound more closely than ever by the shackles of fashion, appears the figure of the milliner.

There she goes, arrogant and self-assured. She has just come from the countess, the duchess or the queen. She has been entrusted with tasks which are as important as state affairs—the trimmings of a dress for the next court ball, for a reception given by the queen, the headdress for the queen herself. Why then should she not be proud, haughty and self-willed?

She is on her way to her shop in the rue Saint-Honoré. Here are the residences of aristocrats and bishops, the elegant palaces of tax-farmers who have grown rich from their ruthless tax collecting.

It is in the rue Saint-Honoré that the famous Mme Geoffrin also lives. In her salon the Age of Reason and the Rights of Man are preached and the myth of the absolute power of kings destroyed. It is the meeting-place of the leading spirits of the age—of Diderot, d'Alembert, Voltaire, of great natural scientists like Buffon and social reformers like Turgot—men as far removed as any from fashion-crazed Society.

But this street is also the paradise of this fashionable, frivolous society. Here women can buy everything they need: perfumes, powder and paint, gloves, fans, fichus and feathers. The shops which sell fashion and beauty articles do not need the street-numbering which the owners of the palaces have opposed for thirty years: they all have their own striking shop signs. At *La toison d'or* you can buy a beauty lotion which banishes wrinkles and hateful crow's feet; at *L'écharpe d'or* and *Au gout de la cour* all manner of enchanting accessories. In the rue Saint-Honoré, too, is the shop of Mme Baret, the wife of a stocking merchant. Casanova once fell in love with her and bought—by no means in vain—so many pairs of stockings from her shop that he no longer knew what to do with them.

A shoemaker comes out of an elegant house. A cobbler? Dear me, no, an artist! In a black frock-coat, beautifully embroidered silk waistcoat and powdered hair, he is on his way to visit one of his customers, a marquise.

'I am deeply honoured, Mme la Marquise,' he says to her, 'that you are willing to be shod by me. I will take the impression of your feet and leave the execution to my foreman.' Some days later the Marquise informs him that his shoes have come apart. 'Oh,' cries the man in consternation, 'I see that Madame must have walked in them!'

What 'lady of quality' ever goes on foot? There is a constant stream of carriages in the rue Saint-Honoré. The coach of the King's favourite pulls up outside the milliner's shop, *Au trait galant*. Mme Dubarry enters to buy fichus, fans and purses from the proprietress, Pagelle. What memories this shop must hold for her! Ten years before it belonged to the famous Mme Labille. Here Mme Dubarry, still a seamstress, sat sewing and embroidering purses and fans almost until the moment when her giddy rise began which made her Louis XV's official favourite and successor to the Pompadour.

The actresses buy their powder and paint from Montclar. In the same street Monsieur Dupont manufactures the all-important rouge. It is as rich in shades as the social status of his clientele: the ladies of the Court pay a louis d'or for a certain little pot of rouge, while lesser fry can get an inferior quality for six livres. The nobler the lady the more artificial the effect of her rouge has to be. It is quite different in the case of the courtesans. For them, M. Dupont has concocted a certain rose-pink, an astonishingly good imitation of real flesh tints; as a result the courtesans can readily be distinguished from the ladies of the aristocracy.

In the show window of the Demoiselle de Saint-Quentin, whose milliner's shop sign bears the title *Au magnifique*, there is displayed one of those Fashion dolls which are despatched every month to London and find their way from there to the cities of the north and south. For how would the Court ladies of Vienna, St. Petersburg or Constantinople be able to dress without a knowledge of the latest Parisian finery and hairstyle?

Through the window panes there are to be seen young, pretty seamstresses, *grisettes*—in those days the word did not yet have the same slightly derogatory flavour it later acquired—bending over their work. Many a young dandy enters the shop and buys a frill or a ribbon merely as a pretext to have a closer look at them. . . .

The arrogant milliner passes the shops of her competitors and at last she enters her own which sports a gleaming gilt sign: *Au grand Mogol.* This is her kingdom and here she rules, the most famous of them all, Mlle Rose Bertin.

She is the forerunner, the ancestress, the first of her race. From her the way leads through other artists, through the decadent genius Leroy to the great founder of Parisian Haute

Couture, Charles Frederick Worth, and from him to the couturiers of the present day. A span of two hundred years, during which, in the glittering lights of Paris, new men and women will rise above the mass of their professional colleagues and will dictate world fashion, a long line of kings of fashion.

How was it that Rose Bertin started this long line, a milliner who furnished only the accessories and the trimmings of a dress? Why not a tailor or a dressmaker? And why did it all start as late as this, about the year 1770? After all, the French language and French polish had begun to dominate the style of life of Europe's elegant society much earlier.

Ever since the Middle Ages fashion dolls dressed in the latest court fashions have travelled from Paris to the English, Spanish and Bavarian Courts. Whoever thinks that the marvellous clothes which enchant us in the pictures of Italian Renaissance masters were at that time the height of fashion is greatly mistaken. In Italy the courtiers of the French King François I laughed at the garish colours, at the ostentatious dresses of the women which, on the canvasses of the great painters, appear to us as perfect works of art. Yes, even at that time, at the peak of the Italian Renaissance, elegant society looked to France for its fashions. Parisian dolls were displayed on the Piazza San Marco to show the rich ladies of the Venetian Republic how to dress with taste.

How important 'La Grande Pandora' in court dress and 'La Petite Pandora' in simple *déshabillé* were in the seventeenth century is proved by the fact that for their journeys they were given an 'inviolable passport'. Nothing was allowed to prevent these ambassadors of French fashion from reaching foreign courts. Even in times of war, when communications between the countries engaged were broken, the Fleet received orders to hold their fire in order to let through ships carrying their cargo of fashion 'babies'.

Only very rarely are tailors mentioned in letters or literary works, and then there is never a reference to the *allure* of their creations, the silhouette or the cut, but always to a particularly ingenious trimming or some very costly embroidery. Thus, for example, when Molière mentions the tailor Perdigeon, in *Les précieuses ridicules*, Mascarille admires a trimming: 'This ribbon is well chosen.' And Madelon replies in the affected speech of the *Précieuses*: 'Fantastically good. Absolutely genuine Perdigeon!'

Mme de Sévigné in one of her famous letters to her daughter describes the material of one of Mme de Montespan's dresses which had been made for her by the tailor Langlée: 'Gold upon gold, embroidered with gold, over-embroidered with gold, and upon that puckered gold, once more embroidered with gold, mixed with pure gold, the result being the most heavenly material that has ever been devised.'

This seems to have been characteristic of that particular tailor. When the king's mistress appeared in the salon everyone cried: *Ah, c'est Langlée!*'

Nevertheless, the tailors were not considered artists and most of their creations remained anonymous. As artisans they were harassed and hampered by rigid mediæval guild regulations and by pedantic limitations which stifled any attempt at originality.

Just as rigid and pedantic were the regulations for the cut, whether it were a case of pompous, richly decorated gentlemen's suits or the ladies' whaleboned bodices, stiff kirtles and petticoats.

The men's tailors sewed damask or brocaded coats for the cavaliers and adorned them with lace, braiding and embroidery; the dressmakers completed the corsages, skirts and petticoats and the trimmings ordered by the customer. It would often be one of the lady's maids who obtained lace, gauze and tulle from the shops and put the finishing touches to the dress.

Up to the last third of the seventeenth century women's clothes were made entirely by men. Women dressmakers did, of course, exist and their fine work was even preferred by the customers, but theirs was still a forbidden and dangerous trade. Time and time again the jealous tailors would burst into their workshops, invoke the statutes, destroy the half-finished goods and impound their materials and stock-in-trade.

At last, in the year 1675, the women plucked up courage to take the decisive step. They sent a petition to the king asking that they should be allowed to make petticoats, peignoirs, skirts and other accessories, with the rider that 'it accorded with the propriety, chastity and modesty of women and girls that they should be dressed by persons of their own sex'.

Bending over the shoulder of the Roi Soleil, his mistress, the pious and prudish Mme de Maintenon, read the petition. There was no more hesitation—the women dressmakers' appeal to morality was decisive. From then onwards they were allowed to found their own corporation.

The years passed, new competitive wrangles arose and new guilds were created, but they were outgrown. The age of Watteau and Fragonard, of scrolls, flourishes and *rocaille*, delicately carved drawing-room furniture, pastel-coloured boudoirs of exquisite luxury, coquetry and amorous dalliance—this age, which as a whim created its own style in art and fashion, also invented a new profession: that of the milliner, of the *marchand de modes*.

The milliners alone were allowed to create as their artistic inspiration decreed. They trimmed the dresses delivered by the dressmaker, designed headgear, caps, fichus, mantillas, delicate lace ruches, falbalas and blonde-lace. They were the artists who gave the dress the correct tone, the flash of wit and its fascinating grace.

The cut changed little in the course of decades, but the change of adornment grew ever more rapid. Milliners brought movement and plasticity into fashion, gave trimmings a whimsical variety which endowed women with that piquant, seductive, almost indefinable something, considered the ideal of beauty in the Rococo age.

Mercier, in his *Tableau de Paris*, sums up the profession of the milliner as follows: 'The dressmakers who cut and sew the individual parts of the female garment are the masons of the edifice. The milliner, on the other hand, who produces the trappings, giving grace and the correct swing to the drapery, is the actual architect and decorator.' Architect and decorator! Words that later apply to Worth, Vionnet, Poiret, Dior. . . .

It needs a colourful imagination to envisage the wealth and scope of these trimmings. Even a glance at a rather dry reference book, the *Dictionnaire historique de la Ville de Paris* of 1779, furnishes the following details: 'In this year there are two hundred different kinds of bonnets, costing from between 10 to 100 livres, a hundred and fifty different trimmings of gauze, lace or fur. . . .'

These trimmings were so luxurious that each one bore its own special name, and many of the names given to them were far more expressive than the often casually chosen designations of the 'creations' in modern Haute Couture. From the mass of charming names of that particular year we need only quote a few: *Plaintes indiscrètes*, *Désirs inassouvis*, *Doux sourires*, *Soupirs de Vénus*, *Signes d'espoir*. . . .

The fashion dolls had long since ceased to announce the latest fashion. Before they arrived at their destination abroad, or even in the provinces, their trimmings were already outmoded. Nor could the almanacs and books of fashion plates such as the *Monument du costume* (1775–1783) and the *Galerie des modes et costumes français* (1777–1787) with their artistic engravings keep pace with the constantly changing fashions.

The new profession of milliner was followed by a second innovation: the fashion journal. On 17th November 1785 appeared the first number of the first 'journal' in the modern sense of the word, the *Cabinet des Modes.* Twice a month, on eight pages of text illustrated with enchanting coloured plates, it recorded everything appertaining to the realm of fashion: dresses, trimmings, jewellery and even interior decoration in all its wealth and profusion.

The Anglomania of the period demanded even more. Five months later the same journal appeared under a new title: *Magasin des modes nouvelles françaises et anglaises.* This journal had its picture reporter in London, who drew all the latest English novelties and sent them to Paris.

In England, Germany and Italy, fashion journals sprang up like mushrooms. The Parisian journal was the fountain-head for the fashion pirates. The French engravings—far less delicately and finely drawn—were reproduced in these journals without the source of origin being mentioned. This first example of piracy was also a symptom of the popularizing of fashion.

None of the trade almanacs of the first half of the eighteenth century mention the profession of milliner, but in Diderot's famous encyclopædia of the year 1765 it is already accurately described and the article closes with the words: 'It is only recently that these tradesmen have established themselves and bear this name; in fact since they left haberdashery and took over the fashion trade.'

In this way their social status was also established, making the milliners, male and female, the ancestors of the Grands Couturiers. They perfected and embellished the dress with finished wares; thus they practised no individual craft and as a result were restricted by no guild regulations. As the offspring of the particularly well-respected corporation of haberdashers—the mercers—they belonged, to a certain extent, to the upper crust of the Third Estate. Thus, as opposed to the tailors who ranked as artisans, they played their part in the rise of the bourgeoisie during the reign of Louis XVI.

Now the period opened in which the bourgeoisie began to understand that thought and creative talent must be transformed into action; that economy was not everything and that a trade was more important than money in the bank. More and more workshops were founded, particularly in Paris, and the French capital became the fountain-head of wit, taste and fashion. Paris furnished embellishments for all the capitals and the provinces; the whole of Europe demanded her luxury products.

At the same time the Third Estate financed the Court and the aristocracy. Industrialists, artists, buyers and milliners—all were the creditors of the aristocracy. The principal debtor was the Court, and the Court was no longer solvent.

Even more than the other tradesmen, the milliners would eventually fall victims to the ruined aristocracy. At the outbreak of the Revolution it would be found that their expensive boutiques, their extravagant standard of living had long been built on shifting sands; for years their customers had owed them enormous sums of money, and their account books showed outstanding debts incurred years before.

But until then the milliners still reigned supreme, strong and proud in the knowledge of their power. The young, extravagant Marie Antoinette held conferences with her milliner at which the new fashions were decreed; 'ladies of quality' begged the favour of being dressed by the most famous of them, and bourgeois women hardly dared to enter their shops. Their showrooms were magnificently appointed: delicately carved *boiserie*, fragile stucco, costly Venetian glass and portraits of their clientele adorned the walls. They employed countless work hands, rode in carriages and led the lives of aristocrats. The power of French fashion, which now extended all over the world, lay in their hands.

### ROSE BERTIN, THE 'MINISTER OF FASHION'

The men and women of Picardy in northern France are tough and industrious, hard-headed and energetic, but at the same time violent and irascible. From this province came the famous milliner, Rose Bertin. A resolute will to work and a readiness to struggle, but also the sensitivity of the artist, were her chief virtues.

Few fashion artists in history have ever risen to such heights of fame. And there are few contemporary memoirs, correspondences of important men or studies of manners in which she is not mentioned. Her art is admired and her vanities are ridiculed, but she is always there, alive and important. The French encyclopædias include her biography, an honour they have never bestowed on Worth, the founder of Haute Couture. And finally there are two voluminous and painstaking biographies of her. Their authors have combed the French archives for all the documents, manuscripts, records of litigation, registers and every scrap of paper bearing her name; but most valuable of all are her letters and account books, collected by the great couturier Jacques Doucet, which are preserved today in the art library of his foundation.

We have the indefatigable researches of the scholars to thank for our knowledge of the facts and dates. We know, for example, that Mlle Rose Bertin (her real name was Marie-Jeanne) was born in Abbeville; that her father had a post in the police and that her mother was a nurse. Rose originally worked in her home town, then with a milliner in Paris, before opening her own shop in 1773.

Rose Bertin's biographers also relate the beginnings of her career. There are no authentic documents for these stories, but they tally most plausibly with her rapid advance and her character: while serving as an apprentice to the milliner Pagelle, she had to deliver the dresses of two young ladies at the palace of Comtesse Conti. In a darkly lit salon she mistook the countess for a lady's maid and began to talk to her so pertly and naturally that the old lady took a fancy to her, and entrusted her with the trousseau of the daughter of the Duc de Penthièvre, one of Louis XV's grandsons. This young lady, soon after her marriage to the Duc de Chartres in 1769, became one of Rose Bertin's most important customers.

The Duchesse de Chartres helped her to found her own establishment *Au grand Mogol* in the rue Saint-Honoré. She and her sister-in-law, the Princesse de Lamballe, were so enchanted by Rose's creations that they introduced her to the Dauphine, Marie Antoinette (this may have been about 1771).

It was about this time that Mercy, the Austrian ambassador at Versailles, wrote to the Empress Maria Thérèsa in Vienna that the Dauphine was neglecting her appearance. But as soon as the milliner appeared on the scene things changed. The sixteen-year-old Marie Antoinette, transplanted to the etiquette-ridden Versailles Court, looked for some distraction. The Dauphin, a year older than she, was a good-natured clod whose only interests were hunting and his own hobby, lockmaking. He paid little attention to his young wife. Marie Antoinette, on the other hand, was gay, high-spirited, young, beautiful and graceful. The milliner stuck pastel-coloured flowers and feathers in her wealth of blonde hair, arranged tulle and lace round her childish shoulders, knew with her able hands how to bring some movement into the stiff waist and the rigid panniers. Marie Antoinette saw reflected in her mirror an image which might have been one of those seductive beauties from Boucher's or Fragonard's *Scènes galantes*.

She sent her latest portrait to her mother in Vienna. The Empress returned it with the comment: 'It is the portrait of an actress and not that of the future Queen of France.'

Two years later Marie Antoinette was Queen. Her mother wrote to her on the 18th May 1774: 'You are both so young and the burden is very great. I am distressed, really distressed. . . .' Hardly a year passed before the old Empress wrote once more of her anxiety: 'I must touch upon a subject which I hear mentioned on all sides. It is a question of your headgear. I have heard that it rises thirty-six inches from the roots of the hair and is built up into a tower with countless feathers and ribbons. . . .'

Mme Campan, Marie Antoinette's devoted lady-in-waiting and confidante, has left us memoirs, in which she relates that the Queen's love of finery and her constant need for change can first be ascribed to the influence of Rose Bertin. 'Now all the ladies want to wear the same finery and plunge their husbands into debt.' And she adds rather sadly: 'It is rumoured that the Queen is ruining the women of France.'

The youthful Marie Antoinette knew nothing of these rumours. She hated the strict etiquette of the Versailles Court and the agonizing formalities of the levée. Hardly had she opened her eyes than she was surrounded by a staff of Ladies of the Bedchamber and ladies' maids. A lady-in-waiting put on her petticoat and a Lady of the Bedchamber her chemise. The handing of each garment and each gesture was an office of honour which even princesses performed: to dress the Queen, pour water over her hands and hand her the basin. Next she was presented with a thick album containing samples of the patterns of her dresses. After the Queen had stuck pins in those she wished to wear during the course of the day and evening, mighty baskets were brought in with the *déshabillés*, the Court robes and the toilettes for the intimate suppers.

Hardly had the Queen's hair been dressed than she hurried impatiently into her private apartments where Rose Bertin would be waiting. Now began the fashion conference and from here the fashion of the day would be launched.

'La Bertin' lost no opportunity of chattering about her 'work' with the Queen. When a lady of rank came into her shop she would say to one of her employees: 'Show Madame the results of my latest work with Her Majesty.' It is little wonder that Rose Bertin is described in several reports as the 'Minister of Fashion'.

Her account books between 1774 and 1792 testify to her aristocratic clientele. To mention a few high-sounding names alone: the Queens of Spain and Sweden, the Princess of Luxemburg, the Duchesse de Chartres, the Comtesse Talleyrand, the Duchesse de Mazarin, the Duchess of Devonshire, the Princess of Nassau, the Duchess of Württemberg, who married Czar Paul I. . . . Even Louis XV's last mistress, Mme Dubarry, who was banished after the King's death but was allowed to return two years later, figured in her books until 1792, a year before she lost her head on the guillotine. At that time she owed Bertin forty thousand livres.

Rose Bertin often refused orders from bourgeois women because the Court and commissions from foreign princesses made too many claims on her time.

Mme d'Oberkirch, the authoress of the famous memoirs, describes how the ladies snapped up Rose Bertin's new creations and the excitement that reigned in her *atelier*. The milliner allowed them an occasional glance at the miracles she had in hand. The models, however, could not be sold until the customers had appeared in them.

'Mlle Bertin,' she writes, 'seemed to me a strange person, very full of her own importance, and who treated princesses as her equals. . . . Her conversation was highly entertaining. It was a mixture of arrogance and obsequiousness, and if she was not held in check it was apt to develop into haughtiness, I might almost say impertinence. The Queen, in her well-known goodness of heart, had allowed her a familiarity which she abused and which she believed gave her the right to be high-handed. . . .'

Bachaumont, the author of the *Mémoires secrètes*, describes how the royal pair drove to a service at Notre Dame in February 1779, passing through the rue Saint-Honoré. Rose Bertin stood on the balcony of her house with thirty of her employees behind her: 'Her Majesty noticed her, "Ah, there's Mlle Bertin!" she cried and waved her hand. "La Bertin" replied with a deep bow. The King stood up and doffed his hat to her; the whole royal family and the courtiers followed suit, all of them bowing to her as they passed.'

Rose Bertin was greatly displeased when her *première*, Mlle Picot, left her and started up as a milliner on her own account. She was so furious that in the Hall of Mirrors at Versailles, just outside the Queen's apartments, she spat in Picot's face. A court case ensued and Bertin was ordered to pay a small fine. She lodged an appeal but the original verdict was upheld. She simply denied the whole incident. 'To think,' runs her statement, which appeared in the form of a pamphlet, 'that I could be capable of such ill-bred behaviour! And in the royal apartments so near to those of the Queen to boot.' Baron Grimm, in his correspondence with Diderot, mentions this affair, which was a subject of conversation in the salons for a whole year. 'Very few ministers,' he adds, 'have remained so long at their posts and at the peak of their fame as this milliner.'

The author of a secret correspondence of 1778 was once

present when a lady of quality from the provinces came to Bertin to order a number of hats. 'The milliner lay in an elegant jacket on a chaise-longue and only deigned to give the customer a slight nod of the head. She rang a bell and a charming young nymph called Mlle Adelaide appeared. "Show the lady last month's hats," said Mlle Bertin. But the lady wanted to see the latest. "That is impossible," replied the milliner. "At my last session with the Queen we decided that the latest models must not appear for a week." '

Over a period of a hundred years we can find similar portraits of the famous couturiers. Their arrogance was doubtless the result of their equivocal social position. They were on confidential terms with the highest of their day, were indispensable and spoiled, yet their social status remained unclarified. They lived in the reflection of the great but also in their shadow, and it is not surprising, therefore, that they tried to smooth out the anomalies of their status by a certain impertinence.

The fact that Rose Bertin features as an allegorical figure in a contemporary play says something for her fame. It is even more significant that she is honoured as a great artist by a famous poet of the period, Jacques Delille, the scholarly translator of Virgil's *Georgics*. In his poem *L'Imagination*, Delille describes Fashion as one of the happiest creations of the imagination, for it embellishes and enhances nature, particularly:

> Quand Bertin fait briller son goût industrieux
> L'étoffe obéissante en cent formes se joue,
> Se développe en châle, en ceinture se noue;
> Du pinceau son aiguille emprunte des couleurs,
> Brille de diamants, se nuance de fleurs,
> En longs replis flottants fait ondoyer sa moire,
> Donne un voile à l'amour, une écharpe à la gloire. . . .

Rose Bertin's account books, with their copperplate-writing entries and elaborate details, embody the whole magic of the Rococo. The mantles, palatines, bonnets, trimmings of taffeta, trains, tulle ruches, silk lace, gauze, gold and silver garlands and sprays, embroideries of beads and coloured stones, tulle flowers, etc., must have been little masterpieces, closely related to the ethereal dainty pastels of the great eighteenth-century painters.

The milliner gave the visible cachet to privileged society because her finery was exquisite, the height of refinement and also the most expensive. She knew precisely the artistic worth of her wares, for when someone found her prices too outrageous she protested: 'Is the painter Vernet paid for his canvas and colours alone?'

Her fame occasionally brought her some very strange customers, such as the mysterious Chevalier d'Eon, who was Louis XV's secret agent and at times carried out his missions in feminine attire. When he returned to France in 1777 and, on strict orders from the King, had to wear women's clothes, Marie Antoinette sent him to Rose Bertin. Much has been written about this curious character, but the reasons for his disguise have never been clarified. Whatever they may have been, Rose Bertin accepted the task and the Chevalier d'Eon reported in August of the same year to the Foreign Minister Vergennes: 'After God, the King and his Ministers, Mlle Bertin must take the greatest credit for my unusual transformation. . . .'

As a literary curiosity I should like to quote the passage in Chateaubriand's *Mémoires d'outre-tombe*, which mentions his meeting with 'La Bertin' in 1786. Chateaubriand, who had been asked by a relative of the milliner's in Rennes to be her escort, had no idea with what a famous person he was travelling to Paris. Nor did 'La Bertin' have any conception that this eighteen-year-old boy would one day become one of the greatest French writers. She laughed at the shy youth who stuttered each time she addressed him, and cowered in the far corner of the coach with embarrassment, 'for fear of crushing Mlle Rose's dress'. They passed Versailles—'the Queen,' he writes in his *Mémoires*, 'reigned in all the splendours of her youth and beauty. . . . The throne, so near its downfall, had never seemed more unshakable and I, an insignificant nobody, was to survive this splendour.' On their arrival in Paris the milliner helped him find a room in a hotel. 'She was in a hurry to be rid of this looby.'

Rose Bertin was certainly a difficult person and puffed up as only very much sought after and indispensable persons can afford to be. Above all she tolerated no rivals or competitors. Her most important competitor was Beaulard, the degenerate, mannered, over-refined fashion artist, a type which will be found down the years among the great couturiers.

An anonymous pamphlet extols him in flowery couplets as a Colbert, an Archimedes of Fashion, describes the brilliant appointments of his shop and his role as an artist of the Mode:

> Beaulard—
> Tant de chefs—d'œuvres si brillante
> Dont tu décores ta patrie,
> Prouvent assez tes grands talents.
> Tu tiens la baguette chérie
> Qui fit de l'Empire des Francs,
> L'Empire heureux de la féerie.

When presented to the Queen by the Princesse de Lamballe, Beaulard handed her a perfumed rose in the middle of which, upon a clockwork spring being released, appeared a miniature portrait of Her Majesty. This was too much for Rose Bertin's ambition. She even refused for a while to continue working for the Princess.

Beaulard's clientele was almost as aristocratic as that of 'La Bertin'. Mme de Matignon, who was ever in the van when it came to crazy fashions—eye-witnesses relate that she went to the scaffold powdered and painted—came to an arrangement with Beaulard that for a monthly payment of 24,000 livres he must deliver her a new headdress every day.

The young, frivolous lovers of fashion were particularly grateful to Beaulard for an expensive yet extremely practical invention. In 1775, when the towering hairstyle reached its peak, the author of the *Correspondence secrète* notes: 'Women kneel in their carriages with their faces almost in their laps.' At this stage Beaulard devised the '*bonnets à la bonne maman*': tall hoods with a hidden spring. When their wearers found themselves in the company of worthy matrons who were inevitably outraged by these monstrous headdresses, nothing was apparent but a low-set, virtuous and modest headgear. But hardly had the young ladies turned their backs than they released the spring and the *coiffure* quickly rose three feet in the air.

An Englishwoman once paid a visit to Beaulard. 'I am an admiral's widow,' she said, 'that is all you need to know. I shall leave the rest to your taste.' Two days later he brought her a 'heavenly creation', as the Comtesse d'Adhémar expresses herself in her *Mémoires*: a choppy sea of padded gauze on which rode a frigate made of ribbons and spangles with a black flag flying at the masthead.

Since the *coiffure*—in 1770 there were 3,744 different hairstyles—still exceeded the dress trimmings in importance, the profession of hairdresser ranked equally with that of the milliner.

This can be seen by the fame of Léonard, the Queen's hairdresser, which extended far beyond the French borders. In contemporary accounts Léonard is credited with being the inventor of the *poufs aux sentiments*, headdresses supposed to portray the personal experiences and feelings of the wearer: butterflies fluttered round the heads of frivolous women, *amoretti* looked roguishly out from the headgear of the sentimental, while tiny biers and urns adorned the hair of melancholy ladies. For the Duchesse de Chartres, when her son was born in 1775 (he later became the Citizen King Louis-Philippe), Léonard designed a headdress on which could be seen a stout nurse with a baby on her arm.

Fashionable adornment alone tells the story of that age. In that peacock age it was so self-willed, independent and detached from the architecture of the dress, that it allowed the milliners to give free rein to their imagination. Great political events, battles and sieges, events at Court and in the capital, trials, theatre premières, salon conversations and gossip—nothing was too important, nothing too trivial to be used as a pretext for a new trimming or a new hair adornment. J. H. Meister, in the *Correspondence littéraire* of 1774, writes that 'one could see the most important events of the age carried on the heads of young women, in the form of allegories'.

The fashionable colours, too, told their tale. The filth in the Paris streets, the streams that poured through them after each shower of rain, were for the ladies in their carriages merely a sensation, something to be laughed at, and for the milliner an opportunity of launching a greyish-yellow silk material: *fond ruisseau*. The well-known milliner, Mlle Lenormand, trimmed the latest bright-coloured Turkish robes with embroideries the colour of Parisian mud: *couleur boue de Paris*. In 1781 the longed-for Dauphin came into the world. The fashionable colour quite naturally and without a shade of embarrassment was christened: '*caca Dauphin*'.

All this was far more than mere craze for fashion; the fevered rhythm of the mode, its breath-taking change, were the expression of an epoch speeding towards its tragic end. To the eyes of the world it presented the spectacle of a ruling society laying claim to an extravagant and frivolous way of life, while the country fell into ruin, the kingly ideal was shattered and the state finances collapsed.

Sensation at all costs, mockery of everything that concerned the people. In 1774 the harvest was disastrous. The following year brought a great rise in the price of flour; a revolt broke out and the bakers' shops were stormed. What was the reaction of the milliners? On the very same day they designed the bonnet *à la revolte*.

It was no less cynical when in the severe winter of 1784 'La Bertin' designed a cap which she ingenuously christened '*Bonnet en sœur grise*' and sold it at the same high price as her ruches and feathered headgear. Simplicity was now the latest sensation in fashion and certainly not because of the hard winter. This simplicity had no ethical grounds. People did not wear bonnets *à la paysanne*, *à la laitière* and *à la Rousseau* because aristocratic society felt a prick of social conscience or because it was influenced by Rousseau's ideas. Nor did they wear dresses *à l'Anglaise* because, in view of their own disastrous state finances, they ogled Britain's solid economic power. The Græco-Roman cut of clothes, which gradually became the vogue, was hardly inspired by a need for purification at the sources of antiquity.

It is the eternal law of fashion: when a peak has been surpassed, reaction sets in. Flourishes and spirals were followed by straight lines; simple garments replaced ribbons, falbalas and farthingales, and garish colours were ousted by pastel shades.

But this new simplicity became a threat to the French economy—one of those paradoxical phenomena which make pre-Revolutionary history so bewildering. From 1780 the hooped skirts made of yards of costly silk disappeared from fashion together with long trains, plumes and high heels. Instead of the flowered masterpieces from the Lyon silk workshops one wore English lawn, batiste and printed cottons with peasant patterns. And while Marie Antoinette and her ladies-in-waiting affected simplicity, idolizing the pastoral charms of the dairy in Versailles park; while the nobility and well-to-do ladies from financial circles aped them, the looms in Lyons came to a standstill and the despairing weavers were left with half-finished silk brocades and damasks on their hands.

In those last years before the Revolution, the fashion artists lost no opportunity of reflecting in their creations the tragic events which followed each other in ever quicker succession. The details of fashion now showed that there was no longer any respect for the royal family. The notorious scandal of the Queen's necklace in 1785, in which the Queen was compromised, produced a hat adorned with strings of pearls, dubbed '*au collier de la reine*'. A straw hat with ribbons in cardinal violet was christened '*cardinal sur la paille*' because the Cardinal de Rohan, involved in the affair, lay on straw as a prisoner in the Bastille. When Parliament freed the cardinal in the following year, thereby almost confirming the rumours that were current about the Queen, the milliners sold in their shops festoons '*au Cardinal blanchi*'.

Despite these ominous events the Queen's orders for clothes and finery did not diminish, and criticism grew ever more outspoken that Marie Antoinette's influence was responsible for the enormous rise in the expenditure of the royal household. In 1785 Calonne, who had been Finance Minister for two years, presented Rose Bertin's exorbitant account to the King. He had to extort a further 900,000 livres from state coffers to pay, or at least cover by instalments, the Queen's debts, which were largely for her toilettes.

It is doubtful whether Rose Bertin's move to the rue de Richelieu in 1783 was due to financial difficulties, as one of her biographers maintains. Not only was the new shop described as being particularly luxurious, but the street itself had now become the smartest for the fashion world and its fame could almost be compared with that of the rue de la Paix a century later.

In 1787 there was a rumour that the great milliner was on the verge of bankruptcy. Mme d'Oberkirch, who was not particularly fond of Rose Bertin, exulted ironically: 'Mlle Bertin, so proud, so arrogant, who works with Her Majesty; Mlle Bertin, whose bills in huge letters proclaim her MILLINER TO THE QUEEN, Mlle Bertin is insolvent. Her bankruptcy, of course, is by no means plebeian, no, it is the bankruptcy of a lady of quality—two million! The ladies of fashion are in despair. To whom shall they turn? Who will arrange their headgear, who will stick in the plumes or design a new fashion in jackets?'

Was it a rumour or fact? In the archives, where the many bankruptcies of those uncertain years are registered, no trace is to be found of Rose Bertin's name. Her contemporaries were soon talking of a *banqueroute simulée*—perhaps she had merely put about the rumour in order to stir up those of her clients who were capable of paying; a newspaper even maintained that it was to extort 40,000 livres from the Royal Exchequer—but perhaps, as certain authors maintain, the bankruptcy was merely an invention of Marie Antoinette's ever-increasing number of enemies.

On the eve of the Revolution the caste spirit was stronger than ever it had been. The French national debt rose by 400 million francs in 1787 and the country was on the verge of bankruptcy. The *Caisse d'Escompte*, which had been in existence since 1776 and was the source of government loans, suspended payment in August 1788. This was a severe blow to the country and an opportunity for the milliners to display their wit. The bank had no funds, so they made hats *sans fonds*, in other words without a crown, and they called them '*à la Caisse d'Escompte*'.

In 1789 the state coffers were empty and bankruptcy could no longer be disguised. But the royal household consumed just as much and the contributions for the King's family alone were 25 millions. When the weak monarch, influenced by Marie Antoinette and his courtiers, allowed the troops to march against the newly constituted National Assembly, revolt broke out. On the 14th July the people rose and stormed the Bastille.

But was the rage for fashion silenced at last? By no means. Bonnets *à la Bastille*, adorned with tricolor cockades, were the mode; but even worse, when the King dismissed Necker from the post of Finance Minister and replaced him by the hated Foulon, who fell victim to the people's rage and was hanged from a lamp-post, a certain milliner sold red ribbons *au sang de Foulon*.

After the storming of the Bastille, Rose Bertin's customers began to fade away. The aristocratic supporters of the ancien régime emigrated, naturally without bothering to pay their debts before they left.

Titles were abolished, church property seized and the power of the radical parties rose. The royal family prepared to flee and actually succeeded in slipping out of Paris in July 1791. Big orders, which can be found just prior to this in the milliner's account books for cloaks and trimmings, appear to be for the wardrobe the Queen wished to take with her.

Mme Campan, the faithful lady-in-waiting, was very distressed by these preparations: 'I watched with dismay the Queen making preparations which seemed pointless and particularly dangerous, and I mentioned that the Queen of France would find enough clothes and shirts wherever she went. . . .' But all her warnings remained unheeded. Mme Campan herself had to procure linen and clothes and complete outfits for them all. An enormous hold-all was made to carry the Queen's toilet table.

Vanity and convention brought the unhappy Marie Antoinette to her tragic fate. These preparations aroused the suspicions of one of the wardrobe women. The royal family was stopped at Varennes and brought back to Paris.

The author of the forged *Mémoires* of Rose Bertin relates that 'La Bertin' herself went abroad at this time with secret messages from the Queen to the Austrian Emperor Franz. One fact is indisputable: on 1st July 1792 Rose Bertin, accompanied by four employees, left Paris for Germany with fifteen cases of finery. An émigré, the Marquise de Lage, reports in her *Récollections* of the coronation of Franz II as Roman Emperor, which took place at Frankfurt on 14th July 1792: 'Mlle Bertin was with us at the time and sold us spangled fripperies and her talents at a very high price. . . .'

In October of the same year she moved to London whither many of her old clients had already fled. There, too, as in Frankfurt and Coblenz, they refused to abandon their aristocratic way of life or to dispense with finery and adornments. Thus we find the famous milliner's name in many memoirs written by émigrés, in which her readiness to be of service is extolled—she must have dressed many of these ladies without reward.

While she was in London disaster followed upon disaster in Paris. The Tuileries were stormed and the royal family transferred to the Temple. The tradesmen had access to the prison and they delivered dresses, fichus, bonnets and shoes for Marie Antoinette and Madame Elizabeth, the King's sister.

In Rose Bertin's account books, which had previously reflected the gay enchantment of a frivolous age, we now find evidence of the tragic last act. Her nephew continued to deliver finery until the 5th October, on which date he appears to have fled abroad. Mme Eloffe, whose account books from 1787 to 1793 were published in two volumes by the Comte de Reiset, brought the Queen the mourning she requested after the King's execution.

When the unhappy Queen herself was led to the scaffold she was no longer allowed to wear these weeds. A black ribbon on her headdress and wearing a white muslin fichu, which perhaps had been made in Bertin's shop, in white chemise and petticoat she was driven in the tumbril past the house in the rue Saint-Honoré where, a bare fifteen years before, her milliner had stood triumphantly on the balcony and received the homage of the King's suite.

Rose Bertin's biographers maintain that she burnt Marie Antoinette's unpaid accounts. As a proof they produce letters from aristocrats which stress her fidelity to the Queen, but I have found no evidence for the destruction of the accounts and no gaps in her ledgers. The milliner's anxiety as to her own fate must have increased day by day, and she seems to have tried to extricate herself from the affair by playing a diplomatic double game. When, for example, she learned that her name, figured on the list of émigrés and that her houses in Paris and Epinay had been sequestrated, she fulminated in her letters to the Paris authorities against the *çi-devants* who had not paid her for her honest work. She, Citoyenne Bertin, had been compelled to go abroad to dispose of her goods in order to pay her faithful workers, who were true *sans culottes*. She had also fulfilled her Republican duties by presenting new shirts to the members of the ultra-Revolutionary Mountain.

Patriotism had become the fashion. Materials, ribbons and trimmings were all red, white and blue, and the tricolor cockade was the favourite form of decoration. As early as April 1791 one can read in the papers that aristocratic coquettes ordered cockades as big as cabbages costing eighteen livres.

On the 13th June 1792, hardly a month before the storming of the Tuileries, Mlle Bertin entered in the Queen's account: 'For a headdress, bows and ribbons in the national colours. . . .'

And now, in the great Revolution which announced the dawn to freedom of the world and plunged its own country into a night of panic and terror, for the first time in the history of Fashion, dresses and political convictions coincided.

The *sans culottes*, in trousers, short jackets and Phrygian caps, the *citoyennes* in simple falling dresses, fichus and bonnets, were the order of the day, designed for political propaganda purposes. The classical style—which had long since appeared on the scene—was proclaimed as the triumph of reason, and simple attire was raised to be the symbol of bourgeois virtue. For the last time, but more clearly than ever before, Fashion told the story of the age.

When Rose Bertin's name was finally struck from the list of émigrés and she could return to France in 1800, her business had not appeared in the trade almanac for two years. Her nephew seems to have transformed her shop into a kind of bazaar, for in the bills are to be found more trinkets and snuffboxes than finery. At last, in 1812, she sold her house to a *restaurateur*. After this, things seem to have gone rapidly downhill and in the autumn of the same year, a few months before her death, she was forced to pawn her watch and jewellery.

# II

# LEROY, THE FASHION KING AND THE SOCIETY THAT CREATED HIM

## THE POST-REVOLUTIONARY NEW LOOK

ON the 27th July 1794, the 9th Thermidor according to the Revolutionary calendar, Robespierre fell and was condemned to death. Already on the following day his name figured in the list of those guillotined.

Let us skim through the *Journal de Paris*. First come the official reports of the Revolutionary Tribunals followed by the endless lists of those condemned to death—for some weeks the details of the charges were still included, but soon there were so many that there was only room for the victim's name and age and the words *condamné à mort*. Next come the theatre notices. *Horatius Cocles* is being performed at the Opera; *Brutus* at the Théâtre de la République and *La mort de Marat* at the Théâtre National. The reality here is comprehensible and vivid, more direct than in the most graphic historical descriptions.

Then suddenly, after the 9th Thermidor, the picture changes. The lists of those condemned to death grow daily shorter; the heroic tragedies disappear from the theatre notices and are replaced by gay comedies.

The Terror is over. The sinister cloud of bitterness and

rebellion still lies over Paris; people are still denounced and condemned; heads still fall under the knife of Madame Guillotine, but already from the depths joy and eagerness for life break through and from one day to the next luxury and elegance have returned.

Is the lady of the Parisian salon a stern Roman Republican, a Spartan who frowns on the joys of life? That may be good enough for the people, for the *dames de la halle* who fetched the Royal couple from Versailles and dragged them to Paris, but certainly not for the ladies of the new society, for the wives of the new rich, the army contractors, speculators and black marketeers.

Plays are running in twenty-three theatres and there is dancing at eighteen hundred balls. People dance in the vast halls of monasteries abolished by the Revolution, in Carmelite convents, in the Jesuit seminary and the educational establishment of the *Filles de Marie.*

At the notorious '*Bal à la victime*' in the Palais Richelieu dance those aristocrats who by a Directoire decree have had the goods confiscated from their families returned to them. Entrance is restricted to those who have lost at least a husband, wife, brother or sister on the scaffold. They go so far in their cynicism as to wear at their throats fine red neckbands known as '*à la guillotine*'. 'Could Holbein's "Dance of Death" have inspired such an idea?' Mercier asks sadly in his *Tableau de Paris.*

At these balls the latest extravagances of the Mode were very much in evidence. Here were to be seen the *Incroyables*, young fops feigning an incredible weariness, in tight, far too tight, knee breeches, ridiculously broad shoulders, shapeless cravats, too short a waist and lank, uncombed hair. Here danced the *Merveilleuses* in Greek garments of flimsy muslin beneath which they wore flesh-coloured tights, trains gathered over their arms and drawn tight to give their limbs an air of plasticity.

Were these transparent dresses, these exposed bosoms, anything more than a sign of protest against the virtuous dictates of the Revolution? The style itself had already appeared before the Revolution with the disappearance of powdered wigs and panniers; long, flowing garments, with high waists, these became the fashion. The new style already existed at least in its outlines, long before the painter Louis David, at the order of the 1793 Revolutionary Committee, produced his drawings for a national costume which was to resemble that worn by the heroes of the Roman Republic. It had to express freedom and the natural shape of the body was to be neither corsetted nor disguised.

The frivolous society of the Directoire turned this Republican freedom into a licence. Mercier notes in his diary: 'The lights from the chandeliers shine on beauties with *coiffures à la Diane* and *à la Psyche*—I do not know whether these dancers have taken the Republican system of the Greek States to their hearts, but at any rate, they have fashioned their dress on the pattern of Aspasia, with naked arms, bared bosom and sandals on their feet. . . .

'The chemise has long since been banished, for it disturbs the natural forms and is, moreover, a completely useless article of apparel. The flesh-coloured undergarment, on the other hand, nestles against the body revealing its most secret charms.'

This post-Revolutionary new look lasted another twenty years. Observers naturally did not conceal their irony, not even the Fashion journals which—then as today—always support the new mode, whether it be beautiful or ridiculous. The *Journal des dames et des modes* mocked: 'When the French reached the Amazon they compelled the women to cover their nakedness with a minimum of clothing. The time has now come when the savages of America take their revenge on France.'

The plain-spoken Kotzebue, who published his recollections of a journey to Paris in 1804, was quite indignant: 'The toilettes which are considered decent here, no prostitute would have been allowed to wear a hundred years ago.' He foresees the time when people will adorn themselves with only a fig-leaf. The chemise was so unfashionable that a dozen sufficed for a trousseau of six hundred dresses. The women in their thin attire of course fought against cold and bad weather, but health was now the mode; they no longer had the 'vapours' and ate with gusto.

The correspondent of the *Journal des modes* of 1802 held a different opinion: he advised his readers to visit the cemetery of Montmartre where they would see many gravestones of young women, who had died as a result of wearing far too thin clothing.

It might be thought that one of the literary-minded coiffeurs of the period invented the short-cropped Titus curls to suit the Minerva and vestal virgin dresses. This, however, was not the case. In the Revolutionary prisons many women had their hair cut off before they were driven to the guillotine in order to give it as a keepsake to some dear one. Among those lucky enough to be liberated—particularly after the 9th Thermidor—there were some who liked this hairstyle; they kept to it and christened it '*coiffure à la victime*'.

During the Revolution the men had adopted Titus and Brutus haircuts in mock heroic pose. This fashion was launched by the great actor Talma who, as Brutus, in Voltaire's tragedy of that name, had triumphed in a Roman toga and short curled hair.

The hairdressers now called themselves artists and tried to

surpass each other in literary affectation. This is wittily described by a journalist in the *Journal des modes*: 'Today I accompanied a friend to a *Perruquier-tondeur*. He wanted some advice on a new haircut. The hairdresser looked at him, made him turn his head to right and left, look up to heaven and fall into a rage, smile, contemplate the picture of a beautiful woman stepping into her bath, look round, mince, dance and blow his nose. He walked round him lost in thought. "Monsieur," he said, "that is enough. I see exactly what you need: a mixture of Titus, Caracalla and Alcibiades. Look at these marble busts. These Titus curls are splendid but it is important to give them a little of Caracalla's strength and to add a touch of gaiety with a few of Alcibiades' silken locks." '

The ladies of fashion were busy from midday until evening adorning themselves. The theatre was often no more than an exhibition, to show off new dresses, launched by the actresses and displayed by the ladies in the boxes. The 'Triumph of the crazy goddess Fashion' however, was the spring drive to Longchamps races where the new toilettes could be admired.

The men of the Directoire were hardly less vain and pleasure-loving than the women; they wore suits designed by David, and while the masses starved displayed a luxury against which public opinion protested in vain.

From hour to hour the value of the paper currency sank and, in 1795, eighteen thousand assignats were paid for a single louis d'or. The speculative fever rose hourly. Everyone gambled. Erstwhile nuns in blonde wigs bought and sold. Everyone dabbled in buying and selling, every deal became a big transaction, and conversations bandied millions. The black marketeer, even when he hawked his wares from house to house, considered himself a financier. The people starved, second-hand clothes were auctioned and the butchers' shops were empty. Pensioners and state employees could no longer buy anything with the worthless assignats. But there were certain restaurants where in *cabinets particuliers*, as Mercier relates, 'at a wink food is brought to the table, where both gluttony and lust can be satisfied. These are the rendezvous of the new society which has waxed fat on robbery and extortion.'

But there are other versions. In the *Journal des dames et des modes*, the handbook of elegance published by La Mésangère, priest, literary man and philosopher, appears a seriously intended leading article which is no less than a hymn of praise to the *cabinets particuliers*: 'Without them,' he writes, 'how could a woman fettered by marital jealousy free herself from her slavery and deceive a tyrannical husband. Without them, how could she reward a tender and charming lover?'

A pagan paradise of eternal carnival. . . . Plebeian queens set the tone in manners and modes, clients of the *grand faiseur*, Leroy, in turn directed and served by him. These queens, too, had their Directoire, Madame Hamelin, Madame Tallien and Josephine, who figured highest and owed most in Leroy's account books.

Who could have foreseen that one of them would become Empress? Josephine, the widow of the Vicomte de Beauharnais, who was guillotined in 1793, looks incredibly beautiful in Gérard's portrait of her. But was it a true likeness? Her contemporaries extol her elegance and luxurious clothes far more than her beauty. The German composer, Johann Friedrich Reichardt, who stayed in Paris in 1802, saw this portrait and describes it in his *Vertraute Briefe aus Paris*: 'One should not look at this flattering portrait of Madame Bonaparte before seeing her in the flesh unless one wishes to be seriously disappointed.'

Barras, the most influential member of the Directoire, the brutal megalomaniac who encompassed Robespierre's downfall, reports in his memoirs the diplomatic way in which Bonaparte seduced 'the widow Beauharnais': 'He began to give Josephine presents of clothes and finery suitable to her inclinations which resembled those of an expensive courtesan; not only shawls and expensive ornaments but diamonds, for which he paid the highest prices.'

Far more than by Josephine, Fashion and the salons were ruled by Madame Tallien, the enchantingly beautiful Thérèse Cabarrus, 'The Madonna of Thermidor', as she was called after Robespierre's fall. From the prison where she had lain during the Terror she wrote on the 7th Thermidor to the influential Tallien, a member of the Convention: 'I dreamed that Robespierre no longer existed and that the doors of the prisons were flung open.' Was it this letter which finally swayed the enamoured Tallien to indict Robespierre?

She was released—she looked quite ravishing with her hair close-cropped from prison—and married Tallien. Her house, La Chaumière, in a Parisian suburb (today it is the site of one of the most important houses of Haute Couture), became a centre for the new society. The Duchesse d'Abrantès, who saw her at a banquet, writes in her memoirs: 'She was the Capitoline Venus, more beautiful than the work of Phidias. She wore a simple dress of Indian muslin, draped in the antique manner, caught at the shoulders with cameos. A gold belt, also adorned with cameos, encircled her waist and a gold bracelet formed the sleeve fastening above the elbow. Her velvety black hair was cut short and curled—a style which in those days was called "*à la Titus*". Round her beautiful white shoulders she had flung a red cashmere shawl, a highly original adornment.'

Thérèse became the arbiter of Directoire Fashion. Not only Leroy but other tailors and milliners worked for her. The wigmakers followed suit, for the Titus hairstyle was soon outmoded, and two of the leading hairdresser-artists vied for the title of inventor of the new fashion—the blonde wig. It was undoubtedly launched in 1794 by Madame Tallien who soon possessed nearly thirty of them. The whole society of parvenus and aristocrats now wore similar wigs ranging from whitish-blonde through ash-blonde to Titian. They were changed several times a day to suit the occasion—whether one drove as a nymph to a *déjeuner*, appeared in the afternoon in the Tuileries gardens garbed as Diana in a poetic Greek chlamys, or decked it richly with diamonds, of an evening at the theatre, above a low decolleté muslin dress.

During the Empire, dress and furniture were still wonderfully suited to each other. David's famous picture of Madame Récamier lying on her chaise-longue in a flowing white Grecian dress, the parlour with its simple furniture—this is the last unity of style before the great chaos of the coming machine age. Madame Tallien's Chaumière, too, resembled a Roman villa with its pillars, halls, frescoes and fountain.

Josephine, who had met Thérèse in prison and had ever since been a close friend, was a constant visitor at La Chaumière. Here, too, were to be found the young Madame Récamier and the intelligent Madame de Staël. From time to time Bonaparte, the swarthy little General, as the guests called him, put in an appearance.

Barras, vain Barras, who ousted Tallien from the Directoire, also triumphed over him in private life. He had originally been Josephine's lover and when she left prison as a pauper after the 9th Thermidor, he provided her with furniture, horses and carriage. Later he conquered the enchanting Madame Tallien.

Thérèse was at the height of her beauty and her power. In her salon was also to be seen the third fashion queen and customer of Leroy, Madame Hamelin, a *Merveilleuse* wearing transparent Grecian attire. The wife of a rich Army contractor enjoying the usufruct of aristocrats' confiscated properties, she is reputed to have launched the chemise-less fashion.

Thérèse was a witness at Bonaparte's marriage to Josephine. When, after the coup d'état of 18th Brumaire, Napoleon was elected Consul for life, an honour which called for dignified surroundings, he turned his back on the corrupt morals of the Directoire. Thérèse was banished from Josephine's salon and even after 1805, when she married Prince Caraman-Chimay and entertained the best Parisian society in her new palace, the Tuileries remained closed to her.

Virtue entered the stage at the Napoleonic Court.

## NAPOLEON'S POLICY OF LUXURY

The storm of the Grande Armée broke over Europe. On the battlefield Napoleon issued his military orders and despatched his economic decrees back home. Silk was to be bought in Lyon, new machines were to be erected in St Quentin for cotton spinning and mechanical looms installed throughout the whole country. Silks and damasks were to be more costly than ever, woollen goods softer than the softest Asiatic cashmere, finer and finer the yarn. . . .

Luxury was General Bonaparte's motto and was the basis of the later Napoleonic economic policy. Luxury was to be the expression of his power, clearer than his shouts of victory, more lasting than his military glory. A contemporary says in his memoirs that an era had dawned in the Tuileries where 'daggers and silk stockings had replaced the sword and the jackboot'.

Luxury would only become productive when it signified no stagnating, stable element in the economic life—it must identify itself with change, the daily mood and evanescence, with everything which created Fashion or was created by it: clothes which one changed three times a day, jewellery designed for each toilette, materials in ever new patterns and fashionable colours. The caprices of Fashion would call industries to life, bring money into circulation and consolidate tottering state finances.

What could be more beneficial to luxury than snobbishness, particularly the type to be found in a society of parvenus and nouveaux riches. Beneficial certainly, provided it raises the production of a country and encourages national industry. But how often does snobbishness merely lead to the quest for the exotic, for what has never been seen before? In those days, too, society women set their hearts to get the fine gauzes and muslins which were mainly imported from England. This was not difficult, for they were so light that they could often slip through the Customs without duty being paid. Anglomania, already a force under Louis XVI, blossomed once more. So powerful did it become that the Parisian button manufacturers stamped 'Made in England' on the back of their wares.

The Revolution had whipped up patriotism to its peak, but hardly had Robespierre been guillotined than pleasure-loving society no longer wanted to hear anything of this virtue. The Duchesse d'Abrantès relates in her memoirs that every dress possessed something 'Turkish, Greek, Mediæval, or Roman, in short a little of everything except good French taste'. And Kotzebue says: 'The whole world has to pay tribute to the toilette of the Parisienne—one wears English cloth, Egyptian shawls, Irish shoes, Roman sandals, Indian muslin, Malines lace, Turin silk, Dutch linen, Prussian-style hats, Russian riding boots and English waistcoats.'

This snobbishness did endless harm to the French economy. Already during the Directoire, Talleyrand, the able diplomat, had outlined an anti-foreign fashion policy. On the invitation card to a ball which he gave in January 1798 to celebrate the triumphal return of General Bonaparte from the Italian campaign, we read: 'I am sure that you will find it decorous to

Rose Bertin, dressmaker and milliner to Marie Antoinette

Eighteenth-century court dress

Caricature of the exaggerated hairstyles in vogue before the Revolution

*Incroyables* and *Merveilleuses*, 1795

wear no article of apparel which comes from the English manufacturers.' Napoleon's trade policy, too, with its slogan 'Freedom from the foreign yoke', began in the Paris salons when in 1806 he wrote to the Governor of Paris: 'Let the women beware if I see them wearing foreign materials.'

In order to understand Napoleon's xenophobic economic policy one must study the political prelude: the Revolutionary Decree of 1793 had cancelled the treaties with the coalition countries under English hegemony which had fought against Revolutionary France, and forbidden the import of certain English products such as velvet, cotton and woven goods. As with every ban, the result was inevitable. Piles of smuggled English goods lay in the warehouses and English muslin and tulle were worn more than ever. After 1805, when the French lost control of the seas at Trafalgar, nothing could halt Napoleon's radical anti-English trade policy. The customs regulations of 1806 brought greatly increased dues, particularly on muslin, cotton goods and linen.

In the same year the notorious Continental System was put into effect, and England was barred access to the European markets. Englishmen in France were made prisoners of war, their property was seized as war booty and no English ships could sail into French ports.

Economic policy and conquests consolidated Napoleon's world domination. The dangerous creed of 'a united Europe under Napoleonic dictatorship' was born. In Rome the same laws were in force as in Paris and the Dutch Provinces became French Départements. North, south and east, French regional commanders were installed and the kingdoms were distributed to the dubious members of Napoleon's family. '*L'Europe—c'est moi.*'

With every means in his power Napoleon tried to encourage French industry and to raise purchasing power. The country was to be modernized and English production exceeded—no mean programme, for in England by the end of the eighteenth century, thanks to the new machines invented by Watt and Arkwright, linen and cotton goods were being mass-produced, and this at a time when France was still weaving with distaffs and hand-driven looms.

Necessity is the mother of invention. Old ossified methods were scrapped overnight. Fulling-mills identical to those in England appeared in Louviers and Sedan. The new machines, which functioned from 1806 onwards in St Quentin, produced such fine linens and muslins that soon the English wares lagged far behind. Valenciennes produced delicate batiste and misty tulle from featherweight linen thread and above all the finest lace which other towns tried in vain to imitate. The reputation of French textiles was soon secure abroad.

In the *Mémorial de Sainte-Hélène*, Napoleon described the import ban on woollen and linen goods of 1806 as a 'coup d'état'. Six years later he could write to General Caulaincourt: 'It was I who founded French industry.' He did, however, participate in the introduction of one foreign article of fashion—the shawl, woven from the soft wool of wild Tibetan goats, that fine, warm, cashmere shawl which protected the ladies' decolletés from winter and the night cold. During the Egyptian campaign Bonaparte sent some of these shawls to his wife Josephine in Paris. She wrote to her son Eugène de Beauharnais who had accompanied the expedition to Egypt: 'I have received the shawls. They may be very beautiful and expensive, but I find them hideous. Their great advantage lies in their lightness, but I very much doubt if they will ever become fashionable.'

Who could ever have surmised that a few years later similar shawls would not only be the fashion but an indispensable article of clothing? Josephine herself was finally so obsessed with them that she soon possessed three or four hundred; when she no longer knew what to do with them she had them made into cushions for her dogs.

Napoleon was quick to intervene. The cashmere shawls should continue to gladden the Empress, the ladies of her Court and all the women of fashion, but they were to be made in France. He searched and found a man who finally imitated them so perfectly that it was unnecessary to import them. His name was Ternaux, a manufacturer who had fled to England from the Jacobins and after the Revolution had brought back to France many of the secrets of the English spinning and weaving machines. The imitation was so good that from 1805 onwards the output rose to more than three thousand shawls a year.

Ternaux also conceived the brilliant idea of breeding Tibetan goats in France. He despatched one of the librarians of Bibliothèque Nationale who could speak Oriental languages to Central Asia. This man returned home with two hundred and fifty goats—a good two-thirds of the herd died on the journey—but breeding was ensured. Ternaux not only succeeded in producing the shawls far more cheaply than the imported article but surpassed them in the elegance of the patterns, shades and fashionable variations. Very soon he was employing nine thousand workers and was given the title 'Baron de L'Empire'.

Napoleon had his own waistcoats and breeches woven of white French cashmere cloth. He set the example for his luxury policy by changing his clothes every morning. After they had been washed three or four times they were thrown away.

We learn these intimate details from Constant who was for sixteen years Napoleon's valet. In his *Mémoires* he reports that his master always wore the finest materials and tells us how costly was the cloth which was specially made in Louviers for his famous grey riding-coat.

The Emperor, however, was reluctant to follow the fashion and Constant had to resort to all manner of ruses. He said his unfashionably long frock-coats gradually shortened by the tailor so that Napoleon should not notice it. The King of Naples, who was always elegantly and tastefully dressed, one day remarked to his Imperial brother-in-law: 'Your Majesty dresses too much *à la papa*. I beg you, Sire, give your faithful subjects an example of good taste.'

When Napoleon married Josephine in 1796 he foresaw the part the 'Salon Lioness' of the Directoire would play in future society. He was not mistaken. As soon as he was crowned Emperor, with every intention of equalling in luxury the courtly brilliance of the Roi Soleil, Josephine was completely in her element. What she lacked in style in her role as Empress, she knew how to atone for by her dress.

Madame de Rémusat, whose husband was Master of the Robes, and who, in her memoirs, has given posterity so many piquant details of Court life, tells us at length of Josephine's passion for the mode, her craze for dresses and her extravagance. She even insists that the Empress constantly exceeded her budget of 600,000 francs for personal expenditure.

For every occasion, however trivial, Josephine ordered new clothes or a new trimming. There was hardly a shop in Paris which did not work for her. The rush of tradesmen knew no bounds. Each day a host of clothes dealers, modistes and jewellers requested audiences. (Of the Court purveyor par excellence, M. Leroy, we shall speak later.) Never before had a ruler been so spoiled. The Emperor burnt incense at her shrine, and selected dresses for her, the colour of which had to harmonize with the new interior decoration of his castles. Luxury reigned, luxury ruled in his household more powerfully and brilliantly than at Versailles. Marie Antoinette's diamond jewel case, which is still on view today in the Petit Trianon, was too small to contain Josephine's jewels.

In order to increase purchasing power and to encourage his newly-fledged French industry, Napoleon desired a new fashion in which luxurious clothes should come into their own again—rich brocades, heavy velvets and silk embroidery. More than one contemporary relates how, while still Consul, he had the fireplaces of the Tuileries bricked up in an attempt to banish flimsy dresses made of gauze and tulle. But, as invariably happens, Fashion was more powerful than the will of the individual: women remained faithful to their muslin dresses.

The Coronation dresses alone brought about a change in fashion. To the flowing high-waisted robes were added full-length cloaks and a ruffle, known as a *chérusque*, rising high behind the head and fastened to both shoulders.

The Court ladies had a hard time under the Emperor, who was constantly demanding a change of dress. It was the patriotic duty of men to ruin themselves for their wives' clothes. To women whom he saw more than once in the same dress he used to say curtly: 'Madame, is that the only dress you possess?' The Duchesse d'Abrantès relates that when Napoleon once saw her in a dress she had previously worn, he ordered her to leave the company.

The history books tell us that Napoleon divorced Josephine because she was unable to give him a much-desired heir. How often do small incidents play a role in political events and become irrevocably entangled with them? While the divorce was being discussed, a milliner, who had been forbidden the palace, was surprised by the Emperor with a number of shawls in Josephine's apartments. Napoleon was furious. Josephine lied to him that the milliner had been sent to her by his mother, Madame Letizia. The Emperor immediately strode off in search of her. The old lady at first tried to protect the Empress but in the end she admitted the truth. This incident, according to contemporaries, finally made the Emperor decide to carry through the divorce.

He appears to have been unaware that the young Austrian princess whom he married two years later was the complete opposite of Josephine and had little interest in clothes. He was most anxious that Marie Louise should not feel the difference between the Hapsburg Court, with its powerful tradition, and the parvenus of the Napoleonic Court. Before her arrival he engaged dancing masters to teach the ladies of the Court some semblance of the aristocratic mode of dancing.

The Emperor sent to Vienna for models which Leroy copied and adapted for French taste. Did Marie Louise appreciate them? Constant, the valet, writes: 'M. Leroy made the dresses ordered for the Empress in his *atelier*. Neither he, nor any member of his workshop, was allowed to approach Her Majesty for personal fittings. When alterations were necessary, the orders were given by the ladies' maids.' Whatever the taste of the young Empress may have been, she was incapable of representing Napoleon's luxury policy. The year of the marriage, 1810, was also the year of the great economic slump.

Napoleon had quite rightly foreseen that, despite the monstrous luxury of the ruling classes, the home market would one day be exhausted; he acted correctly from an economic point of view when he spread the net of French export throughout the whole of Europe. After his great victories, however, his gigantic plans became unrealistic. Instead of founding an economic alliance with the conquered countries, he had made them his economic vassals. As a result of the never-ending wars, raw materials grew scarcer, production fell in many places by fifty per cent and the tragic retreat from Moscow completely destroyed the luxury industry. While armies clashed on the battlefields, people at home traded and speculated, made and lost fortunes overnight.

At first this passed unnoticed in Paris. Even in the gravest times, when the destiny of the nation is at stake, Paris knows how to maintain her gaiety. Trade still basked in some of the brilliance which surrounded Napoleon's waning glory and the country did not altogether sense the threatening economic catastrophe.

Only a few well-informed people knew it and took their precautions. Letizia, Madame Mère, had lost faith in her great son's fame. In secret she placed her money in England.

## 'L'EMINENCE GRISE'

It happened many years before Napoleon became Emperor of France. In the wings of the Paris Opera young 'supers' waited for the call-bell. Rose Bertin emerged from a singer's dressing-room, where she had just cast a last critical glance at the charmingly gathered panniers, drapery and bunches of ribbon—masterpieces from her workrooms. Her professional eye noticed the coiffure of one of the girls, and in the words of a biographer—'this coiffure revealed to her superior skill, worthy of nobler spheres'. The young coiffeur, Louis Hippolyte Leroy, who had created this work of art, was warmly congratulated by the spontaneous Rose Bertin—'and his heart was filled with the vaulting ambition of men appointed by destiny'.

This romantic and affected eulogy from Leroy's biographer, the playwright and journalist Hippolyte Auger, who in 1829 wrote the obituary notice of the great tailor Leroy in *La mode*, sounds sincere. But we possess other, more private, writings by the same author, his memoirs which were never intended for publication and were printed after his death.

In Auger's memoirs a completely different Leroy emerges—a vain, garrulous, arrogant tailor, a genius admittedly, with his flair for the coming fashion and his craftsmanship, but sly and calculating in his treatment of the great, a mountebank to whose sweet piping the new society danced, the '*eminence grise*' of Napoleon's luxury policy. Auger knew him well, far too well, for Leroy's niece had married his brother.

Of Leroy's origins and childhood (he was born in 1763) we know nothing except that his father was a stage-hand at the Paris Opera; at an early age the boy was already well versed in the mysteries of theatre lighting, thunder and mist, and at the age of twelve he decided to become a hairdresser, a profession to which he was irresistibly drawn. It is uncertain how long he remained a hairdresser and to what extent his meeting with Rose Bertin really affected his future as a creator of fashion. Auger's memoirs merely state that he worked on Marie Antoinette's headgear, and that at the Court of Versailles his enchanting hair arrangements, for which Rose Bertin gave him advice, were greatly admired.

The uniformity in dress during the Revolution, and the social levelling process which it caused must have been greatly opposed to his taste for the exquisite: in his own dress he seems to have manifested his loyalty to his former and better-paying clientele. In the streets of Paris he appeared in the despised aristocrats' costume, a striped silk coat with velvet collar, red satin waistcoat, pointed shoes and powdered wig. It is impossible to ascertain the truth of Auger's assertion that he was sent to prison on the charge of being a *muscadin*, a counter-revolutionary fop. On one occasion, when he thought he was being pursued, he is reputed to have vanished into the property clouds during an opera performance.

He was really terrified when he was summoned one day before the Convention. To his joy, however, he learned that he was well known to this stern revolutionary body as an authority on fashion and that his oracle was needed on the problem of Republican garb. In a flash the tailor's love for the ancien régime disappeared in the bright dawn of a new glory. With consummate skill he chose from the designs of various artists those in which patriotic propaganda was most prominent: a costume in the three colours of the young Republic with a belt at the waist bearing the inscription 'Freedom or Death' and a second on the hem of the dress: '*Liberté*, *Egalité*, *Fraternité*'. Leroy's rise was assured.

Personally, of course, he found the Revolution quite repulsive. But how magnificently he played his new part! When he stuck a red, white and blue cockade in the hair of a plebeian it was the symbol of her lowly origin—the same cockade on the head of a Royalist became very much like a martyr's crown. He transformed the inevitable revolutionary cap and, lo and behold, it became an anti-revolutionary turban.

After the fall of Robespierre, Leroy slipped into the new society. Here he was completely in his element. During the Directoire his business in the rue des Petits-Champs had as yet none of the brilliance of his later salon. Nevertheless, he was already a *marchand de modes*, what would today be described as a *visagiste*. He arranged each headgear in so original a manner that it suited the face of its wearer. He knew that arrogance pays in the higher circles and that the customer was impressed when he sold her a hat on condition that it was 'never to go on foot'.

Like all the great couturiers of the past as of the present, Leroy had an infallible flair for the new and the future. Many of the returning émigrés tried to cling to the mode of the ancien régime but his decree was stronger. And since, as the worthy heirs of antiquity, people wore dresses in the colours of Egyptian soil or Greek marble, Leroy, who foresaw the rising power of money and the coming dictatorship of a powerful capitalist society, knew how to introduce into this simplicity the luxury of gold embroidery, artificial flowers and jewels.

Leroy was extraordinarily shrewd in his choice of colleagues. Mme Bonneau, his partner, was only an average dressmaker, but she wore his creations with such chic that she became a living advertisement for them. He was utterly unscrupulous; he lured the best saleswomen and fitters from his competitors, procured the best patterns and gave them out as his own.

Society overlooked these little weaknesses on the part of their '*indispensable*', as they called him. There was not a murmur when he opened a smart shop in the rue de Richelieu with a new partner's money and then threw her out unceremoniously, keeping her employees and her designs. This was the famous Mme Raimbault, a dressmaker who was described in the fashion journals as the 'Michelangelo of Fashion'. People he had imposed upon tried to take their revenge by selling imitations of his clothes at far cheaper prices. It was all to his advantage, for do not copies invariably spread the fame of the originals?

Leroy must also have foreseen the brilliant rise of Bonaparte, since he did everything in his power to get into the good books of Josephine, who had recently married the 'Saviour of France'. He went to work slowly and cautiously, distributing his charming fripperies to her servants, until the doors of Josephine's château, La Malmaison, finally opened and she condescended to receive him.

With great guile he discredited in Josephine's eyes Mme Germond, then the established dressmaker of fashionable ladies. At first he praised her creations, then began to criticize and finally rendered them ridiculous. Gradually the direction of the dress purchases of many elegant ladies fell into his hands and Josephine, too, introduced him to the Merveilleuses, the wives of the parvenus and the aristocracy. And so, through the favour of the future Empress, he rose to *grand faiseur*, to dictator of fashion. 'Leroy's bills cause as much strife in marriage as love letters,' sighs de Jouy, an acute observer of the period.

Leroy was promoted from *marchand de modes* to couturier, when, encouraged by Josephine, he cut one of her magnificent cashmere shawls to pieces and transformed it into a cloak. Within a short space of time he was a great business man with the monopoly of everything appertaining to the toilette—shoes, gloves, hats, linen, lace, flowers, feathers, furs and perfumes. As a willing tool of Napoleonic economic policy, he knew how to apply the necessary degree of patriotism. He bought only French raw materials, Lyon silks, woollen goods from the new manufacturers, muslin and lace from the workshops of northern France and cashmere from Ternaux's factory.

Josephine often allowed Leroy a glimpse behind the scenes. Thus he had more than an inkling of Bonaparte's approaching coronation as Emperor of France. Already he saw himself as the sole creator of the coronation robes, believed that he would furnish all the ideas and drawings, dreamed of future triumphs. But his illusions were dispelled when Napoleon commissioned the painter Isabey, a pupil of the great Louis David, to design the ceremonial coronation dress. It required all Josephine's efforts to persuade her embittered and disappointed favourite to carry out the dresses from Isabey's sketches.

In the last analysis, however, it was these robes that showed the real tailoring genius of Leroy. Isabey had produced hard, stiff designs which Leroy transformed into soft, feminine, ample creations of smooth satin in the daintiest shades, or heavy gold-embroidered velvets, giving them grace and nobility.

David, the great painter, was the *metteur en scene*: at first the rehearsals were carried out with cardboard dolls, then with those taking part in the ceremony, until finally the day came when Napoleon set the crown on his head, which as he said he 'had found lying on the ground' until he crowned Josephine, the former lady-in-waiting, and made a new aristocracy from a mob composed of Corsican middle-class families, of adventurers and *arrivistes*. The Empire style, the Napoleonic new look, are magnificently captured in David's giant canvas *Le Sacre de Napoleon*, and all figure in Leroy's fabulous bill.

Leroy had now reached the peak of his fame and his clientele was composed of the élite of Paris. He designed dresses according to his intuition and a trifle sufficed for him to produce a masterpiece. The Duchesse d'Abrantès describes a visit she paid during the Empire to a lady as she was being dressed by one of her ladies' maids. First came the wonderful embroidered chemise and bodice decorated with fine Valenciennes lace, then an embroidered lace-edged petticoat of batiste; 'the blue satin underskirt from Leroy was followed by the actual dress sewn as only Leroy's clothes could be! White tulle heavily adorned with white silk appliqué embroidery; the pattern of a garland of myrtle with the tiny leaves and buds all in white, the branches growing smaller and more delicate towards the waist. The sleeves were not too flat and not too puffed, and the waist, following the fashion, not exaggeratedly high. The lower hem of the dress was relieved by a large garland of blue and white hyacinths, while a bunch of the same blossoms on one side introduced a perfect harmony.' It is not difficult to imagine the charm of this little chef-d'œuvre.

A fashion article of the year 1810 supplements the picture of Empire fashion: 'The white muslin dresses are worn over blue, yellow or pale pink taffeta. The embroidery is white on white, the waist high and the sleeves puffed. The shawls are either genuine or imitation cashmere. The Italian straw hats are of infinite variety. Curls are no longer worn, and ringlets have taken their place.' Women once more wore their own hair and also hats, since they now drove in open phætons on the Champs Elysées; they actually began to go on foot, which a few years before would have been considered undignified for a lady of quality.

What a difference between the descriptions given by women who frequented the Court and the unfortunately all too rare memoirs of the bourgeoisie. We have the diary of a middle-class woman, a certain Mme Moitte, for the year 1806. She was the wife of a rather insignificant painter and describes her humdrum existence in detail. She could not afford the prices asked by the *grands faiseurs*. She scanned the advertisements in the journals, went to the houses of the advertisers to buy a fabric or a wrap, naturally had her 'little dressmaker' who occasionally made her new dresses but usually remoulded her old unfashionable garments.

One day Mme Moitte, wearing a redingote made out of an old dress, plucked up courage to enter a smart shop; she was treated with disdain; but when, to compare the cambric she intended to buy with the colour of her dress, she opened her shabby cloak and gave the saleswoman a glimpse of her white taffeta dress, dainty white underskirt and watch chain, 'the whole shop beamed at me'.

This simple account is delightfully ingenuous and vivid when compared with the pompous fashion articles of the day—a welcome contrast in an age when, according to Napoleon's decree, a dress could not be worn more than once at Court. Mme Moitte writes: 'This is about the ninety-second time I have worn my padded dress!' And for a new dress she paid less than Leroy asked for the pattern.

The fashion journals, too, were exclusively designed for the 'upper crust'. On the other hand—but only for a short space of time—they were still independent of advertisements and could adopt a critical attitude towards the creations of tailors and dressmakers.

One tailor would be found fault with if he tried to launch a new mode which was in opposition to the prevailing fashion. Another was too conservative; a dressmaker was advised to be more careful with her buttonholes, 'for no detail is too small to be overlooked and the smallest fault can imperil the most brilliant career'. In one account we find: 'This is Mme Mure, with whom we are angry because she created the vogue for cock's feathers and then made the mistake of putting them within reach of all grades of society by her low prices.' A certain Mlle Pepin is advised not to be so prolific in design but to repeat her already successful models; '*le mieux est l'ennemi du bien*' warns the critic.

The fashion journals also criticized the social rise of the tailor. 'Our tailors today,' we read in 1806, 'despise tailoring and only busy themselves with what they call the design of the clothes. Suits no longer need to be solid or to outlive a couple of pairs of shoes which are worn out after a month. These gentlemen merely want to decide on the cut and to busy themselves with selling. When one brings a piece of cloth to a big tailor he says: 'I am not used to working with other people's materials,' and eventually asks more for the making than for the whole suit.

In Leroy's account books we find many references to men's gala suits, some of which cost more than 4,000 francs, and yet his name hardly counted among men of fashion; others were far more in vogue than he: for example, Napoleon's tailor, Chevalier, who provided a series of expensively embroidered ceremonial costumes for the coronation; or Leger, who dressed the elegant members of the clan such as Murat, Jerome

Bonaparte and finally the Emperor himself when, just before his marriage to Marie Louise, he deserted Chevalier whom he no longer considered smart enough.

Neither Leroy nor the above-mentioned *grands faiseurs* worked for the real fashion leaders of the Empire. These young dandies, the successors of the *Incroyables* who were now known as *petits maîtres*, created their own extravagant modes. Their costume is described in the *Journal de Paris*, 1803: 'It is decreed that this year the *petits maîtres* are to have long feet and short arms, the head forward, carry only one glove and wear riding boots in dry weather and white silk stockings when it rains. Furthermore, a young man must not introduce himself without keeping one hand in his pocket and must allow a wisp of hair to fall down on his forehead. It is further decreed that the stockings must be left slack and the waistcoats buttoned incorrectly.'

Lean times had set in for the hairdressers once the wig went out of fashion, as it did just before the Revolution. An exception to the rule were some of the coiffeurs in vogue: Joly, described by Kotzebue as the literary man among coiffeurs; and naturally the Court coiffeurs Herbault, who accompanied Josephine on all her journeys, and Duplan who had a salary of 12,000 francs a year.

The perfumers were in the ascendant and could hardly produce enough beauty salves and toilet waters. At that time the well-known firm of Houbigant was already in existence; it was patronized by Mme Récamier and launched a *parfum Récamier*.

'Millinery and dressmaking,' says the editor of the 1814 *Almanach des Modes*, 'were always women's occupations. When one sees how men have invaded the feminine domain this confusion of taste makes one wonder whether Nature has not made some sort of mistake in them.'

This remark applies perfectly to Leroy. It has a parallel in a passage in Auger's biography: 'Leroy had very beautiful hands and pink fingernails,' he writes. 'He often received his underlings in his bathroom and was reputed to take perfumed milk baths.' His private life, too, was shrouded in mystery. He was said to frequent the notorious gaming hells of the Palais Royal, and some reports maintain that he was powdered and painted like a woman. . . .

All the more *distingué* was his public life. His house in the rue de Richelieu, at that time the centre of the world of fashion, was full of mirrors, bronzes and chandeliers; the costly furniture came from the workshops of the great cabinet-maker Jacob. His calèche had cost him three thousand francs and his four-in-hand cabriolet could vie with those of the most fashionable of the rich London merchants.

His ambition was insatiable. He had begged the Empress to lend him a carriage decorated with the Imperial Arms for the wedding of his daughter, Adèle Bonneau. Josephine at first agreed but when the Emperor heard of it he flew into a rage. According to a contemporary he shouted: 'Let them go in a cab. I will not tolerate shop girls driving in my carriage.' This is in contrast to another remark Napoleon is supposed to have made and which Leroy was very proud of repeating: 'Leroy, for a man like me, there was need for such a man as you.'

At the Court he was trusted, for they knew that he would never show the robes designed for the Empress to another lady, even if she were a queen. For the adornment of certain dresses he was even entrusted with the crown jewels. In order to display these lavish toilettes he organized real exhibitions for which he issued invitation cards to favoured people while footmen stood guard in front of his house.

His aura was enhanced by the fact that people believed him to be privy to the secrets of the Court. His highest bills were

Pauline Borghese, sister of Napoleon, in a dress by Leroy

Early-Victorian dress

Mid-Victorian dress

paid without demur and some ladies figure in his ledger as having spent as much as a hundred thousand francs a year.

That Leroy's affected behaviour and haughtiness were a byword in Paris is proved by the success that de Jouy obtained with his parody *La marchande de modes* on a Parisian vaudeville stage in the year 1808. This ridicules Leroy as the affected M. Crépanville, surrounded by a chorus of his seamstresses who extol him as *le Dieu des chiffons*. Modestly he waves them aside:

> L'éloge est mon antipathie
> Il suffit à ma modestie
> Qu'en tous lieux on dit de moi:
> De la mode, voilà le roi!

Leroy's fame spread far beyond the frontiers of France. When he sent his *premières*—in those days these leading workroom women were known as '*factrices*'—to foreign courts, the diligences were piled tower-high with boxes of dresses and hats. To mention only some of the greatest, the Queen of Spain, the Queen of Bavaria, the Grand-Duchess of Baden and the Queen of Sweden were among his customers, and, of course, Napoleon's sisters too—Elise, Grand-Duchess of Tuscany, Caroline, Queen of Naples, and Princess Borghese, the beautiful, frivolous Pauline whom Canova immortalized in the nude as a marble Venus.

A portrait of Pauline which today hangs in the château of Versailles shows her in a dress which figures in Leroy's accounts: 'A blue wrap over a white satin dress embroidered with little gold flowers and edged with gold fringes, a cameo of Napoleon on its diamond-studded belt.'

When one remembers that in those days the couturier did not create a collection for each season designed for women in general as he does today, and that a man like Leroy never designed two dresses alike, one is forced to wonder where he managed to get such a host of new ideas. Leroy took his models from every source, from antique statuary, from pictures, from David and from all the artists of his age. His first real collaborator was Auguste Garnerey, the designer of costumes for the opera and aristocratic portrait painter of whom the cynical Auger writes: 'He saw everything in pink and pale blue; everything was faked and hazy both in the drawing and the colour.'

Auger's judgment of Garnerey may be correct, but it probably meant a great deal to Leroy to have found a designer who did not encroach on his own personality. Garnerey spent many hours a day in the Louvre copying antique statues and drapery for his employer, who interpreted them in his own way for his clientele; both adapted the costume of Greece and Rome for the Napoleonic Court. Garnery drew the finished dresses for the *Journal des modes*, which was sent all over the world to keep other countries in touch with the Parisian fashions. In addition to this, he painted his portraits of women wearing Leroy's creations and thus they both had the same clientele.

Leroy remained faithful to Josephine, even when the banished Empress lived in complete retirement at Malmaison. He witnessed a tragic scene shortly before the divorce. On entering the salon he saw the weeping Empress on her knees in front of Napoleon. According to Leroy, the Emperor glared at him, but said at last, in a calm and unruffled voice: 'Madame, here is your costumier, whom you should advise never to enter your private apartments without your express order.'

With a heavy heart Leroy finally decided to work for Josephine's successor. It was probably no accident but the effect of his subconscious dislike of the new Empress that on the day the marriage contract was signed between Napoleon and Marie Louise, and her dresses were to be ordered from him, he appeared at Court so late that Napoleon flew into a rage.

Leroy's account books for the years 1812 to 1815, which are preserved in the Bibliothèque Nationale, show that feminine coquetry did not diminish even in the most tragic periods—in the days of Leipzig, during Napoleon's exile to Elba, not even when in 1815 he was finally banished to St Helena.

At the time of the tragic and fateful retreat of the Grande Armée from Russia, Hortense, Josephine's daughter and wife of Napoleon's brother, Louis Bonaparte, gave a masked ball entitled 'Under the sign of the Incas'. The costumes which Leroy designed for Hortense stand in his ledger at a figure of 14,000 francs. For Napoleon's sister, Caroline Murat, he furnished in the same year a fancy dress costume for 20,000 francs. Pauline's craze for clothes seems to have been stimulated by her brother's exile, for her orders poured in during that period. At the same time the abandoned Josephine's unpaid accounts stood at 150,000 francs.

The beautiful Polish countess Marie Walewska, who presented Napoleon with a son, figures largely in his account book for costly dresses trimmed with silver embroidery, fur and lace. During the bitterest fighting in Eastern Europe she paid a hundred francs for a single batiste pocket handkerchief.

Marie Louise, who at first was completely indifferent to luxurious clothes, appears to have undergone a radical change after becoming attached to M. de Neipperg (she married him after Napoleon's death); during the Hundred Days her need for dresses seemed insatiable and Leroy sent countless dresses, hats and *déshabillés* to her in Vienna.

With the return of the Bourbons, after a short break, Leroy resumed his work. He now worked for the Court, the old aristocracy and the returned émigrés. Marie Antoinette's embittered and eternally frowning daughter made her entrance into Paris wearing one of his dresses.

And still the mode did not change, and the high waist, a characteristic of the Empire style, endured. Bourbons and aristocrats of the ancien régime, who despised the Bonaparte family as parvenus, considered themselves lucky if Leroy condescended to dress them.

With the Restoration the English, who had been chased from the Napoleonic Court, also returned. Leroy was able to obtain the custom of many an English lady and in his account books from 1814 to 1820 we find almost more foreigners than French women. For the Duchess of Wellington, the wife of the victor of Waterloo, he made a cloak of silver lamé and a feathered diadem; the Grand-Duchess Katharina ordered her whole trousseau from him on her marriage to the King of Württemberg.

Leroy outlived Napoleon. He outlived the style which had remained unchanged throughout Directoire, Consulate and Empire—that enchantingly erotic style with its refined cult of tender pastel shades, admirable and gay even when it became the Napoleonic Court dress. With this style Leroy's power of invention also died.

How could a creator of fashion who had spent his substance on a mode which had lasted for almost twenty years be expected to give any further proof of his genius? For now the fashion was no longer the joyful expression of a lusty, tempestuous, sensual period. Wasp waists, leg-of-mutton sleeves, towering coiffures and padded hips symbolized the resistance to Napoleon's régime; a new Rococo formed the link with the times which had seen the Bourbons driven into exile.

As he became an old man Leroy relinquished his business to his niece. For another few years he could be seen like a sleepwalker in the garden of his country house near Paris, dreaming of past glories. From time to time he drove into Paris to have a look at his business: *Leroy, Nièce et Compagnie.*

He made one last effort to play his part as a great dress-maker. In 1824 he undertook to make the robes for the coronation of Charles X. 'The artist had sunk well below his own level; he produced nothing new and nothing elegant,' Auger complains in his obituary notice.

Leroy died five years later, forgotten by the society which had created him.

# III

# PRELUDE TO HAUTE COUTURE

## THE NATURE OF HAUTE COUTURE

WHAT does Haute Couture really mean? Can one merely translate this French term, current today in the international world of fashion, as 'the superior art of tailoring', or does it imply more?

It certainly means more, for the art of tailoring has existed for several thousand years in a highly developed form. Haute Couture, on the other hand, applies to a particular industry which expanded and assumed more and more significance from the middle of the nineteenth century onwards until today it has become one of the most important factors in the French economy. The term has been strictly and officially defined by the Parisian *Chambre Syndicale de la Couture*: 'Haute Couture is any undertaking whose most important activity consists in creating models with the object of selling them to a professional clientele which thereby acquires the right to reproduce them. An Haute Couture concern of this nature also reserves the right to repeat these models for private customers.'

This concise definition already shows the distinctions between Haute Couture and tailoring. The dresses of earlier ages were produced for one customer, and were, as we say today, 'made to measure'. With the creation of models, which bear the signature of their creator and, like works of art, are protected by copyright, the couturier has risen to the position of both artist and industrialist.

## THE FASHION INDUSTRY

The histories of costume, which describe the fashions of the last hundred years, maintain that Haute Couture was founded by Charles Frederick Worth. Those members of the Worth dynasty who have taken to writing are even more explicit: In the beginning was chaos, and then came young Worth with his genius and magic wand to conjure Haute Couture out of nothing, the first international wizard of fashion.

But Worth by no means created Haute Couture out of nothing, for all the social and economic prerequisites were to hand. Nor would his smart salon in the rue de la Paix have become a centre of fashion, or the small salesman have risen to be the great M. Worth, had he not, besides artistic genius, possessed sober commercial sense, had he not seen the possibilities of the industrial reproduction of his models.

One searches in vain in the histories of economics for an explanation as to why Haute Couture should have appeared in the middle of the nineteenth century. A variety of different factors played their part: economic conditions combined with elements of the social structure of the times and the national peculiarities of the French.

The production methods, from which Haute Couture developed, evolved gradually and very slowly from bespoke tailoring and 'ready-mades'.

The ready-made trade took a course already foreshadowing our own age: ready-to-wear clothes mean mass production with all its inevitable drawbacks—banality of taste, lack of originality, standardization and uniformity. On the other hand, mass-produced ready-made clothes, with their much lower production costs, are cheap; they make a higher standard of clothing available to all classes of society, and so mass-production has its social function.

In Paris, '*la confection*' had a picturesque origin. In 1820 a few go-ahead second-hand dealers had the idea of buying from the bespoke tailors the suits that had been left on their hands by their customers. These consisted of garments found unsuitable at the final fitting or which, for some reason, did not please some capricious gentleman and were not called for. The second-hand dealers took these clothes to a certain market—the Marché Saint Jacques—which gradually became the centre of this new 'rag trade'.

The trade in fact became a very lucrative one, for soon these dealers not only bought up rejects, but began to order new garments. They soon came up against difficulties. Although the profession of street hawker was legally recognized in the trade register, the tailors considered it disreputable. Thus the second-hand dealers could only find journeymen who were not employed by the tailors of repute to work for them and these were obviously not always the best workers.

After a few years this new trade acquired more solid foundations. This time the initiative came from the well-respected, financially powerful cloth dealers. In 1824 a few of them founded a *confection* house, 'La Belle Jardinière', so called because it was located near the flower market. Its organizers quickly knew how to adapt themselves to the demands of the new age by mass producing working-men's clothing to meet the ever-increasing needs of the Fourth Estate.

The business was soon a great financial success and, in turn, raised the social status of its chief. The small dealer became the big wholesaler, the producer the big clothier, occupations which increased the power of the bourgeoisie.

The mass production of clothes soon found its imitators. In

1833 Ternaux—the man who had made the beautiful cashmere shawl for the Empress Josephine and in the meantime had become one of the most powerful textile manufacturers in France—founded a second ready-made house in Paris, *Le Bonhomme Richard*. Similar concerns sprang up like mushrooms. Soon, in addition to workmen's overalls, they produced men's suits, overcoats, uniforms and ultimately capes, women's coats and wraps. Twenty years later there were already 225 such businesses in France, with a turnover of more than seven and a half million francs.

The ready-made trade started by the old clothes men and developed by cloth dealers, expanded so phenomenally that it soon became a new branch of industry with its own specialist: the outfitter. He now ran the business, bought the material wholesale, had it cut by machine, and sometimes sewn in his own subsidiary workrooms, but more frequently farmed out as homework.

Since the introduction of the industrial production of cloth and accessories, home industries had become seriously threatened. The small tailors had suffered appallingly from the new machine-made output with which they could not compete.

But in 1830 a completely unknown engineer, Thimonnier, arrived in Paris with his invention, a sewing machine. He had conceived it in his home village in the Rhône valley and had worked on it until he had managed to achieve the important chain stitch. He was so poor that he walked to Paris carrying the parts of his machine in a sack.

His fate was typical of that of so many inventors: in his lifetime he achieved neither fame nor profit from his invention.

But the sewing machine had arrived; it was perfected by other engineers in England and America and within a few years of Thimonnier's arrival in Paris was already functioning in countless workshops.

While the hand looms lay idle, the seamstress working at home flourished with the aid of the sewing machine—'the poor man's machine', as it was called.

In other countries, too, since the introduction of the sewing machine, tailoring in home workshops followed its own profitable and independent course, despite the competition from the big manufacturers.

There were as yet, however, no ready-mades for women in the modern sense of the word. Women's clothing 'off the peg' with its standardized sizes, did not develop until the last third of the nineteenth century. At that time any ready-made article of fashion was known as *confection*. Men's working clothes, women's lingerie, aprons, cloaks, spencers, shawls and trimmings for ball and street wear—all appear in the sales catalogues as *confection* or *articles confectionnés*.

Paris taste and Paris chic became known abroad mainly through these graceful imaginative *nouveautés confectionnées* which were important articles of export. At that time almost all clothes had the same cut and even the best made-to-measure tailors worked from a uniform pattern for the whalebone reinforced bodices and the crinoline skirts. If they wanted to shine among the mass of competitors, to prove their talents and creative gifts, they had to do it in the trimmings.

This accounts perhaps for the fact that there is no outstanding personality among the dressmakers of the first half of the nineteenth century.

### THE BIRTH OF HAUTE COUTURE

At the first International Exhibition in London in 1851, French quality goods, especially articles of fashion, aroused great interest. The economist Blanqui—incidentally a brother of the famous socialist—stressed England's supremacy in the field of technology; he praised the excellence of English machinery, its finish, and the cheapness of the raw materials. But France, he said, surpassed every other country in taste at this Exhibition: 'Everywhere we find the immortal flame of French genius which has for us the same significance as iron foundries and coal mines have for England.' How national character persists! Two hundred years earlier Colbert had said, 'Fashion is to France what the gold mines of Peru are to the Spaniard.'

How could fine individual work, which for centuries had been a characteristic of the French race, continue to hold its own in an age when mechanization and standardization were irresistibly spreading?

In other countries the population increased. Factories were founded, industrialization went forward with giant strides and mass goods flooded the market. It was quite different in France. In the 'forties, with its thirty million inhabitants it was still the most thickly populated country in Europe. By the middle of the century the census figure had remained constant and a small number of children was a feature of the French family.

This was due to the pursuit of a better standard of living. The Revolution had raised the bourgeoisie to a higher social status, but hardly had the Fourth Estate come into being than there, too, a desire for a bourgeois existence was born.

Mass production, with its levelling of taste, was and is directly opposed to the French national character. When the first large catalogues of ready-made goods appeared, a murmur ran through the Press: 'We are no longer human beings—we are only widths and heights!'

Obviously there was a certain deficiency in organizing methods such as the machine age demands, a lack, too, of moral courage to be rid of the all-too-beloved past—negative aspects particularly evident in the ready-made industry which lagged behind that of other nations. But once more the French tradition of taste led to the production of quality goods and, particularly in the field of Fashion, to exceptional and unusual peaks of achievement.

Around 1860, when Worth's star was in the ascendant, a clear division appeared between made-to-measure tailoring and the ready-made industry.

Bespoke tailoring went its age-old way. The dressmaker worked for her customers who chose their dresses from an illustration in a journal; she suggested the trimmings or followed the customer's wishes. The ready-made trade increasingly followed the methods of mass-production. The introduction of cut-out patterns from which the dresses were reproduced *en masse*, the standardization of sizes, the resultant lowering of prices, developed into a clearly-defined system. In countries like England and Germany bespoke tailoring was increasingly overshadowed by mass-production.

In Paris, however, a new method of production appeared: made-to-measure tailoring as big business. This corresponded to the demands of an increasingly wealthy middle class for whom elegance became a cult. Increased needs called into life increased production and a new type of employer to master this increased production—men who combined artistic sense and refined taste with business acumen. The head of such a tailoring concern was couturier and cloth merchant, he was—and is—artistic and technical director and entrepreneur at one and the same time.

All the phases of production took place on his premises: from unskilled work to those activities which require a perfect mastery of the craft.

In these workshops there occurred an innovation, which meant a revolution in the history of fashion production: the making of certain models for export only.

The model is a unique creation, a product of French individualism and personal inventive talent. The production of export models began at the very moment when the spreading of mass-production began to endanger the use of the creative imagination in the sphere of fashion.

From now onwards the big couturier sold the model, and it was reproduced in its thousands as the prototype of French taste and French fashion—the unique model was industrialized.

For a century, with few exceptions, the production of fashionable dress had been the privilege of women. Now, when the commercial element became of paramount importance, men took a hand in a new branch of industry. They were better fitted for the competitive struggle than the women. Only with the full emancipation of women in our own time did women work their way up to become heads of such concerns.

The model became the international counterpoint of fashion and the couturier who created it became the dictator of fashion. The knowledge that a woman in Ohio, Sydney or Los Angeles wore an evening or afternoon dress created by him also had its psychological effect. A new race of fashion dictators was born, self-assured and certain of their power.

Haute Couture gradually evolved from a combination of large-scale made-to-measure tailoring for a select clientele and the production of prefabricated models for copying abroad. This was the result of a typically French economic development. Its origin and formation, however, was closely bound up with the rise of a new class of society—the elegant bourgeoisie of the nineteenth century.

## THE ELEGANT BOURGEOISIE

Balzac's *Théorie de la vie élégante* appeared in 1853 but had been written several years before. What a fund of information is to be found in these few pages with their acute and witty definitions of elegance, the more significant as they concern the elegance of the male, who far more than the woman represented the type of the new bourgeoisie.

The bourgeois is no longer the little man fighting for his rights. He is a money-maker, a speculator on the Stock Exchange, an industrialist in a rising machine age. He is the man who invests his money in works of art and choice libraries. And since he has no escutcheon and no title he must assert himself in society by other means.

The costume of the bourgois is completely new. The aura of gold braid, lace jabots and brocade is a thing of the past. In a changed society the bourgeois has to play the part of the well-dressed gentlemen.

A curious age in which the machine worked miracles in industry, while the workers went hungry; in which class arrogance and social ideologies faced each other; in which Karl Marx wrote *Das Kapital* while Balzac proclaimed his apologia for the elegant idler.

For Balzac was anti-revolutionary and anti-social. 'After the revolution,' he wrote, 'in exchange for a ridiculous and effete aristocracy we have the triple-headed aristocracy of gold, power and talent. . . .'

'Intelligence is the crux of our culture. For the man of the new age is not born rich but needs intelligence in order to become rich. The man who makes a fortune by the sweat of his brow cannot possibly be elegant.' Marx writes, 'Who does not work should not eat.' And Balzac: 'No one who works understands anything of elegance with the exception of the artist, because for him work and leisure are the same.'

Balzac divides men into three categories: the workers, the thinkers and the idlers. The last-named are the sons of those who have grown rich. Only the idlers aspire to an elegant life, 'for elegance is the art of knowing how to enjoy one's idleness'.

The idlers had to keep up their prestige, manifest their elegance in subtle shades, *savoir vivre*, distinguished speech and exquisite gentlemanly attire.

Dress was the most expressive of all symbols. Balzac's aphorism, 'Elegance is not so much simple luxury as the luxury of simplicity' characterized the claims, which the smart man-about-town made on his tailor. In the first half of the nineteenth century there were still refined combinations of colour in frock-coats, trousers and waistcoats, but men's costume soon slipped into that uniformity from which it has never really recovered.

All the more important became the cut and the more delicate the work of the tailor. His art, his very intelligence had to show itself in the skilful tailoring of the back, the curve of the waist and in the lie of the pleats.

Men's costume was already made up of the elements which it possesses today—tails and frock-coat, waistcoat and long trousers. Nevertheless, dress could still express a man's political convictions. By wearing long trousers one made it clear that one approved the basic principles of the Revolution. Knee breeches, on the other hand, were an admission of Royalist sympathies. Years after long trousers had established themselves in France they were looked upon as revolutionary in the German states. When some gentlemen who were invited to the Court at Dresden in 1833 asked whether they could appear in long trousers, they were informed that 'one would have expected from them more attachment to the Royal House'.

The clumsy administrative machine of the first half of the nineteenth century produced a special type of bourgeois—the bureaucrat. He wore very high starched collars with lace sprouting from his neckcloth. This stick-up collar or 'parricide', as it was called, became the symbol of the middle-class pedant.

Balzac also stresses that simplicity in fashion came from England. It would be a mistake, however, to think that the French Rococo gentleman simply discarded the wig and exchanged his flowing garb for a cloth overcoat and redingote because he was under the spell of English fashion. Despite the strong influence from across the Channel, fashion in France followed a social development which was just as sudden and revolutionary as the political and social upheaval.

In England, no bloody revolution had been necessary to strengthen the middle classes and allow them some participation in power. That the Revolution in France was so vehement and took such a terrifying course was because the privileged classes wanted to put back the historical clock, and because the aristocrats, whose power lay in the possession of real estate, could no longer participate in the economic progress of the country.

In England, the power of the crown had long since been curtailed, Parliament strengthened and the economic system founded on a capitalist basis. Thus it was the logical path of social development if the outward signs of a new class of society manifested themselves earlier than in France and in the most obvious manner—in dress.

It is also a mistake to think that the king of the London dandies, George Bryan Brummell, invented English elegant simplicity and launched a new fashion for men. 'Beau' Brummel did no more than raise the already existing fashion to its peak. To a certain extent he set the seal of aristocracy on the bourgeois male costume.

Beau Brummell spent nine hours a day at his toilet, transforming it into a religious ceremony with rigidly prescribed rites. The climax was the tying of the gleaming white starched cravats which had to be done according to certain laws. His friend 'Prinny', the future George IV, often appeared to watch the miracle of this cravat tying.

Balzac laments the fate of Beau Brummell who had to flee from his numberless creditors to Caen where he later died: bald-headed, he now wore a wig and tied an odd strip of black silk round his throat because the laundress, to whom he owed a fortune, refused to iron his white cravats.

In 1837 the eighteen-year-old Princess Victoria came to the throne. The power of the merchants and manufacturers increased. Huge, solid fortunes were amassed and with them arose a new middle class intent also upon showing its weight in society by its outward appearance.

This English middle class needed no bejewelled mistresses and wives to display the latest fashions. Quite the contrary. The gentleman's independence had to be expressed in his unobtrusive dress and in his wife's discreet elegance. In contrast to the previous ruling classes, Victorian society affected simplicity, discovering the concept of elegant Puritanism and fashionable virtue.

The rites prescribing the correct costume to be worn at different occasions were observed ever more rigidly, and greater demands were made on the tailors for perfection when they had to dress a lady. She must not appear old-fashioned, nor was it permissible for her to be ahead of the mode.

The French middle class, whose rise proceeded more rapidly, was entirely different. It hurried ahead of the fashion, and for a lady it was the height of elegance to be the first to wear a new cut, a new colour and completely original trimmings.

In spite of this, the snobbishness of Parisian society was affected by customs which had come from England. The distinguished gentleman had to be a sportsman, belong to the Jockey Club and ride in a steeplechase; his lady had to appear in a tilbury and keep a groom who was usually engaged from England.

In France, however, the monied classes lacked the solid foundations which were a distinction of the English middle classes. The Napoleonic Wars had done irreparable damage to the country; the rhythm of the economic machine had been disturbed, the credit system was insufficiently organized and in this sphere France lagged far behind England.

Ideologists stirred up unrest. The democrats wanted to realize the positive conquests of the great Revolution; the militarists forgot Waterloo and stressed the Napoleonic victories, and the Bourbon clique desired the return of an aristocracy dressed in the pompous attire of their ancestors.

From these contrasts one tried to escape into the past. Typical was the unbelievable success of the fancy-dress balls, where one could revel in historical memories: people appeared as Mary Stuart, Charlotte Corday or Catherine de Medici.

The time lacked its own style and the soil was prepared for historical reminiscences in fashion, architecture and interior decoration. People became hypersensitive and sentimental; the vapours were a sign of good breeding and women were particularly attractive when they swooned.

The new romantic ballet, with stars like dainty Fanny Elssler or Taglioni who, in *Les Sylphides*, introduced the *tutu*, still worn today, was a furore. People raved about de Musset's passionate poems and Chopin's love pangs set to music.

To produce the dresses which combined romantic sensibility and historical recollections it needed a new type of cultured dressmaker, among whom the best known were Palmyre and Victorine. They visited exhibitions, rummaged about in the print room in order to be historically accurate in their style and trimmings and took their inspiration from Oriental ballets and historical tragedies.

Literature invaded Fashion and vice versa. There is hardly a novel, whether by Stendhal or Balzac, in which the smartness of a man and the toilette of a woman is not described. Balzac was the first great novelist to recognize the spiritual ego of the wearer in a dress: 'Her toilette was for her what it is for all women—a permanent revelation of her most secret thoughts, a language and a symbol.' (*Une fille d'Eve.*) A human being revealed his character and his intellect in his dress. And Balzac went even further: a dress may determine a character's fate, because it brings to light the slumbering urges of the subconscious.

Balzac also eulogizes the art of the dressmaker. In *Le deputé d'Arcis* he writes: 'Her dress, trimmed with three rows of fringes, fell in enchanting pleats, clearly denoting the skill of a Parisian dressmaker.'

The famous Victorine was even mentioned by Stendhal in his *Souvenirs d'egotisme*: 'I often admired the old Duchess when she wore one of Victorine's ravishing dresses. I am quite obsessed by a well-made dress and for me it is a true delight.'

A perfectly cut piece of clothing, the cunning pleating of a material, the way a well-bred woman wore a dress—all this took on the same significant importance as an angelic face or a beautiful soul.

Towards the end of the 'thirties, the historical element waned both in art and fashion. Dresses became ever wider, petticoats were stiffened and increased in number, their lower parts reinforced with horsehair, '*crin*', and broadened with goffered or wired lace and flounces. The crinoline was born. Its production developed into an industry and the wearing of it into a way of life.

France's new middle-class society which had consolidated its wealth needed a bourgeois way of life and a bourgeois king. But Louis Philippe, despite his petit-bourgeois behaviour, his umbrella and civilian suit, was not popular. The economic crises shook the country too severely and the workers had too grim a struggle for their daily bread.

His reign lasted eighteen years, and eighteen years are long enough to crystallize a change of fashion and behaviour which had already begun.

During this period of crises, middle-class society created for itself a comfortable life—a humdrum yet cosy existence. The women were happy at their cooking and housekeeping; at home they wore a small silk apron and a lace cap. There was plenty of room for the vast crinolines in the broad armchairs.

The walking dress was buttoned high, the head disappeared beneath the bonnet and a mantilla was worn round the shoulders. The evening dress was décolleté, but the shoulders were modestly swathed in lace or tulle shawls. The summer cotton frocks with the girlish flower patterns on a white ground were modest and respectable.

These 'good old days' were even more pronounced in Germany and reached their highest charm in Imperial Vienna. Prince Metternich's strong administration saw to it that the people and the bourgeoisie were kept in ignorance of political problems. From this idyllic existence was born the Biedermeier style with its own individual charm in interior decoration and fashion.

Ever new types evolved, leaving their mark on the age only to disappear as quickly as they had come. The sensitive romantics, the lovesick swains, held the stage of Parisian society, soon to be followed by new types—the 'lion' and the 'lioness'.

The 'lion' was naturally a member of the Jockey Club, wore the latest clothes, was an eccentric, constantly striving to be original. His conversation was exclusively of horses and mistresses.

The society lady was now a 'lioness'. She was wild and excitable, could ride and fence, smoked and drank champagne and knew all the racing jargon. She wore an Amazon dress with shell-shaped buttons and Brandenburgs. Through the open bodice a glimpse could be caught of a jabot-trimmed blouse; the half-length sleeve ended in a long cuff which was covered by yellow leather gloves. Although she aped everything English by day, she was exotic by night. Her evening dresses were made of Oriental fabrics with Bedouin or Persian sleeves, a bunch of curls fell down her neck, and her headgear was either a Greek cap or a lace scarf. It is often said that George Sand must be numbered among the 'lionesses', but this shows a misunderstanding of the meaning of the word *lionne*. The *lionne*, with her exotic urges, led an empty, extroverted life. She never read, for reading or intellectual occupations were alien to her way of life. George Sand, on the other hand, the important writer and friend of great men such as Chopin and de Musset, with her masculine intellect and preference for male attire, was already a forerunner of the modern, emancipated woman. It is merely that her romantic adventures furnished material for gossip in the drawing-rooms of the 'lionesses'.

Madame Ducrest notes wistfully in her journal: 'I wonder what is the origin of the word lioness, which has become a kind of honorary title for any woman who wishes to set the tone. Our sex would have done better to have sought its success in the qualities of other beasts and left those of the lion to the men. And there are even women who sport a lioness couchant on their coat of arms!'

The 1848 Revolution brought no change to bourgeois society or to fashion. A glance at the journals of that year suffices to show that Fashion remained quite untouched by the political events.

The din of the fighting on the barricades filled the streets of Paris. Louis Philippe fled to America. In the March number of *La Sylphide* we read: 'On the avenues of the Champs Elysées one sees beautifully dressed ladies whose exquisite dresses and good taste are a demonstration of protest against fear and distrust. If the women so wished they could be of great assistance in helping France out of the crisis into which the perfidy and machinations of the King have plunged her.

'Nothing is without significance today: ribbons, feathers, flowers, lace and pearls, for behind all this finery there is bread for all who work for their living. Paris teems with working girls who spend a great part of their days and nights in toil —weaving muslin, making lace, fashioning flowers and painting all the finery we admire so much in the reflection of the crystal chandeliers.'

In December of the same year Prince Louis Napoleon was elected President. Two years later he pulled off his famous coup d'état, and in December 1852 proclaimed himself Emperor as Napoleon III.

From then onwards fashion and fashion creation were dependent upon the impetus received from the court society of the Second Empire, and last but not least from the brilliant energies of the most Parisian of all Parisians, the Englishman Charles Frederick Worth.

# IV

# AN ENGLISHMAN—FOUNDER OF PARISIAN HAUTE COUTURE

## HARD TIMES

CHARLES FREDERICK WORTH was born at Bourne in Lincolnshire. In this bleak and humdrum manufacturing town he spent his early childhood—a sad, disconsolate childhood, a jungle of torments and early humiliations.

Money troubles at home and tyranny at school . . . . Every flight of the imagination was prohibited. Dickens grew up in similar circumstances and the sufferings of his youth find their echo in his novels.

In *Hard Times* the squire says to the teacher: 'Now, what I want is, Facts. Teach these boys and girls nothing but Facts. . . . You can only form the minds of reasoning animals upon Facts: nothing else will be of any service to them.' A hard school for a boy like Charles Frederick, for whom later the words luxury and fantasy meant the whole world.

His early boyhood, too, might have been a plot for a Dickens novel. He had to look on while his father, a lawyer, wasted and gambled away the little money his profession brought in.

The family was up to its ears in debt. The rent was in arrears and the school fees could not be found. Charles Frederick had to interrupt his schooldays and help to support the family. At the age of eleven he joined a printing works, where he had to slave for very little money.

Child labour was at that time a commonplace and the fact held no terrors for the boy. But it was a different matter when it came to the tragedy at home. In that calm, provincial world with its stable bourgeoisie, to which the Worths belonged, the family disgrace must have made a profound impression upon him. For years he suffered from the humiliations his mother had to endure and he often referred to them in later life.

A year later the boy went to London. We do not know whether he was on the look-out for a fashion shop or whether he got the job by chance, but he started with Lewis and Allenby, a shop which sold materials, shawls and cloaks.

A new life began, a breathing space after a period of terrible tension. Charles Frederick was now allowed to handle the most superb Manchester velvets and English cloth. He could observe how the young London girls draped themselves in shawls or how one laid a mantilla over the shoulders of a lady.

He could also see how a well-ordered business was run, could stand at the tall counting-house desk and learn the mysteries of debit and credit.

What a pleasant change from his childhood with its tribulations and chaotic family conditions. How carefree and unembarrassed were the well-dressed women who came into the shop. Sometimes they came alone, sometimes accompanied by gentlemen in smart blue frock-coats and silk top-hats. They inspected the wares, made their choice, and the shawls or mantles they bought were carried by a servant to the fine houses in the West End of London, or were packed and despatched to their country seats.

In the shop, that well co-ordinated world of sales and purchases, of careful book-keeping and a strict love of order, he was surrounded by the calm atmosphere of a respectable old-established London business house.

In the evening, however, when Charles Frederick left the shop, life looked quite different. To reach his wretched rented room he had to walk through mean streets, past tall houses in which families lived in misery and filth—rookeries undreamed of by the beautiful ladies who came to Lewis and Allenby's shop.

This precocious boy was already acquainted with two sides of life—the one comfortable, contented and bourgeois and the other full of unrest, affliction and appalling misery.

Whenever he had a free moment he went to the National Gallery. He stood fascinated in front of the pictures, making notes and drawings. The colours and ornaments of the costumes made a deep impression upon him. He kept returning to the portrait of Queen Elizabeth to admire the beautiful brocade dress, embroidered with symbolical eyes and ears and snakes on the sleeves. Twenty years later he used these motifs in the embroidery of one of his own creations. His enthusiasm was aroused by these pictures. He succumbed to beauty, luxury and magnificence and in his thoughts he was already living in another world. The boyish dreams took shape and content. He would and must find a way—the way which led to that world.

A flight from reality, from the intolerable contrasts of Early Victorian England with its dreary, puritanical middle classes, its sober world of trade and the romantic mediævalism of the London slums.

The Pre-Raphaelites, too, fled from this reality when they painted their dreams of the Italian quattrocento; when they projected a past age of beauty into the materialistic, sober present.

The young Charles Frederick was no romantic. He dreamed

of magnificence and wealth but he never lost himself in his dreams. He went forward step by step along the sober path of book-keeping and accounts. At the age of thirteen he was already cashier in Lewis and Allenby's shop.

But the years went by and he remained a cashier; his small salary did not allow him to put away a little money or to better his condition.

The days brought forth nothing new and nothing changed —neither the shawls in the shop nor the cloaks and mantillas— not even the dresses of the most fashionable customers. The mode seemed to have come to a standstill except that skirts grew longer and more voluminous. And why? Because the young Queen Victoria had injured her foot and received her visitors at St James's Palace lying on a divan, covering her foot with the hem of her skirt. This had sufficed. Two days later all the women of London wore longer skirts.

Charles Frederick looked through the fashion journals; *The little Messenger of Parisian Fashions*, or the *Monthly Selection of Parisian Costumes*, or the genuine Paris fashion paper, *Estafette des modes*, which had a branch for London subscribers.

How different the mode looked in the French paper. It lived, it moved, it vibrated with change and daring discoveries. The most beautiful dress of the most elegant London woman was a mere pale reflection of Parisian chic.

On the other side of the Channel lured a world in which the source of all fashionable events seemed to spring. And there, perhaps, a crock of gold would be waiting for a young, capable English business man.

He made up his mind. In 1845, Charles Frederick Worth, a boy of twenty, left his secure post in the shop and shook the dust of foggy London from his feet.

After paying his fare he had only a hundred and seventeen

francs left and not the slightest knowledge of the French language.

## THE FIRST PARIS PERIOD

His beginnings in Paris were not easy. He worked like a slave twelve hours a day in a draper's shop.

Materials—nothing but materials. . . . There had been more variety at Lewis and Allenby's.

But now luck took a hand. At the right and decisive moment came the lucky break which Fortune so often gives to men who have the iron will to succeed; Charles Frederick obtained a job with the firm of Opigez and Chazelle, the Maison Gagelin, where materials, shawls, cloaks and other fashionable ready-made goods were sold.

The shop was located in the heart of the smart fashion quarter, at 83, rue de Richelieu. A few steps away had once stood the house of Leroy, *grand faiseur* and couturier to two Empresses, and before that, in the very same street, Rose Bertin's millinery.

Worth's biographers—and naturally first and foremost the members of the Worth dynasty—try to play down the importance of the Maison Gagelin in order to stress his brilliance. They are wrong. This firm at the time was one of the most famous in Paris. It figured in all the exhibitions and its name always appears when three or four of the most important fashion firms are mentioned. The best writers were often encouraged by high fees to give their services by describing in their *feuilletons* the newest toilettes to be seen at the Opera or the races. No flowery conceit was too precious, no effusion too heartrending to extol the magnificence of the dresses. And then as though quite by chance the name of the fashion house was inserted.

How often one comes across the name of the Maison Gagelin in these articles—time and time again in *La Sylphide*, the paper founded by Emile de Girardin who counted the greatest writers of his age, such men as Balzac, Alexandre Dumas and Théophile Gautier, among his contributors.

Charles Frederick was now transplanted into the very world for which he had longed so many years. All around him were French materials and trimmings which only trickled into England as rare and costly imports—brocades, silk ribbons and lace.

For twelve decisive years Worth worked with Gagelin. His value to the firm was recognized, his talents encouraged, and he was trusted. He could exercise his creative talents. He drew, designed and produced new ideas. His technical capabilities also revealed themselves. He improved the art of cutting out by following the run of the cloth, so that the material could mould itself to the body and its movements.

It was the Englishman in him which inspired this reform. Although English tailoring was completely lacking in chic, it was superb when it came to cut. He now took special care in the cut with the result that French dressmaking was soon to triumph abroad.

In 1851 an event of international importance took place—the Great Exhibition in London. The Crystal Palace of glass and iron, a miracle of modern engineering, was erected in Hyde Park. Every nation displayed their industrial products. France sent the most beautiful luxury articles—priceless silks from Lyons, tapestries from Beauvais, carpets from Aubusson and porcelains from Sèvres.

The exhibits from the Maison Gagelin—Indian-type shawls and smart dresses—featured prominently in all the reports. That year the firm sold more than 350,000 francs' worth to the leading houses abroad.

The firm won the only gold medal awarded to France at the Great Exhibition of 1851. Not without justification, Worth's biographers attribute a great deal of the firm's success to him.

The next world fair took place in Paris in 1855 when the splendour and luxury of the Second Empire began to flourish. This exhibition, too, was of extraordinary brilliance; there were fêtes and countless pageants.

Queen Victoria and her Consort came from England and Bismarck from Germany. The English Queen was full of praise for the exhibits, but Bismarck found much to criticize and maintained smugly that the level of Court society in his country was far higher than it was in Paris.

This exhibition brought young Worth his first personal triumph. A court train in gold and bead-embroidered silk moire made from one of his designs won first prize. More than thirty years later Worth admitted that, unwittingly, he had nearly offended Napoleon III with his design; the motifs of the embroidery, carried out in Renaissance style, were interpreted by one of the Court officials as lilies, the Bourbon emblem. As a result of this the train, which Worth had shown to the Emperor, who was delighted with it, was not sold to the State as had been planned. Nevertheless, this model of a court train was imitated and became an indispensable article of international court dress.

Worth consolidated his position more and more with Gagelin. He persuaded the firm to found a branch for ready-made dresses, to open sale-rooms and to enter into closer contact with the Lyon manufacturers.

He rose from employee to partner.

The Maison Gagelin employed a host of cutters, seamstresses and *vendeuses. Vendeuse!* This was no profession for a middle-class girl. Moreover, what respectable bourgeois girl would have worked in those days or thought of earning her own living? And yet there was one at Gagelin's—the daughter of a tax collector from the Auvergne. Her destiny seemed to link her with Worth, since poverty had forced her, too, to fend for herself.

The grace with which this *vendeuse* draped the firm's shawls round her shoulders may have attracted the young man as much as her youthful beauty.

It was a romance with a happy ending. The shop-girl became Mme Charles Frederick Worth and his indispensable collaborator. He designed dresses, hats and draperies for her, and she knew how to wear the gowns and cloaks, how to display his creations with so much charm that the customers were quite bewitched. Orders poured into the Maison Gagelin.

Unfortunately the firm was old-fashioned and traditional. For a time the partners had been galvanized by Worth's youthful drive, but he came to them daily with new projects. He proposed to make dresses for individual customers, to start a department for high-grade made-to-measure dresses and to improve the export models. These plans, which were far in advance of the times, were turned down.

Worth left the Maison Gagelin in the winter of 1857-8. He started his own firm, with a colleague, a young Swede named Otto Bobergh from whom he later parted company.

### WORTH INVENTS THE RUE DE LA PAIX

He moved into 7, rue de la Paix, and installed his family and his business in the same building.

The rue de la Paix! For more than half a century this street was to be the focal point of Parisian elegance, a centre for the finest jeweller's shops, the most admirable fashion shops and Haute Couture. A street whose name became the symbol of luxury and fashion.

But in those days it was merely a quiet respectable street in a smart residential quarter. An occasional carriage made its way down the street or a military parade was held in the Place Vendôme. Worth's son, Jean Philippe, remembered standing as a three-year-old boy—it was in 1859—at the window watching the victorious troops on their return from the Italian campaign marching through the rue de la Paix.

The leading fashion houses of the period were on the *grands boulevards*, round the Palais Royal, in the rue Vivienne and the rue Richelieu.

At the end of the rue de la Paix there were one or two shops: at no. 20 they sold gloves, at no. 23 linen, hats *Chez Grafton* at no. 25, and no. 17 was Doucet's lingerie shop. But there were no business houses and no shops adjoining no. 7, so near to the aristocratic Place Vendôme.

It was somewhat of an adventure to install a dressmaking salon there, on the first floor. Was it boldness or speculation on his part?

Some way off, where the silent street ended, throbbed the pulse of new life. In the distance could be heard the sound of hammering and sawing, houses being pulled down and small alleys being reduced to rubble. Deep breaches were being made in Balzac's '*paysages noirs*', in the mysterious romantic Paris so beloved by poets.

Napoleon III wished to transform Paris into a modern city. The slums were to be razed and the children given light and air. Peace, wealth and the grandeur of France were to be expressed in broad avenues, noble squares and delightful parks.

But this was not on æsthetic and social grounds alone. The Emperor was thinking of the fighting on the barricades in the '48 Revolution and of the rioters who rebelled in the streets against his coup d'état. Those dark alleys in which the people lurked were dangerous.

'Together we will do great things,' the Emperor said to his prefect, Haussmann, when he received him in audience for the first time in the Château de Saint-Cloud. He was not mistaken. The *artiste-demolisseur*, as Haussmann called himself, realized the Emperor's brilliant plan and built modern Paris.

In the same year that Worth moved to the rue de la Paix a decree was issued giving permission for the building of a new opera house. Not a stone's throw from his house the big square, which was now to be cleared, would become the hub of Parisian society—the *Place de l'Opera*.

It is a clever piece of calculation to start something new where the future will soon reside; and this is just another indication of Worth's flair.

The broadened streets and the new houses going up brought an opportunity for bold speculation. More and more new shops were opened and new businesses founded; shares rose, and on the Stock Exchange the barometer was set fair.

It often happens when an employee or partner sets up shop on his own that the customers follow him. The Maison Gagelin saw with consternation that many ladies who admired Worth's talents were drifting to the rue de la Paix.

Worth soon had a very smart clientele, but the Court was not yet within reach. The Empress patronized two of the best-known dressmakers, Palmyre and Vignon. She had ordered fifty-two dresses for her wedding from them. All the French textile manufacturers had been requested to produce their most beautiful materials, taffetas and antique moire silks.

The most eminent lady of fashion of the Second Empire still knew nothing of its greatest couturier. But soon there were, among the smart women who frequented the Court, some who were Worth's customers. Hardly two years after his installation in the rue de la Paix the Empress's eagle eye for fashion discovered these ladies among her guests.

To dress the Empress meant more for Worth than a mere personal triumph, more than merely his appointment as purveyor to Her Majesty. This great lady was for him a means to an end, linking him to the Imperial economic policy—with her assistance he became able to help the Lyons silk industry to attain a brilliance such as had not been seen since the time of Napoleon the Great.

The steam-driven machines threatened the hand-looms so dear to the hearts of the Lyons silk weavers, on which they wove their delicately shaded floral marvels. Worth realized the danger and did everything in his power to protect the Lyons quality goods from the drab levelling of mass production. But since the Empress had deigned to order dresses of Lyons silk, her example was followed by the Court, the ladies of high finance and the rich bourgeoisie. Lyons could once more produce quality goods. The Imperial economic policy triumphed and superior tailoring acquired both brilliance and an individual character. The Empress, who for many years wore the heavy silk brocade dresses which Worth made for her, even though she often disliked them, called them '*mes robes politiques*'.

The results are evident in the statistics: between the years 1860 and 1870 the number of Lyons silk looms was doubled.

A few years after Worth moved to the rue de la Paix, the highest in the land flocked to him—the Empress, queens and princesses of several countries, the noblest ladies of *le grand monde* and the most exquisite from the demi-monde.

The pulse of fashion beat in the rue de la Paix. High up in the attics were the workrooms. Here hundreds of girls were busy from early morning to late at night, cutting out, sewing, embroidering, gathering ribbons into ruches, ruches into flounces, flounces upon flounces into bells which were to be worn over the crinoline scaffolding. Plumes were stuck on toques and birettas, flowers were arranged and veils as light as a breath of wind were attached to tiny hats.

Light two-wheeled cabriolets and tilburys rolled through the streets, the coachmen's and valets' liveries matching the colours of the upholstery. Carriages waited outside the shops, a lackey on the running-board waiting to open the door for the lady. The owner could be recognized by the carriage, the colour of the upholstery and the livery of the lackeys. The dandy at his vantage point could say: 'That is Princess Metternich's carriage and that one belongs to La Païva. . . .'

The rue de la Paix was the fashion. In each house a new business was opened: the most elegant modistes, the largest jewellers, makers of hand-made shoes, court hairdressers and other Grands Couturiers established themselves in the shadow of the fashion dictator.

## WORTH AND THE CRINOLINE

Worth maintains that the Empress introduced the crinoline to disguise her pregnancy. Her son was born in 1856. Queen Victoria, who was pregnant at the same time, immediately adopted this fashion.

It is a bold assertion, since the crinoline had already been in vogue in the 'forties.

The crinoline originally evolved from a political reaction—a new Rococo that suited the rightful heirs of the Bourbons—and thus its exaggerated form in the Second Empire also had special grounds: the luxuriating, swelling shapes of clothes, their pomp and splendour were intended to disguise a lack of style and to show off the pretentious wealth of the new society, in the same way as the stucco façades and the overloaded salons.

A great deal has been written on the eighteenth-century

hooped skirt and its revival in the form of the crinoline. Today, in the Anglo-Saxon countries, costume has been subjected to a psychological analysis. James Laver calls the crinoline an 'instrument of seduction' because it made women appear unapproachable and thus had an alluring effect.

James Laver goes so far as to say that the crinoline 'was from one point of view the first great triumph of the machine age—the application to feminine costume of the principles of steel construction'. He overlooks the fact that a hundred years earlier the hooped dress also had a mighty frame of wire and whalebone and that the use of steel bands had nothing whatsoever to do with the fashion.

The crinoline was a subject of great controversy in its own time. Théophile Gautier, one of the wittiest and most celebrated writers of his age, devoted a small brochure to it which appeared in 1858 in an edition of three hundred copies. In it he says: 'Dresses with hoops, dresses with springs, which have to be repaired like watches when they no longer function—is that not hideous, coarse, abominable, a contradiction of art?' But then he continues: 'We, however, do not hold this opinion. Women are right when they cling to their crinolines, in spite of jests, caricatures, vaudeville skits and teasing of all kinds . . . the waist rises elegant and slender from the wealth of pleats. . . . This rich mass of material acts like a pedestal for bust and head which, now that nudity is no longer the fashion, have become the most important parts of the body.'

The crinolines grew ever more voluminous. The factories could hardly fulfil the orders on account of the vast quantities of material required. For a very simple crinoline ten lengths of silk or velvet were needed, and when the dresses were adorned with ruches and flounces they consumed thirty yards and more.

Worth speaks later of such a dress: 'I once produced a crinoline which needed a hundred yards of silk. It was made of satin taffeta in three different shades, ranging from dark violet to pale lilac. When the dress was finished it looked like a gigantic bunch of violets.'

In order to give it the right breadth countless petticoats were needed, and these too had to be stiffened with whalebone, crimped and ruffled lace and flounces. Worth was, therefore, delighted when an inventor came to him one day with a collapsible steel frame—he must still have been at the Maison Gagelin—which made petticoats and horsehair padding superfluous. Worth immediately used these frames for his creations and the inventor earned more than a quarter of a million francs in a few weeks.

Petticoats were now limited to one or two muslin underskirts, whose fine lace was visible when the lady walked. But hardly had this steel frame been introduced than the wider and more cumbersome the crinoline the smarter it was considered. This cage-like foundation with the billowing skirts above, so wide that the wearer could hardly go through a door, became a magnificent target for caricatures and jokes. The magazines were full of them, from harmless stories like the one in which the landlord says to a lady: 'Here is your room Madame and the one next door is for your dress,' to highly obscene jests.

It is amusing to note that during the time these monster dresses were the rage, bathing costumes were worn on the beach which, from the time of the crinoline's disappearance to the First World War, would have been considered thoroughly indecent. We find drawings of them in various fashion papers: short knickers ending well above the knee, a little jacket and a sporting scarf round the head. A fashion reporter writes from Dieppe: 'It seems as though the bathing belles' legs knew that they are rid of the burden of the crinoline.'

In 1860 there was a rumour that the Empress had abandoned the crinoline. The fashion reporter of *L'Illustration* informed readers that at the last Tuileries ball there had been a noticeable attempt to limit the size of this object of apparel, not because of its extravagant use of material but because it was already being worn by ladies' maids. Queen Victoria in England and the Empress Elizabeth in Vienna had already discarded it. But only for a few days. Then both of them learned that the great Parisian couturier had decreed that the crinoline should continue to be worn.

## 'L'EMPIRE S'AMUSE'

Napoleon III, like his more famous uncle, loved pomp and splendour. With every means available he tried to give the right éclat to his power. Fêtes disguised his political incompetence, and became State occasions. Pomp and splendour were the basis of Worth's ostentatious toilettes.

The parvenu nobility and finance magnates hobnobbed at Tuileries receptions. The women revelled in elegance and flaunted a luxury of dress which had hardly ever been seen before: the gentlemen, when they were not in uniform, had to appear in court attire—knee breeches and silk stockings.

And then the balls! Paris had rarely witnessed such a display of feminine coquetry since the fêtes at Versailles, such a splendour of dress. The billowing crinolines in which the ladies swayed like harebells, necks, heads and arms laden with diamonds and precious stones which sparkled in the gleam of the giant chandeliers, the bright uniforms. . . . Truly the Rococo age had returned. But the Offenbach melodies and Strauss waltzes brought a movement and gaiety into the company such as the eighteenth-century court balls with their rigid etiquette had never known.

The names of the guests one reads in the papers of the time are almost the same as those one finds in Worth's account books—the Comtesse Pourtalès, the Comtesse Montebello, the Duchesse d'Alba, the Duchesse de Morny, the Baronne Alphonse de Rothschild. Worth's masterpieces were on view at these balls, dresses which have become part of the annals of the Second Empire: the silver lamé dress in which the Duchesse de Morny appeared as the morning star, La Castiglione's devil's costume, the feathered dress that transformed Baronne Rothschild into a bird of Paradise, Princess Subaroff's ball dress which had cost 30,000 francs.

These fancy dress balls cost the Court enormous sums of money. The director of the Louvre sighed that his museum was given a grant of only 7,000 francs for its yearly purchases while the Empress received 100,000 francs a month.

But for this world—'*le monde où l'on s'amuse*'—there were no crises and no menacing wars. Nothing but garden parties and balls, the big horse races, love affairs and fashion.

Artists and poets were in the swing. One has only to look at the newspapers of the period. Merimée, Alexandre Dumas fils, Octave Feuillet; the composers Gounod, Meyerbeer, Rossini, Auber, and the painter Meissonier, to mention only a few of the best known.

Industry and the steam engine brought speed and mobility into life. The railway lured the elegant Parisians to seaside resorts and spas, to Baden-Baden, Dieppe and Biarritz. The railway carried everyone who had a full purse to Paris. Thomas Cook's tours flourished.

People hurried from the provinces to admire the elegance of the Parisians and to see the latest fashions at close quarters. From abroad came Americans, Russians, Turks, Egyptians and Chinese. Everyone streamed to Paris.

'Barbarian invasions', wailed the Parisians, and grew rich from the foreigners who bought dresses and jewels, lace and shawls with extravagant irresponsibility.

In Paris the intellectual life flourished. Here were staged the great art exhibitions and the great opera premières. Parisian wit, Parisian gaiety, Parisian taste. . . . And 'God's own company of actors', as Heine called the Parisians, also ruled the world stage of fashion.

The Paris Exhibition of 1867 was the final peak of luxury, a last lull before the storm of war, the swan-song of the Second Empire. The rulers of the Great Powers came to Paris—the Tsar, the King of Prussia, the Italian King, the Austrian Empress and the Sultan. Bismarck reserved his seats by telegraph for Offenbach's operetta *La Grande-Duchesse de Gerolstein* in which Hortense Schneider appeared in dazzling Worth dresses.

## MONSIEUR WORTH

M. Worth's reputation increased from day to day. Every lady who visited him for the first time trembled for fear that he would dismiss her, finding her unworthy to be dressed by him. 'M. Worth said this, M. Worth said that. . . .' Each of his pronouncements and judgments became gospel. His respectful son maintains that Worth recognized only God and the Emperor as his superiors.

It is only too understandable that a man who towered so high above all his competitors should have a host of enemies. Many of these pleaded Puritanism and found it indecent, even scandalous, that a man should be present when dresses were tried on. His weaknesses were brought to light and his little peccadilloes parodied.

Jean Philippe, who worshipped his father, only hints discreetly at these hostile attacks. For example, a newspaper article, describing a new firm whose owner was a young man, who received his clients with a velvet cap on his head and his feet on the mantelpiece. A harmless enough story, which makes it difficult to understand from Jean Philippe's account why Mme Worth should have gone weeping to her client Mme de Girardin, to tell her of her distress. Emile de Girardin, the famous newspaperman, who was present, consoled her: 'But Mme Worth, these things happen to everyone who is successful.'

But we know the real reason of Mme Worth's distress, which Jean Philippe does not mention. No less eminent a figure than Hippolyte Taine himself had satirized the great couturier in his enchanting skit on Parisian life, *La vie et les opinions de Thomas Graindorge*: 'He receives in a velvet jacket, lounging on a divan, cigar in mouth. A society lady comes to him to order a dress. "Madame," he asks, "who has recommended me to you? In order to be dressed by me you have to be introduced. I am an artist with the tone scale of a Delacroix. I compose, and a toilette is just as good as a picture." To another client he says: "Move about, turn round . . . come back in eight days. By that time I will have composed a dress suitable for you." '

More biting and elaborate is the article written under the pseudonym of 'La Vicomtesse des Trois Etoiles'. In this, the salon of a couturier, Monsieur X—once more unmistakably Worth—is described. It does not ridicule him but the lady customer who slavishly begs for the maestro's favours: 'In his innumerable salons the *vendeuses* slip among an elegant and busy crowd, trailing their long silk trains with a majestic serenity. They have learned from autocratic customers. With a pinch of dignity and a little condescension an inexperienced visitor tries in vain to reach this *bon faiseur*. Soon she has to put on her most seductive smile and plead for an audience.

'It is as difficult to see X as to obtain an audience with a Minister. But to what lengths would not one go to possess the first edition of one of his dresses? Great ladies have been seen waiting patiently in rows like lackeys in his antechamber. From time to time X walks past them, motions to them to be patient, only to disappear in the most graceful manner. . . .

'That is power, that is real autocracy. Ladies may be allowed to put on arrogant airs and despise women who do not belong to their set, but to reach the man who possesses the magic formula of their elegance and beauty they have to leave their arrogance in the anteroom, or at least at the cash-desk.'

A few years later Monsieur X becomes Monsieur Chose. The anonymous reporter pays a visit to his salon. 'I climbed stairs covered with soft black carpets. Hothouse atmosphere and fragrant perfumes. . . . Exotic plants, dwarf palms, camelias and a procession of ravishing women like angels on a Jacob's Ladder. . . . On the first floor a great coming and going, the rustle of frou-frous and sophisticated perfume in the air.'

Fabrics and patterns are displayed in four huge salons.

'The salesmen are worldly-looking young men. When the ladies ask about shades and trimmings they reply in dignified monosyllables with the absent, bored expression of melancholy poets.'

The reporter goes into the big salon where Mme de M. is having a fitting. 'The salon is in darkness but a lamp of twelve gas flares with movable shades lights the lady exactly as she will appear that evening at the Tuileries.'

In the adjoining salon Monsieur Chose is checking the toilette of Princess S. and condescends to say: 'A masterpiece!'

And now the maestro in person enters the room where Mme M. is being fitted. 'Hair parted down the middle, his plump pink and white face gleams, with the drooping moustaches that almost look like a piece of sculpture; his thick white throat is hidden in an outsize collar with a wide pale green cravat. He is wearing his set smile and greets the client without bothering to bow. His voice is strange and his accent quite incredible. . . .

'At a single glance he recognizes what is the matter with the dress. "What are you doing there, Esther?" With her waist Madame must only wear draped material. It's too décolleté. Let the material lie diagonally across the shoulders. The spray on the corsage is far too big.'

'He is brilliant, sober and knows exactly what he wants. He has been known to dismiss a customer because she wanted too low cut a dress.'

Then the *essayeuses* appear in a great variety of dresses. 'The ladies are enchanted, their enthusiasm knows no bounds. The maestro remains cool and languid, accepting compliments with melancholy indifference and a strong English accent.'

What fashion reporter today would dare to paint such an ironical portrait of a great couturier, and what newspaper would print it?

But irony and ridicule could not harm the famous M. Worth. Slightly over forty, he was already at the height of his fame.

The fact that a man dictated women's dress aroused some criticism here and there. In a report on the Paris Exhibition of 1867 we read: 'The biggest dressmaker of society and the demi-monde is a man—and a man who knows how to treat courtesans and duchesses disdainfully, one might almost say with unparalleled rudeness.' And another reporter complains: 'Now men dictate ladies' dresses and are arbiters of fashion, a custom which we hope will not become general.'

As opposed to these opinions, Ernest Feydeau goes so far as to say that the revolution in fashion—this is how he described the transition from the crinoline to the narrow skirt—should not only be ascribed to Worth but to the fact that men had now taken over women's fashions.

In his book *L'Art de plaire* (1871) he writes: 'M. Worth has today a world-wide reputation. Nothing is lacking in his fame, for he is mocked, ridiculed and envied, as many innovators, even men of genius, would wish to be. With a wooden doll, a few yards of choice material and a pincushion, he improvises, composes and creates according to his own inspiration. But one must be a man in order to be able to dress women.'

And yet what do we know today of Worth's creations? Of the clothes he designed, transitory works of art which vanished as rapidly as the few hours during which they were worn? Neither the publication of Worth's dresses in the fashion papers nor photography enable us to form a valid judgment. All we can do is to assess his fame, not only from the applause of his contemporaries but also from the hostility he aroused.

There may have been good reason for his being portrayed so often as a parvenu, even by his admirers. His rise from humble, even poverty-stricken conditions, was far too rapid, and his taste, which displayed itself in his creations in an extraordinary assurance of style and refined elegance, often seems to have let him down in private life. His house—he later used the rooms at no. 7 rue de la Paix entirely for his business and moved with his family to a luxurious *hôtel particulier* in the Champs Elysées—is described as overloaded and pompous. His villa at Suresnes, on which he spent 800,000 francs for the building alone, seems to have been a typical example of a nouveau riche palace. He even went so far as to have huge strips of silken brocade from the dresses of his royal customers inserted in the upholstery of the chairs.

Worth's social rise aroused much hostility in certain conservative circles. It seemed hardly possible that a dressmaker and his wife should be invited to big receptions; that he was at home in salons frequented by the highest society of the age.

Today, in retrospect, we know that it was not the creator of individual toilettes who had risen to a higher social status, but the big businessman, the prototype of the modern Grand Couturier; the man with the foresight, the innovator who conceived the idea of industrializing fashion by linking up with a foreign clientele of merchants and clothing manufacturers.

### THE DICTATOR OF FASHION

Worth directed Fashion so absolutely that it became his private domain, that much which had already been in existence was ascribed to his inventive talent.

But even without Worth, Fashion would have followed its own mysterious laws of change. The wide crinolines had reached their maximum extent round the hips and so a new development was due. The hoops were lowered and made oval-shaped so that the skirt only stood out at the back. Hips grew smaller and the fullness of the skirt sank ever deeper. The logical development of a wealth of pleats behind was obviously the train.

Worth's genius lay in his mastery of the fashion and his intuition for the development of style. Even had he not invented it, he understood how to add details which belonged so justly to the style that the whole image of the fashion might have been his brain child. It is undoubtedly a fact that the train appears for the first time on one of his 1866 models.

The introduction of the tunic (about 1868) has also been ascribed to him. He gives certain details as to how this came about. One day on a walk he noticed a woman of the people crossing the road. She had hitched her skirt up backwards so as not to get it dirty and it fell down like a tunic over her petticoat. Worth found the swing of the folds very attractive and began to design models with the gathered skirt and the petticoat, which now became visible, carried out in two materials of contrasting colours.

In the same period there also appeared the *polonaise*, a kind of heavily padded tunic which also showed the petticoat. The similarity of the polonaise to the 'paniers' worn in the late Louis XVI period has made some philosophers of fashion wonder whether this analogy in fashion at the close of two dynastic epochs could be a pure coincidence.

During the 1870 war the House of Worth was closed and his workrooms transformed into a hospital. Worth had remained in Paris, but during the siege made his escape in a balloon. During the war it was considered chic to dress carelessly, but shortly after the armistice Worth returned. He created new materials, toilettes to fit the situation, ordered coloured satins which corresponded to the news. He christened a deep grey shade '*cendres de Paris*' and a flaming orange '*Bismarck enragé*'. During the presidency of MacMahon there were fêtes and receptions which almost competed in brilliance with those of the Second Empire. Worth could once more give free rein to his imagination.

From a combination of the tunic and the polonaise evolved the bustle: above the skirt, which fell sheer or in pleats, an overskirt was draped behind, padded out with material and lengthened below into a broad train. The bodice was cut like a man's waistcoat and its retreating line was stressed by a fichu ending at the waist.

Fashion decreed that the dress should daily become more complicated. The skirt was draped more and more and the trimmings elaborated. Twenty flounces at the seams were not unusual and there could never be enough ribbons, frills and velvet. The fringed, looped-back, velvet curtains at the windows and doors showed an undeniable kinship with the full gathered beribboned bustle and its train.

In those years, which changed all the natural lines and deformed the female body while articles of everyday use lost their functional shape, shapeless hairstyles with additions of false hair were the fashion once more as in the Baroque age. In 1875, in France alone, 320 lb. of false hair were made up, and in the same year 182,500 lb. of hair from the Near East, China and Spain were registered in the harbour of Marseilles. The old clothes trade suddenly became very lucrative, for the dealers collected false hair as well as old rags and remnants.

Towards the end of the 'seventies fashion took a strange turn. Suddenly there were no more bustles, and clothes became so tight that women could hardly walk. Slimness was the order of the day. The vanished bustle was now only suggested by a slight gathering of the dress at the back.

In 1880 a new fashion appeared, for which Worth was responsible—the crinolette. Under the skirt a short steel cage, open in the front, was worn close over the hips. Once more this provided great material for the humorists and caricaturists. *Punch* did not let the opportunity slip by. In the year 1881 it published a poem entitled *The Chant of the Crinolette*:

Who's responsible, I ask you, for this strange portentous birth
Of an ancient hideous fashion, and an echo answers 'Worth'. . . .

The crinolette disappeared. And then in the middle of the 'eighties, by another curious caprice of fashion, the bustle returned. And as though it wanted to be recompensed for its banishment, it was mightier and more accentuated than it had ever been, exceeding all proportion, more arched and protuberant with the help of ribbons, frills and sashes.

It was now known in international fashion jargon as the *cul de Paris*. Its mighty arch, the tightly laced bosom, seemed like a last appeal to femininity which the rapid advance of women's emancipation threatened to destroy. But when women took up sport, and in 1890 the discovery of the bicycle made the bustle impracticable for everyday use, it finally disappeared from fashion.

By that time old Worth had already retired from business and left it to his sons. If he had been superstitious in his youth he became far more so in his old age. He still believed in the fatal influence of the moon and certain lucky dates. When he saw the new moon through glass or through a cloud he was convinced that there would be business difficulties until the following new moon. If he saw the moon in its first quarter in a cloudless sky success was assured.

He had also determined his own private and personal Ides. Every year he was terrified of the 10th March.

And he died on the 10th March 1895.

# V

# GREAT CLIENTS OF THE HOUSE OF WORTH

## THE EMPRESS

THE year 1860 brought Worth his great triumph: the Empress Eugénie became his customer.

For the first time the Grand Couturier entered the Tuileries. He made his way up the stairs which led to the Empress's apartments, through the green salon where the Court officials were arrayed, through the pink salon where the visitors waited and the blue salon which was a riot of Sèvres vases, crystal chandeliers, sculptures and gilt. The lackeys suppressed a smile. M. Worth had not appeared in tails which were de rigueur for any visit in the Tuileries, even in the early morning. He wore, as though at home or at his business, the black velvet jacket and dark trousers, which in those days already had become almost the uniform of the head of a big house.

The last door opened and Worth entered the Empress's boudoir—her study, as she called it, because it was lined with books. Evil tongues maintained that she had not read a single one of them. The Empress seemed to like Worth's lack of convention and she greeted him with great cordiality. Worth knew that Eugénie had already exercised her influence on fashion. She had introduced the Spanish lace mantilla which was worn in her country and it was perhaps no coincidence

Charles Frederick Worth, founder of the first great fashion house

Caricature of the crinoline, invented by Worth

The Empress Eugénie, Worth's most important client

that the loud colours she affected had become the rage. The Empress was reactionary in politics but not in questions of fashion. Worth realized this as soon as he sought her favours for the Lyons silk industry. Shortly after her first order, he had brought her a dress of magnificent Lyons silk brocade with an enchanting ancient Chinese pattern of flowers.

At first she refused to put it on.

'But won't Your Majesty wear it for the sake of the Lyons manufacturers?' asked Worth.

'And why should I, pray?' She smiled ironically. 'Have they ever showed themselves particularly favourable to us?'

At this moment the Emperor entered the room. Worth was very eloquent and emphasized how important it was to encourage the Lyons looms and thereby to win the heart of the Lyonnais. The Emperor was susceptible to such arguments and the Empress had to comply whether she liked it or not.

She has been described as a 'fashion fiend' by all her contemporaries. Her fickleness, her constant desire for innovation and outward splendour, made her always wanting to be in the van of fashion.

Baron Hübner, the Austrian Ambassador in Paris at an earlier period, had known Eugénie before her marriage and we can accept this serious man's portrait of her as credible. At that time she was still Doña Eugenia de Montijo, Countess of Tebà. Hübner remarks in his memoirs: 'She is crazy for the new, the wondrous and the original. Both outwardly and inwardly she is constantly on the quest for movement.'

Louis Napoleon fell in love with this beautiful twenty-eight-year-old Spaniard and wrote her long letters while he was still Prince Regent. She replied with long, witty letters, but she had not written them herself. Merimée, the famous author of *Carmen*, an old friend of the Montijo household, had done her the favour of drafting them.

Eugénie's main preoccupation was to avoid committing faux pas. Shortly after her marriage to Napoleon III she took lessons with Rachel. The great actress had to show her how she had to behave as an Empress at audiences, in her carriage, in the ballroom, and how to wear elegant toilettes with natural *grandezza*.

There is no doubt that the false and artificial had a particular attraction for the Empress. Pauline Metternich saw her for the first time in Biarritz, and noticed to her astonishment that her eyebrows were dyed brown and the eyelids painted in with a black pencil. Eugénie was a blue-eyed natural Titian blonde, an inheritance from her Scottish mother. To quote Pauline Metternich once more, she insisted that fair eyebrows and lashes gave the face a stupid washed-out expression.

The witty and biting Maxime du Camp, who lashed the superficial and frivolous society life at Court in his memoirs, often had an opportunity of observing the Empress at close quarters: 'She had dyed hair, a painted face, mascaraed eyes and rouged lips. To have been really in her milieu the only thing that was lacking was the circus music. She dreamed of playing great parts, but she was never more than a "super" who has been given a role which she is incapable of playing.'

'Her greatest achievement,' he adds, 'is her collaboration with her couturier.'

From the outset clothes had been the focal point of her life. In the Tuileries life-sized dolls had been installed, on which the Empress's clothes were put when she did not wear them lest they receive the slightest crease. She held real conferences with dressmakers and milliners, modistes and jewellers. On her table lay a list of Marie Antoinette's dresses; it had been found in the archives and she considered it one of her greatest treasures.

The Emperor, who had tolerated the crinoline craze at Court

for several years, suddenly lost his patience. He looked about for some radical means of weaning the Empress and the other ladies from this absurd, exaggerated fashion and thought that at last he had found it. He commissioned two vaudeville poets, Dumanoir and Barrière, to write a farce which would kill the crinoline by ridicule.

After a few weeks the skit appeared at the Théâtre du Gymnase. It was called *Les toilettes tapageuses.* The Empress, the Court and *tout Paris* were present. It was a slight, innocuous farce. A wife tells her husband that she urgently needs a new dress, but it must be of Lyons silk, a yard of which costs no more than twenty francs. The rash creature gives his permission but learns to his horror that nearly twenty yards are necessary. In spite of this the wife has her own way and appears in her new dress with a gigantic crinoline supported on an iron frame. The astonished husband stammers: 'Look at my armoured wife!' The public roared with laughter. The lady also has a very low-cut corsage. The chorus sings:

> So much material used in the dress
> That nothing remains to cover the breast!

Finale:

> Crinolines with false petticoats
> With often naught beneath but dry sticks,
> Up men and wage a Holy War
> Against the world of crinolines.
> Change the fashion for the better
> And end the reign of crinolines.

It was of no avail. The world of the crinoline did not collapse. The laughter which this gigantic crinoline provoked made not the slightest impression on the Empress. On the day after the performance Pepa, the Empress's maid, paid a visit to the actress, asking her to lend the costume so that her mistress could take its measurements. Three days later Eugénie appeared in the same giant crinoline and naturally the other ladies of the Court followed suit.

That was in 1856. Only from the moment Worth became Eugénie's couturier can one sense from the fashion reports that the distinguished Englishman had succeeded in transforming the eccentric Spaniard into a smart Parisienne. Princess Metternich had been able to influence Worth with many of her extravagant ideas, which for all their audacity always remained in exquisite taste. But the Empress completely yielded to Worth's impeccable guidance—to her own advantage.

In the few autobiographical sketches which Worth left behind he tells of the first dress he designed for the Empress.

'The first of my creations for the Empress was a town dress of grey taffeta adorned with black velvet ribbons. Dress and jacket formed an ensemble, a novelty which later became the general vogue.

' "M. Worth," she said, "I do not want to appear in such a novel costume. I must wait until it has been worn by someone else. In my position I must not set the fashion: I must be content to follow it."

'And so it was the Comtesse de Pourtalès who took over this dress; not until six months later was I able to make its match for the Empress when she was in half mourning for the Duchess of Alba. At the same time I delivered her a house dress in black moire antique, in the "Princess cut" which means the skirt and the corsage in one piece. This was the first dress of its type that had ever been made.'

Photographs from now onward give evidence of the Empress's aristocratic, thoroughly Parisian toilettes. Even from the dry descriptions one can feel the attraction that the great couturier was able to give to her attire. In *La vie parisienne* of

1863 we read: 'Her dress was of regal beauty, grave yet at the same time gay, majestic and idyllic. The skirt was of violet taffeta cut on the cross with an open fan-shaped front, so that one caught a glimpse of a violet and white striped petticoat adorned with flounces.'

For the opening of the great Paris Exhibition in 1867, the last success of the Second Empire, Worth designed a sensational gown for the Empress, a triumph for his long efforts on behalf of the French silk and lace industries. The dress was carried out in specially woven Lyons silk, a lemon-yellow faille with charming Rococo flowers; it was trimmed with real *point d'Alençon* and lavender-coloured satin ribbons. And for the first time it had no crinoline.

The Empress never wore this superb dress. A few hours before the opening ceremony she learned the news that Maximilian, the Emperor of Mexico, had been taken prisoner and condemned to death—a tragic fate, for which she was not without blame. It was at her instigation that the French expedition to Mexico had been undertaken. Without her unhappy influence Maximilian, the brother of the Austrian Emperor, Franz Joseph, would probably never have been persuaded to accept the Mexican Imperial Crown and to embark upon this ill-starred adventure.

The Empress's appetite for dress remained as insatiable as ever. A year later, for the opening of the Suez Canal, she took with her no fewer than two hundred and fifty dresses.

Worth remained true to her until his death. She had once given him a violet from a posy, and each year until he died he sent her an enormous bunch of violets.

Many years after the Franco-Prussian War, old Worth visited the Empress in her villa in the South of France, where she lived in complete retirement.

Eugénie was very melancholy and all her memories seemed

to have died. The old man told her of the latest Paris fashions and of the latest creations of the House of Worth.

The old Empress roused herself from her lethargy and a gleam came into her eyes.

### THE ENGLISHMAN AND THE AUSTRIAN LADY

Princess Pauline von Metternich once encountered her couturier, Charles Frederick Worth, at a ball in 1867. With great emotion in his voice he said to her: 'To think that it was I who invented you.' And the Princess adds in her memoirs: 'Perhaps he was right.'

Complete self-assurance and pretty native wit can be read in this admission. She had not been tempted to say: 'It was I who invented you.' For after all, it was thanks to her that Worth had become Grand Couturier to the Empress.

Her memoirs are as spontaneous and witty as she was. With great frankness she portrays the people she met, whether great political personalities or insignificant rivals in the arena of feminine vanity. She mentions great events and fleeting gossip.

Pauline, the daughter of Count Sandor, who became almost a legend in Austria on account of his wild picaresque life, married Prince Richard von Metternich, the son of the famous statesman, whose name has gone down to posterity as a symbol of reaction and oppression.

Pauline and her husband, who was Austrian Ambassador in Paris from 1859, soon became the leading figures in society. A strange anomaly for the period, they were fond of each other and their private life afforded no material for the *chronique scandaleuse* at the Court and in the capital.

As a true Austrian she loved music and poetry. She adored Heine, introduced the Court to Wagner and Liszt, and was not averse at the same time to catchy tunes and popular ditties.

She used to sing Styrian songs to the Emperor, who was enchanted. At the Empress's informal evenings she sang the latest hits which Thérèse, the café-chantant star, had launched, such as *La femme à barbe* and many others.

Despite the gaiety she brought into society she was looked upon with a certain mistrust. She was a foreigner, and an Austrian into the bargain. France had not always had the happiest experiences of Austrian women. When she appeared one day, most unconventionally, in Thérèse's box it was enough for this *chanteuse* to be accused of being one of Bismarck's secret agents.

Pauline could give free rein to her exuberance at the fancy-dress balls. She set no store by coquetry and appeared at one of them as a woman of the people selling hot Vienna sausages.

She was not beautiful, in fact according to many of her contemporaries almost ugly. Intelligent and witty, Pauline herself stressed the fact: 'I am not ugly, I am far worse.'

Photography already existed at this time, and its veracity is stronger than the interpretations of portrait painters. The faded daguerrotypes show a broad mouth, a chin and nose that are slightly too short and a thin face with big, intelligent eyes.

'I was so thin that I could have made a matchstick jealous,' she says. But this frail slimness was part of her chic, of her aristocratic manner of wearing her clothes. Count de Maugny, in his *Souvenirs du Second Empire* says of her: 'A great lady to her fingertips, with breeding and a natural distinction.'

Pauline Metternich relates that one day—it was in 1860—she was sitting in her salon, deep in a book, when her maid appeared with an album.

'A young woman begs Your Highness to glance at the drawings of the dresses her husband has designed. He would like to make a dress for you, and you yourself shall name the price.'

'What is his name?'

'He is an Englishman called Worth.'

'What, an Englishman who presumes to dress Parisiennes?'

The Princess was about to return the album, but cast a glance at the drawings, and with her flair for everything artistic was soon enchanted. She received Mme Worth, who told her that her husband had been employed by Gagelin and had now started up on his own in the rue de la Paix.

And now the Princess wanted not one dress but two, one for morning and one for evening wear, and for both of them she would pay no more than six hundred francs. Mme Worth was overjoyed, for the evening dress was to be worn at the next Tuileries ball.

The two chefs-d'œuvre were delivered to Pauline the same week. 'Both of them were perfect in every respect, and I sent my congratulations to the artist whom I had not yet met personally, for the fittings had taken place at my house. I can truthfully say that I had never seen more beautiful or better made dresses in my life.'

The evening gown was of white, silver-threaded tulle, a completely new material, with bunches of pink cowslips half hidden in tufts of grass. At the waist was a broad white satin sash. Pauline Metternich adorned this dress with a wealth of diamonds for the evening, 'and Worth had his first success'.

The Empress's sharp eye immediately spotted the genius of this toilette and asked who had made such a wonderful dress. 'An Englishman, Madame. A new star who has arisen in the fashion firmament.' 'Such a star must have satellites,' said the Empress. 'Tell him to come and see me at ten o'clock tomorrow morning.'

'Worth was made,' writes Pauline Metternich, 'and I was lost, for my dresses in future no longer cost three hundred francs: Worth was fantastically expensive, more expensive than any other couturier.' This was the start of their collaboration. They thought out new fashions, launched bold discoveries they had worked out together, as Rose Bertin had once done with Marie Antoinette. The Princess wore these fashionable innovations at Longchamps and other women followed suit.

But her sharp tongue did not spare the indispensable couturier. She ridiculed his wife for playing the great lady, and laughed at Worth's servants who were dressed in knee breeches and silk stockings. And his house!

'I confess, I would rather live in a whitewashed room,' she writes, 'than in the many salons of which poor Worth is so proud, and which are a riot of gold, satin, plush, embroideries, gilded furniture and bric-à-brac.' She goes on to relate that he was inordinately proud of a silver bath-tub and perhaps most of all of the little retreat where a small fountain of Eau de Cologne constantly played.

Pauline was assuredly as mad on fashion as the Empress, but with far more charm and a more subtle intelligence. At Court she was nicknamed 'Madame Chiffon' and everything she wore was copied. There is hardly a journal between 1860 and 1870 which does not describe one of her dresses—at the races, at a Tuileries ball or on a summer holiday at Trouville.

The wide crinolines demanded small heads, and tiny hats known as *bibis* or *cabriolets* were worn. Not too much of the hair was to be shown: it was not fashionable, and so it was hidden by a so-called *bavolet*, a ruche that welled backwards and sideways out of the hat. Worth had once persuaded his wife to go to the races without the inevitable *bavolet*. The public forgot to look at the horses, and could not take their eyes off Mme Worth and her sensational hat!

But this was not enough to enforce the fashion: it had to be adopted by Princess Metternich. When she passed the couturier's wife she cried: 'Mme Worth, what is that delicious hat you're wearing?' Worth triumphantly tells us that from that day onward *bavolets* disappeared from fashion.

When creating his ball dresses it was Worth's custom to make last-minute retouches like an artist who adds some final strokes of his brush when finishing a picture.

Princess Metternich with some other ladies once arrived for one of these dress-rehearsals just before a great ball. Worth was unwell. Everything was in a panic. What was to be done? At last the Princess invaded his private apartment. Worth was lying on a chaise-longue with cold water compresses on his forehead and eyes. She entreated him for so long that he finally allowed the other customers to come in. He took one look at them and groaned: 'Appalling, ridiculous, terrible!' Not one of the dresses satisfied him and all the ladies were in despair.

'I suddenly had a splendid idea,' writes the Princess. ' "M. Worth," I cried, "this proves that you have had your day." '

At this he sprang up, tore off his compresses, and began to put matters right. A train was fastened differently, the position of a ribbon changed, and in an hour everything was in order.

That her greatest enemy, Countess Castiglione, was also a client of Worth's could not make her go elsewhere. She showed a certain courage, however, when she did not invite this official favourite of the Emperor to her receptions at the Austrian Embassy.

Photographs bear witness to the classical beauty of this Florentine who was known in Italy as *la contessa divina.* Cavour sent the Castiglione to the French Court to win the Emperor as an ally for his anti-Austrian plans. 'You must succeed,' he said. 'Use all the means you have at your disposal.'

Her principal weapon was her dazzling beauty, which the Emperor found irresistible. It was generally accepted that she had encouraged him in his campaign against Austria. In any case the secret treaty with Cavour was signed. The Austrian armies were defeated at Magenta and Solferino, and a year later (1860) Italy ceded Nice and Savoy to France.

Pauline saw the Countess for the first time at a Tuileries ball. 'I was spellbound by her beauty,' she admits in her memoirs. At a fancy-dress ball the Countess Castiglione appeared in another of Worth's masterpieces. Flaubert's *Salammbo* had just been published. The Countess had stuck to Flaubert's description of the young priestess. She wore a cloak of black velvet over a pink tricot; the cloak was open to the waist and left her beautiful legs free. This dress caused far more sensation in Parisian society than Flaubert's novel.

'She had the figure of a nymph,' writes the Princess. 'Neck, shoulders, arms and hands seemed to be of pink marble. Her features were regular, her eyes of green velvet, her teeth like pearls . . . in short a Venus descended from Olympus.' But Pauline adds that she had no character and was so conscious of her beauty that when you had feasted your eyes long enough she got on your nerves. So studied was every movement 'that you were disgusted by her affectation'. Pauline writes quite frankly: 'She was popular with no one except the Emperor.'

The whole splendour of the Court fêtes during the Second Empire comes to life in Pauline's souvenirs. At a ball given at the Austrian Embassy Johann Strauss conducted the orchestra. One imagines a whirl of crinolines, but no; the princess notes that he conducted the quadrilles so slowly that the dancers had to keep asking him to speed up the tempo.

The luxury in dress of Worth's customers knew no bounds when they were invited for a few days to the Château de Compiègne, the autumn residence of the royal couple. The guests went by rail. To find seats for the ladies in their wide crinolines was quite a problem. An extra truck was attached to the train for their wardrobes, which were packed in enormous wooden boxes. The princess relates that she once took eighteen of these boxes with her and that many of the ladies took as many as twenty-four.

Pauline's dependence upon Worth was well known at Court. One day she appeared very late for lunch at the Tuileries. All the guests were at table when she came in very languidly and said: 'It's not my fault, you must blame Worth. He did not deliver my dress on time.' The Emperor and his wife laughed heartily.

She was Worth's ally in the campaign against the crinoline. Her slender waist and small hips were advantages which were lost in a crinoline. She conspired with her couturier to end the reign of women with voluptuous curves.

1870–71, the Franco-Prussian War. . . . The Empress went, and Princess Metternich remained. Thiers became President of the Third Republic.

Pauline paid an official visit to the President's wife. The aristocrat made fun of the dowdy middle-class woman. 'The cut of her dress and the shape of her hat seemed to be a protest against what the President's wife described as the corruption of the Empire.'

Under MacMahon, who became President in 1873, a rich pleasure-loving society came into being again and the receptions at the Elysée were hardly less brilliant and elegant than they had been at the Tuileries.

Princess Metternich had been the first to wear Worth's bustle at the races. Now she was also the first to adopt his bold creation—the ankle-length skirt.

And why did all the smart Parisiennes suddenly carry bright coloured sunshades? One day, some years after the war, Pauline Metternich visited Worth who asked her if she were going on the following day to the Grand Prix at Longchamps. 'No,' the Princess replied. 'I haven't a suitable dress and I can't show myself on a bright spring day in a black one.'

'Wait,' said Worth, 'I've an idea. A red sunshade. The very thing for a black dress.'

It was a sensation. The Princess appeared with a poppy-red sunshade at the races. Within twenty-four hours a few red sunshades were to be seen here and there on the promenades. At the next race-meeting graceful sunshades in all colours swayed above the ladies' heads.

## QUEENS, EMPRESSES AND PRINCESSES

With great pride Jean Philippe Worth enumerates nine queens among the customers of his house. As far as court robes were concerned the Russian princesses were undoubtedly the most exacting. The etiquette at the Tsar's Court was so rigid that each dress had to be passed by a master of ceremonies appointed for that purpose. At court functions, even the petticoats had to be costly; diamonds or precious stones were de rigueur instead of buttons.

The length of the train was also stipulated. The most costly and richest in trimmings that had ever been ordered at Worth's was the train for the wife of the Russian Ambassador in Berlin. This man had a passion for luxury and pomp and any dress his wife wore had to be lavishly adorned with precious stones and heavy embroideries. The train which Worth finally made for a court reception was in fact so heavy that the Ambassador's wife, when she left her carriage and tried to enter the vestibule of the Palace, stood there fixed to the ground and quite unable to move a step. Finally, the unfortunate woman had to be taken back to her carriage and driven home.

The Grand Duchess Marie, sister of Tsar Alexander II, often visited Worth's establishment in the rue de la Paix. She was steeped in the strange atmosphere of Russian ceremonial and always accompanied by six ladies-in-waiting. Worth made a suggestion, giving her a long explanation of design and cut. The Grand Duchess nodded majestically and replied: 'I should like it in white.' The six ladies-in-waiting also nodded and ordered the same model, each one in a different colour.

For the ball which took place each year in the palace of Princess Sagan, Worth had to use all his imaginative resources. We can read on an invitation to an Animal Kingdom ball: 'You are invited, for the 2nd June, to choose a costume from Buffon' (the famous *Histoire naturelle des bêtes*).

It is almost impossible today to conceive the fantastic realism of these fancy-dress balls. La Fontaine's fables came to life. Hardly had the orchestra struck its first note than a hive opened and women, dressed as bees in gold lamé, swarmed out. Then came the supper, served by fifty lackeys. An ostrich would dine with a lioness, a lobster with a cat and a leopard with a swallow.

Baroness Rothschild, one of Worth's customers, appeared as a tigress in a real tiger's skin with black claws on her gloves and Princess Sagan in a peacock costume, made by Worth. This famous dress was of white velvet with a tulle wrap decorated with pearls and silver peacock's feathers falling from the shoulders in a train, which on closer inspection turned out to be a folded peacock's tail.

Another great customer was Princesse Mathilde, who played an important role in society. Her salon was a centre of attraction, thanks to her intellectual independence, frankness and originality. Not only were the great literary figures of France her constant guests—Saint-Beuve, Renan, Alexandre Dumas, Flaubert and Merimée, but the crowned heads of Europe, the Queen of Holland, Victor Emmanuel and the ex-King of Bavaria Ludwig never failed to visit her when they were in Paris.

And even Worth, the self-assured M. Worth, lost his arrogance when he came to discuss clothes with her and was delighted when she visited him in his villa at Suresnes.

Jean Philippe relates that she looked superb in low-cut dresses, and displayed her charms till the end of her days—a bosom and shoulders which became famous in literature. Sainte-Beuve describes them as being beautifully smooth and white, like marble. Photographs and even the most flattering portraits which artists painted of her show her even when she was young as a stout, comfortable, far too plump lady with a precociously fat neck but a fresh healthy face and lively intelligent eyes.

As a girl Princesse Mathilde had been in love with her cousin Louis Napoleon. A marriage was planned but it came to nothing. Later, the future Napoleon III met Eugénie de Montijo in her salon. Had it been within her power the princess would have hindered this marriage, which she quite openly referred to as a *mésalliance*. She was rude to Eugénie and a reconciliation only took place after the marriage, but purely for the sake of appearances. Mathilde remained bitter and piqued; so much so that later she encouraged the Emperor's liaison with the beautiful Castiglione in order to infuriate Eugénie.

Throughout her whole life she considered herself fortunate and never forgot the fact that she was a niece of Napoleon I. Her adoration of her great uncle was positively idolatrous. When Marie Louise proved unfaithful to him, Princess Mathilde began to hate all Austrian women. Hence her hostility against Princess Metternich, whom she called 'a little histrionic monkey with her thirty-six flounces and her forty trunks'. Mathilde could not be too scathing about her extravagance in dress. It was exceedingly awkward that they both went to the same couturier.

At a performance of Sardou's *Madame Sans Gêne* she left her box during the scene where Napoleon's sisters are quarrelling—she had heard them often enough in real life—banged the door and cried: 'I refuse to listen any more to the way they're talking about my family.'

But despite her pointed remarks about the fashion-loving women of the Court, she herself enjoyed dressing well and elegantly. Hers was a personal note of costly simplicity. 'The fashion does not concern me,' she used to say. 'It is a kind of slavery for people who have no personality.' Worth therefore designed dresses for her which hardly differed from each other and corresponded to the prevailing fashion only in a vague and general way.

The colours of materials and trimmings she chose herself. Since she painted and was quite a talented water-colourist, she liked to have the same colours in her toilettes as she used on her canvasses. Pauline Metternich did not miss the opportunity of ridiculing her in her memoirs: 'Princesse Mathilde always dresses in her water-colours.'

As an old lady, Mathilde lived so much in her brilliant past that she did not bother to follow the changes of fashion at all. In his novel *A l'ombre des jeunes filles en fleurs*, Marcel Proust describes meeting her in the Bois de Boulogne.

'An elderly but still attractive woman cloaked in a dark mantle and capped with a little bonnet tied beneath her chin with a pair of ribbons.' Swann draws Proust aside while Mme Swann talks to the Princess. 'That is the Princess Mathilde,' he told me, 'you know whom I mean, the friend of Flaubert, Sainte-Beuve, Dumas. Think of it, she's the niece of Napoleon I. She had offers of marriage from Napoleon III and the Emperor of Russia. Isn't that interesting?'

'She was,' Proust goes on, 'clothed in a dress so typically Second Empire that, although the Princess no doubt wore it simply and solely, from attachment to the fashions she had

Eleanora Duse, who was dressed by the younger Worth

Princess Metternich, one of the elder Worth's clients

Midinettes in the rue de la Paix. The establishment with flowerboxes is that of Worth; the one with

Fashions at the Longchamps races in 1908

loved in her youth—she seemed to have deliberately planned to avoid the slightest inaccuracy, in order to satisfy those who looked to her to evoke another age.'

The Queen of England seemingly remained true to her own country and only very occasionally ordered dresses in Paris. Nevertheless, Queen Victoria wore Worth models. The Worths made them according to her measurements and sold them to the English Court dressmakers. And they were delighted to see the Queen in their models, which she wore, it is said, quite unaware of their origin. Particularly after the death of the Prince Consort the Queen preferred to dress extremely severely and simply. Her dressmakers, however, have revealed that she was extraordinarily exacting and never wore the same dress twice. Since the Queen was particularly careful of her reputation, the clothes had to resemble each other so closely that the uninitiated believed she wore the same dress year in year out. Only her widow's bonnet, which she never laid aside even when she wore the crown, remained the same.

With the old Empress Augusta, the wife of Wilhelm I of Germany, the same comedy took place as with Queen Victoria: Worth sold certain toilettes intended for her to the Berlin dressmakers, who passed them on to the Empress. But, unlike Queen Victoria, she only liked magnificent and very richly decorated dresses.

The Austrian Empress Elisabeth ordered two or three dresses a year from Worth, but never actually visited Paris. She was beautiful and elegant, always dressed in the latest fashion, yet her dresses had to be quite individual and simple. She chose only colours which reflected her dreamy romantic personality—white, pearl grey or very pale lilac.

Queen Margaret of Italy once received a dress from Worth which she was to wear on the occasion of her visit to Russia. The couturier, however, before despatching it forgot to remove a paper label on which was written in huge letters 'Worth, 7 *rue de la Paix*, blue satin embroidered with silver and pearls, for Her Majesty the Queen of Italy.' When she entered the throne room the Emperor Alexander asked her: 'What is that? Are you a walking advertisement for the House of Worth?' Margaret noticed the strip of paper and laughed with the rest of the company until she cried.

It was never very easy to deal with royal clients from far-off lands. Once a very funny misunderstanding happened. The Empress Eugénie told Worth that she wanted to send a present to the Queen of Madagascar and had decided to send two dresses in the latest European fashion. Worth produced two wonderful creations, one of silver-embroidered red velvet, the other of green velvet with white and gold beads. He naturally added the indispensable steel-framed crinolines in colours matching the dresses.

When the dusky Queen received the dresses she immediately sent for the French Ambassador to thank him for the costly gifts. He found the Queen bare-footed, standing under a tree, in the magnificent red velvet dress, whose hem lay in a wide circle round her on the ground. Above her in the tree, as a canopy, hung the red cashmere crinoline.

### BOURGEOIS CUSTOMERS

Money and titles were on an equal footing in the Second Empire. The rich commoner was an aristocrat, particularly if his wife was rich enough to be dressed by Worth. Artists and literary men without titles haunted the salons of great aristocratic ladies, who were only too proud to have them as guests. The wife of a novelist knew her debt to society—just as the Empress or Princess Metternich she went naturally to the leading couturier.

To Señora Errazu, a Mexican, Worth sent new dresses three times a week for her visits to the theatre, and her invitations to parties and balls. Until one day she came to him and said: 'M. Worth, I have made a vow before Our Lady of Carmel never to wear silver again, and in future only to wear brown wool.' The Señora carried out her plan, which sorely taxed Worth's imagination. Ball dresses, afternoon gowns and dinner toilettes were all carried out in brown woollen materials, that often had to be specially woven in Lyons. But the vow was never broken.

One comes across a host of references to meetings with the famous couturier in the memoirs of middle-class women. . . . There is for example Mme Octave Feuillet, the wife of the famous novelist and popular playwright. In her memoirs she describes how she became his client.

It was in the year 1860, when she was to be received at Court for the first time. She went to a very well-known dressmaker in the smart Faubourg Saint-Germain and ordered a dress, which was delivered at eleven o'clock on the evening before the great event. It was a great disappointment. It looked like a widow's weeds and she herself in it 'like a spindle bound up with ribbons'. What was to be done?

Very early next morning, as the sun broke through the morning mist and the greengrocers were bringing their dew-covered wares to Paris, she drove in a fiacre to the rue de la Paix.

The concierge opened the door. 'M. Worth, please.' 'He lives on the first floor.' Mme Feuillet went upstairs, rang the bell and a sleepy nursemaid with a baby in her arms opened the door. 'M. Worth, please.' 'He's still in bed.'

She sent her visiting card in and Worth appeared in his dressing-gown. He showed her into his wife's bedroom, insisting that she had to be present when any new dresses were ordered.

Mme Worth lay in her four-poster bed 'in a sea of lace and charming ribbons. I thought I was attending the Queen's levée.' Mme Feuillet implored Worth to make her a dress for that evening.

The couturier, leaning against one of the bedposts, closed his eyes like a poet in search of inspiration. 'A dress of lilac silk,' he whispered, 'swathed over and over with clouds of tulle, in which nestle clusters of lilies of the valley. Then a white tulle veil, a sash with fluttering ends like the ribbons of cupids on Venus's chariot.'

Mme Feuillet remained the whole day at Worth's. She had grown up far from the fashionable bustle of Paris and was intimidated and impressed beyond measure by her surroundings. During a moment's relaxation she wrote to her old nurse in Saint-Lô, her home town. 'Just fancy, I've been up since four o'clock this morning merely to get myself a dress. I am writing to you from the couturier's house, for it is a man and not a woman who today makes dresses for all the fashionable ladies. . . . The dress is like a bouquet of flowers; it has a train which I can see falling behind me and it makes a delicious frou-frou. God grant that when I curtsy before the Emperor I shall not tread on this train! This M. Worth is a very amiable man, and he assures me that I have "chic", a word you have probably never heard, and which means that I have a certain personal elegance.'

The chandeliers were lit in Mme Worth's bedroom and two pretty women fitters appeared. Worth came in, and after rearranging a bow, which was not graceful enough, declared that he was satisfied.

Mme Octave Feuillet arrived at the Tuileries as night fell. The Empress was wearing a white tulle dress trimmed with black velvet bows, in each of which was a cluster of real diamonds. She stopped in front of Mme Feuillet and said:

'Will you please tell me the name of your dressmaker, Madame?'

'He is a man, Your Highness, an Englishman named Worth. . . .'

## THE DEMI-MONDE

In a French nineteenth-century thesis, an analysis of the economics of the tailoring trade, the feminine connection is divided into two categories: society ladies, to whom the couturier must give long credit—which often entails a risk—and the ladies of the demi-monde, from whom, taking no chances, he asks an important payment in advance.

How did this new split into the world and the half-world come about in the middle 'fifties?

Alexandre Dumas fils's play *Le Demi Monde* was performed in 1855 at the Théâtre du Gymnase. Three years earlier, his *La dame aux camélias* had aroused great interest. A new world, the world of 'fallen women' had been introduced into literature; Dumas had given it a name—the half-world.

In this play two young men discuss the 'shipwrecked' women. Raymond asks: 'Whence comes this strange world?' And Olivier replies: 'It is a phenomenon of our age. Adultery as we understand it did not exist before our time.'

And indeed, *la grande cocotte* was a phenomenon of the bourgeois age. Certain writers were greatly mistaken when they maintained that the Second Empire with its cocottes and cocodettes was an immoral one. On the contrary it was extremely moral and puritanical.

Even *La dame aux camélias* had to pay very dearly for loving a young bourgeois. The great role in society played by a Madame Tallien in the frivolous Directoire would have been impossible fifty years later.

It was puritanism, too, which decreed that no fallen girl, even from a respectable home, could contract a bourgeois marriage. Puritanism and prejudice made it impossible for such a girl to have a profession which would have made her acceptable in society. If she was beautiful and attractive, well-mannered and cultured, she had only one chance in life —to become a *grande cocotte*.

The well-respected man of the world lived in two distinct spheres of life: among his peers and among the demi-mondaines. In both of these worlds he had to make his position felt and give some display of his fortune. Thus his life in the demi-monde was certainly no hole-and-corner affair. His position and repute were just as evident if he went into society accompanied by his wife bedecked with jewellery and wearing the latest dresses as it was when it was common knowledge that he kept a mistress who appeared in a smart carriage with liveried servants, lived in a smart residential quarter and entertained writers and artists.

With this separation the outward and visible virtue of the society ladies increased and in virtue they found their raison d'être. Virtue expressed itself in fashion, and the very fashion was virtuous. The dress was high-necked, the lady with her hooped skirt, puffed sleeves and all-enveloping mantilla was unapproachable.

The woman of the world was *distinguée*. The cocotte followed suit, affecting great simplicity in her toilette. A famous demi-mondaine of the Second Empire once said: 'Society ladies go to this or that couturier to be dressed like cocottes: I go to Worth's to be dressed like a lady.'

The most distinguished of all couturiers was greatly in demand by all the ladies of easy virtue. All of them wanted dresses to equal those worn by 'La Metternich' or other fashionable ladies. Worth relates that they were very pleasant customers, for they never bothered about the price and nothing was too expensive for them.

If the demi-mondaines copied the distinguished behaviour of the society ladies, the latter did their best to fight these dangerous competitors with their own weapons. For these ladies, who liked playing the role of being more frivolous and coquettish than was the custom in respectable salons, the word cocodette was coined. These cocodettes were to be found at Court rather than in bourgeois society, and there were times —towards the end of the Second Empire—in which they set the tone, and many aristocrats like the Comtesse de Pourtalès, the Princess Sagan, the Marquise de Gallifet and even Pauline Metternich called themselves cocodettes.

That many ladies wanted to rival the demi-mondaines caused a great deal of disapproval. At a session of the Senate in 1865, the attorney-general thundered against women's mad extravagance in dress and against the demi-mondaines, who were aped by the ladies of society. As a newspaper put it: 'Unfortunate Paris. Once upon a time you were the lamp that illumined the world, but now you are only the little candle of the half-world.'

Like the ladies of society, the demi-mondaines appeared at Longchamps in their latest creations. But however distinguished they might look, they were never allowed to enter the grandstand. If a gentleman escorted one to the *tribunes* he risked being black-balled at his club. Thus one saw the cocottes in their magnificent flower-laden carriages on the other side of the course.

To offset this their return from the races was a triumphal procession. Reclining languidly against the cushions of their four-in-hands, with two liveried lackeys on the box, they drove from Longchamps to the Place de la Concorde and then back to the lake in the Bois de Boulogne until night fell. The whole of Paris turned out to admire these fabulously beautiful women.

Today it seems quite incredible how strongly the gap between society and the half-world was emphasized at the races, and how easy it was for a woman, if she had no legitimate husband to give her his name and reputation, to be numbered among the demi-mondaines.

There was for example Mme Musard, one of Worth's richest clients. Every Friday she sent him her emeralds and rubies to be used for trimmings for her new dresses. She was the daughter-in-law of Musard, who had risen to fame as organizer of the Parisian balls. Her incredible wealth came from a piece of land in America, a present from the King of the Netherlands, on which oil had been found. She appeared at the races in her white satin-upholstered carriage, drawn by the most magnificent thoroughbreds. Her lackeys wore pale-green liveries and powdered wigs.

But her princely retinue did not help her. She had a 'past' and could not show herself on the stands. On one occasion she caused a great scandal by dressing as a man and driving her own carriage to Worth's. The press of people was so great in the rue de la Paix that the traffic was brought to a standstill.

Cora Pearl, too, one of the most famous of the Parisian cocottes, caused immense excitement when she visited Worth. The upholstery of her carriage was yellow satin and her lackey's liveries were yellow, to match her golden hair.

Whether the unbelievable amount of clothes that Cora Pearl ordered from Worth were paid for is a matter of conjecture. One thing is certain: her lingerie maker sued her for a sum of nearly ten thousand francs.

Cora Pearl suffered the same fate as so many of these women. Hardly had her youth and beauty passed than she became poor and had to sell her furniture and works of art.

One of the most celebrated demi-mondaines who went to Worth was La Paiva. Her life reads like a novel; the stories about her were legion.

Her real name was Thérèse Lachmann, and she was the daughter of a poor weaver and had grown up in a Moscow slum. At the age of eighteen she married a French tailor. But she yearned for wealth and adventure. Conscious of her blonde beauty she left her husband and child and went to Paris, where she led the life of a pauper in the Russo-Polish quarter.

Henri Herz, the celebrated pianist and piano manufacturer, rescued her from poverty. They fell in love and he introduced her everywhere as his wife. Under Herz's tuition she became a good pianist. They lived in lavish style and soon famous writers, like Théophile Gautier, and above all a number of great musicians frequented their salon. Here Hans von Bülow once played Bach, and Wagner discussed his plans for *Lohengrin.*

Herz was eager to introduce her to the royal couple in the Tuileries. She put on her parade toilette and her finest jewels.

In the lists of the Tuileries, however, they figured as a *faux ménage* and they were not admitted.

Herz went on a tour abroad. Did he think of abandoning Thérèse? In the meantime his family learned that she had been living with him in sin and, in his absence, was leading a highly irresponsible life. She already had a bad reputation so they ordered her to leave the house. Once more Thérèse was faced with poverty. She went to her dressmaker Mme Camille—Worth had not yet set up his own establishment. She made her the most magnificent wardrobe on credit. Thérèse travelled to London, not without previously having begged Théophile Gautier for a phial of chloroform in case her journey proved a failure.

But it was successful. Thérèse returned to Paris wealthy and elegant. Henceforth this beautiful, intelligent, cultured woman became a focal point of Parisian life. Her husband, the little French tailor, died and she married a frivolous, passionate Portuguese who gambled on the Stock Exchange, but had a magnificently sonorous name: Marquese Albo-Francesco Aranjo de Païva. Two months later he vanished from her life, but she kept his name. Until the end of her days she was called La Païva.

She became the greatest courtesan of the Second Empire. Her box at the Opera was just opposite the Imperial Box, which amused the Emperor but infuriated the Empress. Her carriages and liveried servants were the height of elegance. As to her toilettes—Worth now became her couturier and excelled himself in dressing this beautiful woman. It did not disturb him in the least that his bills became astronomical: these were investments.

Her distinguished behaviour, culture and originality allowed her to hope for the arrival of a Prince Charming. He appeared in the guise of the fabulously wealthy Count Guido Henckel von Donnersmark.

The Count built her the palace in the Champs Elysées, bought her a castle in the country and enabled her to live the life of a queen. The house in the Champs Elysées still stands today, swamped by modern buildings. In a guide-book to Paris, published in 1897, it figures as one of the sights of the city.

The staircase was of onyx, but its false proportions disturbed La Païva's artistic friends even then. The high-spot of the house was the bathroom—Théophile Gautier calls it worthy of a Queen from the Arabian Nights.

When Worth came to see her she told him, as she showed him round, that her hunger for luxury was the effect of the misery of her childhood.

The War broke out. In 1871 Count Henckel was appointed Governor of Metz by Bismarck. In the same year Henckel and La Païva were married, since her union with the Portuguese Marquis had been annulled.

The couple returned to Paris and once more her salon was the centre of art and literature. Thérèse was invited to supper by the President and the great Gambetta dined with her every Friday evening.

La Païva, the great courtesan, had won her place in society. Until the outbreak of the First World War the ladies of the demi-monde played a leading part in society. With the complete social upheaval after the war they gradually disappeared. They had been the exotic blossoms of a luxury-loving, and at the same time puritanical, age: the society which conceived, envied and ostracized them, shrouded them in a fragrant perfume of romantic mystery. Their ostentatious drives to the races, their appearance at premières or at the Opera, and their presence in the most fashionable summer resorts inspired many of the great couturiers to produce their most remarkable creations.

# VI

# HAUTE COUTURE ON THE STAGE

## STAGE AND FASHION

THE actress and her couturier: fifty years ago they worked in close co-operation; they sat together for hours on end poring over sketches, discussing, discarding and creating.

In the third quarter of the nineteenth century, and until the outbreak of the First World War, the French theatre was the mirror of society. The drawing-room comedy, which gave the leading lady every possibility of displaying her elegance, dominated the repertoire. The romantic play, with its exaggerated sentimentality, was finished and vaudeville flooded the stage. When we read the plays which at that time were colossal successes, it is almost impossible in our problem-fraught age to see how the public could have adored these shallow comedies or insipid moralizing plays.

With the drawing-room play, contemporary dress also came to the foreground. And since the ever more uniform male costume could offer no fashionable sensations, interest was concentrated on the women's dresses. In fact so great was the fashion craze among actresses that they appeared, even in historical tragedies, in dresses of the latest style. In the Second Empire it was not unusual for the partner of a Roman, clad in tunic and toga, to enter in a crinoline with a low-cut corsage and high-heeled shoes, while the peasant girls and shepherdesses appeared in velvet, silk and lace.

The smaller parts were usually played by women who were not professional actresses—for them the stage was purely an opportunity for displaying their charms. Heine relates that these *femmes entretenues* were often unsalaried and even paid the director for the right to appear on stage—'it is difficult to tell where the actress and the courtesan change roles, where comedy ends and nature in the raw begins once more, where the six-footed Alexandrine changes into four-footed lechery'.

In Paris, more than ever the world centre of fashion, people went to the theatre not only to see light comedies and stories of adultery; they also wanted to learn what was the latest fashion, what new toilette the leading lady and her couturier would launch. After each première, papers and magazines published two criticisms—one from the literary critic and one from the fashion reporter.

One of the most famous fashion reporters, the Vicomtesse de Renneville, in the *Gazette rose* of 1882, stresses the importance of fashion on the stage: 'The success of plays is certainly not purely literary. In most cases the theatre can be certain of big crowds when sumptuous dresses can be seen on the stage. One has only to consider how many people are employed in the dressmaking trade alone. Hardly has the rumour gone round that in a certain play many new toilettes will be shown, than a considerable part of the population is in a frenzy of excitement—dressmakers, modistes, makers of lingerie and designers.'

When French actresses were invited to play abroad, they were often used by the fashion houses for advertizing purposes. In the cities where they appeared they organized special exhibitions of the stage costumes so that the public could see these masterpieces of French tailoring art at close quarters.

In the last quarter of the nineteenth century stage costume became a veritable cult. There were actresses of whom it was said: 'If they are entrusted with Racine or Corneille they present Paquin or Doucet.'

While criticism continued to be levelled at the luxury of the dresses on the stage, the creation of stage costume was the best advertisement for the couturiers. They continued to send their mannequins to the races, but here only the expert eye knew how to differentiate between the creations of the great fashion houses. They passed and received only a fleeting glance. It was quite different in the theatre. The name of the couturier stood in black and white on the programme. And on the stage were the beautiful dresses, framed by a décor expressly designed to suit their splendour—the pastel-coloured boudoir to the fragile muslin negligee, the elegantly furnished salon to the evening gowns, the gardens with their flowering shrubs to the dainty summer dresses. Here the audience could look, and, if they missed the dialogue, what did it matter so long as they could take in all the details of the dresses, get some inspiration from them, or even dare to order these models from the same couturier?

For the creative couturiers, such as Jean Philippe Worth, Redfern and Doucet, co-operation with the actresses and the dramatists meant far more than mere advertising. Saturating themselves in the role and in the atmosphere of the play, they ranked themselves as artists with the man who designed the sets and the director who produced the play. Sarah Bernhardt, who designed her own stage costumes, must be numbered among these.

These names belong to the history of the theatre, just as they belong to the history of Haute Couture. For more than half a century the stage was for high society what modern Haute Couture collections are today. During this period the history of stage costume is one with the history of fashion and of the great couturiers.

## REDFERN

Redfern was another Englishman who played a great part in Parisian Haute Couture. His real name was Charles Poynter, and he came to Paris as the representative of the London House of Redfern. This British fashion house had been founded in 1842 by John Redfern, who for years had been dressmaker to the aristocracy and included Queen Victoria among his regular patrons. No less talented and capable was young Poynter, whom he sent to Paris in 1881. He made his name there. Charles Poynter Redfern founded a branch in the rue de Rivoli with such success that ten years later he was employing a staff of five hundred.

It was soon considered chic to be dressed *à l'Anglaise* by Redfern. It was part of Redfern's chic to affect a strong English accent and to behave in as English a manner as possible. Apart from the accent, he had a lot in common with Charles Frederick Worth, combining British distinction and a Parisian refinement of taste in his creations. 'As cool as an Englishman and capable of a Frenchman's enthusiasm,' is the judgment of a contemporary. His hair cut *à la brosse* and sporting a small fair twirled moustache, he was to be seen in his smart fitting-room in a high-chair wearing an Arab burnous. 'Like a general in mufti', he had the models paraded before him, and decreed alterations with the aid of a long conductor's baton.

Redfern was the first to introduce the tailormade, the English lady's suit of dark blue woollen material, which was an unqualified success for several decades. And, perhaps it was because he endeavoured to bestow a line of clanic distinction to his customers' clothes, that he had a passion for creating dresses for the stage; it gave him an outlet for his imagination.

Redfern's historical stage costumes conformed to the taste

of the day. The closer they adhered to documents and pictures the greater was their success with the public. When he dressed Jane Harding as the Marquise de Pompadour (in the play *La Pompadour* by Émile Bergerat) he was congratulated on all sides at the première like a stage star. '*Voilà Redfern auteur dramatique*,' one critic wrote enthusiastically. Redfern had studied pictures and Rococo engravings and had caused the materials for the costumes to be woven from contemporary patterns.

His success was almost as great with Mary Garden's costumes when she played a young Galilean courtesan in the musical drama *Aphrodite* (adapted from Pierre Louys' novel). Taking his inspiration from Greek statues, Redfern transformed the American singer into a charming Tanagra figurine. In the opening scenes she wore a classical dull gold peplum, and when, in the final act, she appeared in a transparent flesh-coloured robe the applause was directed at Redfern who was sitting in one of the balcony boxes.

Redfern was very proud of his collaboration with the playwright Henry Bataille. Bataille's light, lyrical plays were a tremendous success at the time, in France and in other countries. On one occasion Redfern created the dresses for Berthe Bady, who played the part of a middle-aged woman in love with one of her son's schoolfellows. A letter which Bataille wrote to Redfern a few months before the first night of this play, *Maman Colibri*, bears witness to this collaboration.

Bataille writes: 'I am fully in agreement with you that for the second act a mauve dress is right. Autumn tints for the fourth, provided the mauve shade is not repeated. I think that a reddish and a bluish mauve combined in the embroideries would be effective and would correspond to the mood of the act.

'For the grandmother's dress (she is now resigned to her

fate) in the fourth act, I think that russet brown with dark sable is appropriate. Rather loose and heavy, but that I leave to your infallible taste.

'For the first act, brilliance, for the second charm.

'And don't forget that in the third act the woman is at home, and thus unfortunately obliged to wear a dressing-gown; but for goodness' sake try and get away from the dressing-gown . . . it must be a transparent and clinging négligé.

'I am exceedingly grateful to you for this truly close collaboration. Anyhow please do what you consider best, and may the gods inspire you. I am convinced that you will flabbergast *tout Paris.*'

## SARAH BERNHARDT AND HER TOILETTES

Zola's social novels had shaken the world; naturalism pervaded art, literature and the theatre. There was now an end to painted stage sets. A salon on the stage was now furnished with real furniture and the soup served at table had to steam. Historical dramas had to be historically accurate and the stage costumes really authentic.

In France the naturalistic theatre in its mature form was introduced by Antoine who, in his *Théâtre Libre*, took the utmost care to show the stage as a true reproduction of life.

The great tragedienne, Sarah Bernhardt, was completely under the spell of this new trend and interpreted it in her inimitable grandiose manner. When she played a sixteenth-century courtesan in a gold dress hung with pearls and flowers in Victor Hugo's *Angelo*, or Lucrezia Borgia, for which part she had studied countless Renaissance pictures, it was as far removed from the Renaissance as a neo-Gothic nineteenth-century church is from the original Gothic.

Histrionic genius, intelligence and subtle femininity—a

combination of these qualities gave Sarah Bernhardt an unlimited power over the parts she played. Her love for the grandiose, the intoxicating and the ecstatic, was realized in the glittering precious stones, the colours and riotous splendour of her stage costume. Her costumes belonged to her acting, to the colour with which she imbued the characters she portrayed.

However dithyrambic might be the articles published in the papers about her, at times they took exception to the lavishness of her stage costumes. Many critics even maintained that her knowledge of costume and choreography far exceeded her talents as an actress.

Who were her couturiers? In 1880, when she suddenly broke her contract with the Comédie Française—she had to pay a hundred thousand francs damages—and went off on a tour, she ordered twenty-five dresses from Laferrière. This was a fashion house founded by Mme la Ferrière which had been in existence since 1849 and was still very much in vogue. For half a century one can hardly find a newspaper or a magazine in which her name does not appear.

Sarah Bernhardt had her historical costumes made by Fred, the famous theatrical tailor. For her costumes as Phèdre she had ordered the embroideries, which alone cost four thousand francs, from Lepaul, a young costume designer. He worked for three days and nights on end and fell seriously ill as a result. As she relates in her memoirs, she was so upset by this that she never wore this richly-embroidered costume.

Sardou's *Fédora* (1882) was one of her greatest triumphs. Her toilettes in the latest fashion, which she changed five times in the five acts, were the highlight of the evening. 'Soon we will be wearing Fédora hats,' wrote a critic. 'Fédora dresses, combs, trimmings and jewellery inscribed with the name Fédora.'

Some of her critics insisted: 'Her toilettes bear the signature of the Grand Couturier.' This could only have referred to the all-powerful Worth. Sarah Bernhardt had approached Worth and told him that the dresses for a play, which had been made by a well-known couturier, were a complete disaster and that within the next three days she must have two new ones without fail. In the course of the conversation Worth realized that in this particular play five and not two dresses were to be worn. He therefore gave her to understand that he was by no means prepared to share the honour with another firm, and Sarah immediately ordered the other three dresses. Worth went to the première, and saw that only the first two dresses worn came from his *ateliers*. On the following day he sent his cashier with the bill to Mme Sarah Bernhardt, telling her that if the bill were not paid immediately he would attach her salary. Mme Bernhardt never set foot in his establishment again.

When the divine Sarah obtained her own theatre—it is still called the Théâtre Sarah Bernhardt—she supervised every detail of stage sets and decoration. For hours on end she perused art histories and books of costume and held conferences with artists. Naturalistic décor was carried to extremes. When she played the leading role in d'Annunzio's *Francesca da Rimini*, a real tree in blossom, chemically treated to prevent it from withering, stood on the stage.

She played the young Duke of Reichstadt in Rostand's *L'Aiglon*. For this she travelled to Vienna, studied the royal apartments in Schönbrunn in which Napoleon's son had lived, and made countless sketches. The sets for the second and third acts were almost complete replicas of the salon in the Palace of Schönbrunn. She also collected drawings and engravings in order to have the Austrian uniforms copied in Paris: even the materials were authentic. For weeks she walked about in uniform, to get used to it, so that she should appear free and untrammelled on the stage.

A great deal of gossip was rife about her private life, and it was said that she constantly wore men's clothes and smoked thick cigars. Thus she once received a letter from a tailor, begging her to wear one of his suits. 'He wanted no payment,' she writes in her memoirs, 'and offered me a hundred pounds into the bargain.'

In describing the preparations for her big tours abroad she sometimes mentions the name of the great couturier Doucet. Just as she was surrounded by great architects who carried out her plans for the sets, by jewellers who made her stage jewellery, by tradesmen, coiffeurs, masseuses, modistes and shoemakers, so she was also surrounded by Doucet's seamstresses. He himself never appeared. For her, the Grands Couturiers were merely tools who had to work to her dictates.

The reporters swarmed round her. 'What are your favourite colours?' 'Golden yellow and pale green.' 'What are your passions?' 'I have three: one for cloaks, one for hats and one for shoes.' 'How many dresses are you taking with you?' 'Oh, not many. . . .' She began to count. 'Twenty-six theatre costumes, twenty-five town dresses, eight furs and, of course, evening dresses and peignoirs. . . .' Not many. On occasions she had taken far more. For her tour of the United States: a hundred and twenty pairs of shoes and forty dozen handkerchiefs.

Gigantic baskets surrounded her, gigantic trunks, coffers as tall as a man, and special baskets for her own bedding, mattresses and pillows. An apartment was reserved for her in each hotel, rooms for her dressers, maids, masseuse and valets.

Never before had an actress experienced such triumphs. Wherever she went—in Paris or abroad—she was received with huge ovations. Enthusiastic crowds waited for hours to see her, and when she left the theatre there was a frenzied jubilation and her carriage horses were unharnessed.

There was hardly any difference between her life as an actress and her private life. She was as much obsessed by her own ego as by the theatre. For years she slept in her coffin of costly West Indian wood upholstered in white satin. According to her own express wish she was buried in this coffin. Even beyond the grave she was her own stage-manager.

In the history of Haute Couture she, whose costumes were copied by so many actresses of her age, must be ranked among the creators of fashion.

## JACQUES DOUCET AND RÉJANE

In the year 1815 a man and his wife could be seen selling bonnets in an open porch in one of the busiest business quarters of Paris. The man's name was Doucet. He had chosen the right moment, for bonnets were the height of fashion. From the voluminous variety current during the Revolution had developed an enchanting little frippery, and even the hats were bonnet-shaped. They were either made of lace or trimmed with lace.

Many of the women who came to Doucet's stall and examined his bonnets closely asked: 'Is the lace genuine?' For the first bobbin machine had only recently been invented with which real lace could be well imitated and at much lower cost.

Doucet's professional knowledge increased, thanks to the demands of his customers. Already in the following year he had a business on the boulevard Beaumarchais where he sold the finest Brussels and Malines bone lace, the finest Valenciennes and the rare and expensive *point d'Alençon* with its attractive patterns on cobweb-fine backgrounds. His clientele changed from day to day. More and more elegant men and women from the elegant residential areas in the west of the city visited him. Since Doucet lacked neither goods nor capital he rented his own shop in the rue de la Paix. This was in 1824.

He could have had no idea that this street would eventually become one of the smartest business centres. Doucet's move to the rue de la Paix was the result of his wish to be closer to his patrons, to have a smart setting for his new goods and to be able to raise his prices.

His calculations proved correct. Twenty years later he had rented the upper storeys. In one department the ladies bought the fine laces; in a second the gentlemen chose their shirts and cravats. This department was particularly successful, for the more uniform men's dress became, the more stress the dandies laid on finely frilled ruches, a relic of the jabot. In fact, the beaux of those days had become so exacting that they even sent their linen to England, for only on an English lawn could it really be bleached, only in English laundries could the right quantity of starch be given, indispensable to the semi-stiff smart shirt.

Doucet's son Edouard had the bright idea of installing a fine linen laundry on the premises to compete with the British and eliminate the tedious transport from Paris to Dover. It proved very profitable. Over the next few years he had as clients the smartest Parisian dandies and aristocrats, English gentry, Russian grand dukes and also the crowned heads of France—Charles X, Louis Philippe, Napoleon III.

Ten houses away from Doucet's elegant haberdashery and lace shop ruled the all-powerful king of fashion Charles Frederick Worth. Why should Doucet not try and become a competitor, since Jacques, Edouard's son, had, at an early age, evinced an interest in the refined elegance of women's dress? A new department was founded and entrusted, not long after the Franco-Prussian War, to the young Jacques Doucet. Almost overnight he became a king in the realm of Haute Couture.

Jacques Doucet, the finest connoisseur of painting and expert in feminine elegance, one of the most fastidious collectors of art works, became couturier to the most beautiful demi-mondaines and the greatest actresses. . . . He carefully kept his two main interests apart, so that his customers should know nothing of his passion for art and the circles in which he moved nothing of his profession. Only one of his patrons knew both sides of his life—the charming actress Réjane whom for many years he dressed for the stage and the salon, and who became his life-long friend.

Réjane, a synonym for gaiety, joy of life, vivacity, inborn talent, naturalness and complete merging into each part; and also exquisite taste, refined femininity, tactful elegance—'courtesy' one writer called it, for Réjane gave her public not a shade less than the mood of a play demanded nor a tone that was too shrill.

Her elegance was that of a graceful, shapely, born Parisienne. At the school of drama she had not even enough money to order the dresses for her first audition from a little dressmaker. She was nearly seventeen and her mother had to make the dress for her. 'I shall never forget that short printed cotton dress,' she writes, 'for which we laid out exactly ten francs.' She wore a spray of jasmine in her hair and her fellow pupils immediately copied both her dress and hair adornment. A year later, for the last great audition at the Conservatoire, one of the teachers ordered a dress for Réjane (at that time she was still Gabrielle Réju) from the smart fashion house Laferrière. This expensive dress, however, was as Réjane wished it, only a simple cotton frock, and once more she wore jasmine in her hair.

She did not win the first prize or the engagement at the Comédie Française, for she looked too gentle and insufficiently heroic. So she went to the Théâtre de Vaudeville and appeared in those light shallow comedies, which flooded the theatres of the world in the latter part of the nineteenth century.

The public was delighted. The house was always sold out. The critics praised her charm, her delicious appearance and her elegance. Her first leading role was in Augier's *Les lionnes pauvres* in 1879. Her teacher Régnier, one of the best actors of his age, wrote to her at the time: 'You were perfect, your dresses were impeccable, in exquisite taste and hit the right note.' The right note was so much Réjane's speciality that when in 1888 she played the role of a poor servant girl in *Germinie Lacerteux* by the Goncourt brothers she appeared on the stage in a shabby, creased ball dress, a real maid's dress, her arms red from much washing of crockery and without a trace of feminine coquetry. The public was astounded and displeased, for here was no longer the elegant Parisienne whose dresses they had come to see. There was no applause and it was a total failure. And yet in this particular part Réjane s acting had been superb.

At this time she was already a client of Jacques Doucet. The cultured couturier with his interest in art—he originally wanted to be a painter—and 'the most Parisian of all Parisiennes', both would immerse themselves in the part which Réjane was to play, in search of clothes suitable to the gay tone of a comedy in which the heroine moved so airily between a husband and a lover. The result could not fail to be a perfect chef-d'œuvre of Haute Couture.

If the house of Worth was famous for its dignity, Doucet was the couturier for the seductive woman. As though the shades of his lace-making ancestors stirred within him, he created his most exquisite toilettes in lace. They were like themes from Rococo pictures, with their delicate skirts, their floods of pastel-shaded silk-dainty dresses which seemed to have been taken straight from the *Fêtes galantes* of Watteau or Fragonard.

The eighteenth century was his favourite period and his collector's passion was concentrated on it. His house was full of pictures and drawings by Watteau and Fragonard, pastels by Fantin-Latour, landscapes by Guardi, genre pictures and still-lifes by Chardin. His drawing-room furniture had been made by the best cabinet-makers of the eighteenth century: Riesener, Leleu and Charlin. The art of his own age was alien to him. He sold the few pictures of the Impressionists in his collection in order to buy new Watteaus and new Chardins. Degas, whom he knew quite well, learnt of these sales. Doucet once met him in the street and was about to approach him cordially, but the painter cut him. 'Don't you know me, M. Degas?' cried Doucet, 'I'm Jacques Doucet.' Degas looked at him coldly and replied: 'I once knew a Jacques Doucet, a man of taste. He's dead.'

Surrounded by his art treasures, by the magic of the Rococo, Doucet himself became a *grand seigneur* of the eighteenth century. He was in quest of everything precious, rare and choice, and he also liked to dress in exquisite taste—a little too precious, according to those who knew him and described his appearance in white spats, white waistcoat and beard 'trimmed like a royal park'. He had his shoes relacquered daily and left in the oven to dry.

Everything in him cried out for perfection, whether in the field of his profession as couturier or in his activities as a connoisseur. He read all important books on art to give a solid basis to his passion as an art collector, thus laying the foundations for his art library, today the most important in Paris.

A circle of writers and poets formed round him. Among his friends he counted Paul Valéry, Pierre Louys and Henri de Régnier. When he was with them he never mentioned his profession; dresses and clients were never discussed and he behaved as though his fashion house did not exist.

And yet he was devoted to it. Here he was the practising artist, lovingly watching his creations and attending to the smallest details.

Doucet was godfather to Réjane's son, who was christened Jacques after him. This boy later wrote his memoirs and tells us a great deal about the relationship between his mother and the grand couturier. Whenever Réjane tried on a new dress in his workroom in the rue de la Paix, Doucet would arrive in his two-in-hand, which he drove himself, anxious not to miss the fitting. For hours on end they remained together in the fitting-room with the whole of his staff at their beck and call.

Jacques Doucet arranged the dress, and while the *essayeuses* were on their knees around Réjane, he gave 'orders to his girls in his strident nasal voice'. Jacques Porel writes: 'He began by draping my mother in velvet silk and taffeta, while she "held" her smile as a singer holds a note.' It is not difficult to imagine Réjane standing there, weary but still smiling, with that smile which belonged to the dress as much as did a train or a bunch of flowers. On her return home she would say: 'Doucet has made me another masterpiece.'

In 1892 Réjane had married the actor-manager Porel, and Doucet was on friendly terms with both. Doucet greatly liked Réjane's house, which was furnished in perfect taste; for everything that surrounded her had to be elegant—her theatre, her home and her street clothes.

Her most popular role in Paris and abroad was Catherine in Sardou's *Madame Sans-Gêne*, the laundry girl who delivered Bonaparte's linen and married Corporal Lefèbre, whom the Emperor later made a Maréchal de l'Empire. As Madame la Maréchale, Réjane retained the primitive coarseness of a woman of the people. No one who saw her in this part will ever forget her impertinence, the way she kicked aside the uncomfortable train when she was received at Court.

Doucet made the dresses, but the ideas were to a great extent produced by Réjane. In an interview she once told how she had looked for precedents to make the laundry girl true to style on the stage. She examined contemporary engravings and genre pictures, and studied the washerwoman's profession in a handbook of arts and crafts dating from 1773. 'The corsage is décolleté, with a loose kerchief at the bosom; the sleeves reach only to the elbow; the apron is adorned with frills and she wears a muslin cap on her head.' Réjane also read the works of the Comte de Caylus, a famous eighteenth-century antiquary who, typical of his age, wrote light literature in his spare time. Here she found the description of a young laundress who danced a minuet so enchantingly in a tavern that all the women were jealous. 'Have you noticed what short skirts she's wearing?' one of the women asks. 'Because she's pretty, is that a reason to wear such a low-cut dress and a hooped cape?' remarked a second.

And Réjane goes on: 'Then I saw exactly how I had to make my entrance in the scene where the handsome Corporal Lefèbre defends me against the rude advances of a soldier.'

After her triumph as *Madame Sans-Gêne* her range as an actress increased. Antoine, the founder of the *Théâtre Libre*, called upon her. They discussed new plays and new parts. Doucet now had to create for her a different type of dress—serious dresses for serious women.

Now Réjane was no longer the virtuoso who moved about

at her ease in an 'eternal triangle', but a woman faced with a host of new problems. She played in Henri Becque's *La Parisienne*—a play far above the heads of the ordinary public —and she played Nora in Ibsen's *A Doll's House.*

In 1906 she founded her own theatre, the Théâtre Réjane. Doucet now also made costumes for other actresses in her company. Réjane was furious when a costume was not completely in character with the part; when an actress, following some personal whim, was dressed by some dressmaker who did not know the play.

She had already divorced Porel, and her son, without giving the reasons, reports that her relationship with Doucet cooled considerably. The couturier suddenly disappeared for a long time. When he appeared on the scene again he had already decided to sell his collection—everything that bound him to his past was to disappear out of his life, even his beloved Rococo. 'For years I have amused myself with the eighteenth century: now it is the turn of modern art,' he said to Réjane. The collection was displayed in a big art gallery; the Paris dealers were at fever pitch and the prices rose daily. The final result: twenty million gold francs. With the proceeds Doucet turned his house into an art library for students.

Réjane visited him in his new home in the Avenue du Bois de Boulogne. The rooms were decorated with modern furniture and on the walls hung pictures by Manet, Cézanne, Van Gogh, Monet and Degas. He had his first editions of the great classics bound by young artists he discovered and encouraged, such as Legrain and Rose Adler.

Doucet was one of the first collectors before the 1914 War to buy canvases of the still unknown Picasso, Bracque and Matisse. Picasso's *Desmoiselles d'Avignon*, today one of the highlights of the New York Museum of Modern Art, adorned the hall of his new dwelling, and le Douanier Rousseau's *La*

*Joueuse de Flûte*, which he later presented to the Louvre, hung in his study.

Doucet was undoubtedly one of the greatest couturiers of his age, but when Réjane wore one of his creations on the stage the credit went to her and not to him. A novel jacket in velvet and pleated satin became the fashion as the 'Jaquette Réjane'. Women wore hats *à la Réjane* despite the fact that they had been created by the famous milliner Caroline Reboux, whose customer Réjane had been for many years.

'I often get my ideas from the public,' Réjane once told a journalist. 'For example, for Zaza's corsage [Zaza was a very common *chanteuse* in some dreary provincial music-hall] I was at the theatre with Albert Lambert—a famous actor from the Comédie Française—when I noticed a very ostentatiously dressed woman in the balcony. "What is she wearing on her blouse? Is it a piece of iron from an old junk shop?" I asked Albert. "No, it's a kind of braid." "Sketch it for me, *mon ami*." And Lambert, who was a talented artist, sketched the dress for me, which I wore later as Zaza.' For the fourth act, Doucet made the cloak in which the heroine wants to make an impression upon her former lover. Young Poiret, who at that time worked with Doucet, was entrusted with the making of this garment. He described it thirty years later in his memoirs: 'All the sadness of the romantic ending, the whole bitterness of the fourth act, was expressed in this cloak.'

So famous were Réjane's stage costumes that, when she died in 1920, her elegance was referred to almost as much as her acting. 'No other actress has had such a gift for harmonizing colours and endowing her body with fantasy, wit, charm and grace. Our great couturiers have lost in her not only a friend but a most valuable collaborator.' Our great couturiers! That meant Doucet, and no one else.

Shortly before Réjane's death Doucet visited her at her

sick-bed and remained a whole afternoon with her. Jacques Porel relates: 'As he left I saw a strange gleam in his eyes, and when he embraced me I felt the tears in his perfumed beard.'

## ELEONORA DUSE AND HER COUTURIER, JEAN PHILIPPE WORTH

'When you do not help me the magic leaves my roles,' complained the thirty-six-year-old Eleonora Duse in a telegram to her couturier.

This is a relationship between couturier and customer unique in the history of the tailoring art: the great, perhaps the greatest actress of her age and her couturier were so closely united in their common task of stage costume that the actress could not play without his help; that her magic vanished, and the finest tools of her art were lacking.

Jean Philippe was the son of the great Charles Frederick Worth, the founder of Haute Couture. Already as a boy he had filled the margins of his schoolbooks and notes with sketches of the dresses he had seen at home and in his father's workshop. Lace, tulle, silk, cloaks and crinolines were his companions since early childhood. His father sometimes took him along when he went to the Tuileries, and on one occasion the Empress, thinking of her delicate and ailing son, had looked sad and said with a sigh: 'I wish my son were as tall as you.'

His early contact with Corot was of the utmost significance for him. Corot, the painter-poet, the 'man with the fortunate eyes', had struck a chord in Jean Philippe which would echo for the rest of his life. The ageing artist was often a guest in the Worths' house. During the Siege of Paris in 1870, when Jean Philippe's father left the city in a balloon, the fourteen-year-old boy was allowed to visit Corot on Sundays and learn from him. 'These Sundays with Corot were worth at least fifty years' experience in my own profession,' he wrote. Corot gave the boy a feeling for painterly values and taught him how to put an idea or a mood on to paper by means of a subtle drawing.

Contemporaries who had worked in his house for many years speak of Jean Philippe's perfect taste. As his predominant colour he had chosen a shade of blue, so special that he would suffer no other. This colour had to reign supreme down to the last detail, and even the string with which the dress boxes were tied had to be this particular shade of blue. He once ordered a thousand balls of this string from the makers, but when they arrived they were not of the right colour. He returned the whole consignment.

Even the bottle of his perfume *Dans la nuit* was a dark blue star-spangled ball designed specially for him by the glass artist Lalique. He had commissioned the scent to his precise requirements from a chemist—it was to have the same subtle intoxicating scent which he had breathed for one whole summer in the Borromean Islands.

Duse's biographer and friend, Eduard Schneider, wrote in 1924 that she had been dressed for thirty years by Worth. Her first appearance in Paris was in 1897. A reporter who visited her in the Grand Hotel wrote: 'See, there she sits on the terrace of the Grand Hotel, a small distinguished-looking woman in a smart dark cloth costume, collar and sleeves in single coloured linen and her face covered with a veil of tulle and lace.' On the same occasion another journalist wrote: 'We have been told that she knows nothing of our elegant ladies, but behold, we have an artist before us who knows all the houses which cater for the Parisienne and strange to relate dresses nowhere else except in Paris. That is a charming discovery.'

When she appeared in Berlin in 1893, her outward appearance aroused the enthusiasm of the great critic, Paul Schlenther:

'Although Mme Duse's dress standards are very costly,' he writes, 'her aim almost invariably is simplicity. Her dresses are like her acting. With the greatest subtility she achieves the effect of natural ease. In *La dame aux camélias* she appears only in shimmering white dresses. . . . No jewellery is used to relieve the eye, no ring burdens the mobile and eloquent hands. In Duse's art what she wears subordinates itself with a kind of joyous humility to what she has within her.'

And yet in Paris Worth took exception to this simplicity. When the Duse told him that she wore no jewellery he protested: 'In Paris you must wear jewels in this play, for we cannot imagine *La dame aux camélias* without them. We must make it clear to the public that Marguerite Gautier was showered with gifts of jewellery.' So he lent her a magnificent pearl necklace, which he says was worth between thirty and forty thousand francs. 'You'll see how useful this necklace will be to you.' And indeed, the day after the première she came to him in great excitement and said the necklace had saved her.'

But it was not the pearl necklace that made the Paris audiences weep, that caused the rapturous applause she received from the very first performance, that aroused the enmity of her rival, Sarah Bernhardt; it was her incomparable acting, the magic of her simplicity and her renunciation of all theatrical artifice.

Worth was so enthusiastic about her acting that he followed her to London to admire her once more in *La dame aux camélias*. He had also sent her a new, very low-cut dress which at first she refused to wear until he produced a tulle veil for her. She knew how to give a particular significance to this veil. In the scene when Armand Duval insults her, flinging the banknotes in her face, she shrouded herself in the tulle veil as though trying to defend herself against him.

For the Duse the dress she wore on the stage was not merely a theatrical costume. It was part of her and part of her theatrical vocation. Her stylish dresses must have put Sarah Bernhardt's flamboyant attire in the shade. At this period the great stage designers like the Swiss Appia, the Englishman Gordon Craig and the Russian Stanislawsky had lured away conventional décor. They created an entirely new kind of set expressing the spiritual content of the piece—lyricism or passion, gaiety or dark tragedy. For the Duse, costume, too, was analogous to the dramatic action; it formed the tone-scale of her acting just as subtle shades of colour formed the essence of Impressionist painting. The mood of the play was already expressed by her costume.

Her couturier understood her magnificently. We possess a correspondence, even if somewhat fragmentary, and merely the last chapter of a long exchange of ideas about the choice of stage costumes, colours, materials, style and atmosphere. It is hardly conceivable that Worth's letters from earlier years were more tender and tactful than those he wrote to the ageing actress. And the Duse's telegrams—for she seldom wrote letters—are as she herself must have been—passionate, stormy and bubbling over with spontaneity. Each sentence, each word was a message.

After her last appearance in Ibsen's *The Lady from the Sea* in Berlin, in 1900, Eleonora Duse retired from the stage. Her great tragic love affair with Gabriele d'Annunzio had come to an end and she was sick in body and mind. She could not go on. But after a twelve years' retirement she was compelled to return to the stage. A sixty-two-year-old, grey-haired woman once more played *The Lady from the Sea* to a wildly enthusiastic audience. She played in Rome, Turin, Florence, Paris and America, and then again in Italy and Paris.

Her impresario demanded the impossible from her, wanting

her to give five performances a week, but Eleonora would have preferred to play in a whitewashed cellar to workers and students; she felt too old to be a star. She immersed herself in the writings of the mystics, reading the Gospels, the Confessions of St Augustine, the letters of St Catherine of Siena, her eternally questing spirit always hoping for a revelation of the truth.

Violent attacks of asthma racked her tired body. She was in great financial difficulties and was soon no longer able to pay the cast she had assembled.

Schneider and his wife visited her in her Paris hotel. She met them with a smile. 'Look,' she said, 'I've put on a Worth gown to receive you in,' adding, 'but I would have you know that it's not yet paid for. Worth,' she said to Schneider, 'has behaved admirably in all my tragic situations. I wrote to him, saying that I was in such difficulties that I could not pay my last bill. He was the only one who replied that I could pay him whenever I liked.'

An eternally youthful passion for acting still glowed within her. Now she chose mainly maternal roles, and Worth helped. She must not look too old, not even as a white-haired mother, for the public would not like it. And in her other parts, on the other hand, she must not look too young, only a trifle younger. With unfailing sensitivity he shared with her the tragic approach of age, tactfully helping her over a host of difficulties. Even when his letters deal only with professional advice on clothes, trimmings and materials, his loving care for her shines through. He closes his letters with a mark of homage: 'I kiss your beautiful hands.'

'My dear and great lady,' he writes to her, 'I must insist that you neglect no means of making yourself as attractive as possible, as youthful as possible—even in *Ghosts*. Never forget that the public is a young creature, eternally young (even younger than Sarah Bernhardt). The public, you must remember, although it ages, is constantly renewed; it is pitiless, and artists are well advised to bow before it—they must make concessions to this terrible judge whose first impression is always that of a spontaneous and ingenuous child. You must always reckon with this most important element and try to win the hearts of the public as soon as you step on to the stage. A great foreign singer who made her début in Paris said to my father these words which I have always remembered: 'M. Worth, I require only one thing from you, that I look beautiful when I make my entrance on the stage. The rest is my affair. You know from experience that you have conquered when you can hold the audience's attention at your entrance. After that you can even make mistakes, but you have won the public and it will applaud you.'

Although at the time of her affair with d'Annunzio—and also later—the Duse considered it her mission to make his work known to the world, Nordic harshness, the grey and white colours of Ibsen, suited her better than the bright sensuous colour of the Italian poet. In *The Lady from the Sea* she identified herself with Ellida Wangel, the doctor's wife, who cannot forget the sailor, who is to her a symbol of vast horizons and freedom. Her impresario wanted her to play this part in gorgeous Parisian dresses. She wrote to Schneider: 'Can you imagine the wife of a poor Norwegian doctor in wonderful Parisian gowns?' But she also knew how perfectly Worth would understand her when in one of her rare letters she wrote and explained how she envisaged Ellida's clothes. 'Only one word, my dear good friend, eminently true! I am expecting the three white dresses for the 28th November [1922] in Milan. We must also think of the two dresses for *The Lady from the Sea*. The one in the first act, a bathrobe of white woollen tricot; the dress below this bathrobe (don't forget the two dresses I left with you) should consist of part of the blue muslin dress (a kind of Madonna robe in make), and of the green muslin lined with ultramarine taffeta (decorated with white beads). Out of these two dresses you wanted to make a single one which I can wear under the woollen bathrobe. Décor of the first act: a bright morning. I am coming from the bath and could perhaps wear something on my head. A scarf? I leave the decision to you. The dress for the second act should be of the dark bottle-green shimmering taffeta which I tried on with you; it needed a little trimming on the corsage to make it smarter, less severe and lacking in poetry. We discussed a sea-blue trimming.

'For the second act: Night, outside in a garden. Please find me a headgear, something coloured which suits the dress (shimmering dark bottle-green taffeta) in one of your own cuts.

'In December I sail for New York. You realize that for New York it is very important that you "make me beautiful". The rest is then, as you wrote in your letter, "my affair".

'Please fulfill my requests. With all my heart, your Eleonora.'

The Duse also identified herself with Mrs Alving in Ibsen's *Ghosts*, living the tragedy of the mother who has to watch her son gradually lose his reason. She would have liked to resemble the women whom Whistler painted. With sure instinct she had selected this artist with his twilight and his discreet range of tones.

She telegraphed to Worth: 'Please read over text in Nordic atmosphere. Need single beautiful austere dress, period between 1860–80. Perhaps some portrait of Whistler's would be useful. Exists enchanting picture of woman in black bell skirt material with broad stripes, broad sleeves, lace adorned dress must be of heavy black satin or velvet as you prefer. Send wig too with white curls like an aura and beautiful white lace falling from shoulders, austere though elegant.'

And here is Worth's reply:

'I went today to see Whistler's portrait of his mother. I will send you a sketch of it. I am not very certain about the white scarf on the white hair. I think it may look heavy. I should prefer a black one, which will give an even more austere effect to the whole.

'For the period I should suggest between 1860 and 1870, for a decade later the fashion was too striking and would be ridiculous on account of details such as the bustle. We all know what effect the ridiculous can have: better to do away with it and retain only the beautiful silhouette you find in Whistler's portrait. Material: poplin or velvet, since they are not making heavy silk any more.

'I have read *Ghosts*. I am convinced that you will lend all the expressive powers of your acting to this tragedy. I regret that this Norwegian genius with his amazing talents has never been able to help us in our existence. After reading it I felt most dispirited. My only consolation is that this play will afford you the opportunity of giving a beautiful interpretation.'

Eleonora Duse played the part of Anna in d'Annunzio's *La citta morta*. Décor: In ravaged Argolis, before the ruins of golden Mycenae. Anna is blind; with the sensibility of a loving wife she realizes that her husband loves a young girl. She wants to give up life and to fade away into old age. 'Look, nurse,' she says, 'and see if you can find any white hairs. I must already have white hairs here at my temples.'

Worth worked on the costumes for blind Anna. 'I am all yours, devoted to you, and more than ever I will do what lies in my power to help you, and I admit frankly that I am proud. That I am fortunate enough to be considered by you as a friend gives me the additional delight of admiring and understanding you. Your telegram spurred me on and I have already begun work on the two costumes for *La città morta*. I intend to make both dresses on the same model for I feel this corresponds to the spiritual content of the role. First act, a dress in off-shades of cream, white and gold with a slight touch of blue. You will remember that you yourself always suggested this—an atmosphere of heavenly light. . . . Act two: the same dress in dark green, black and silver. I am convinced that the feeling of melancholy which combinations of these three colours inspire in me will also capture the audience and emphasize even further the powerful tragedy of the last act. Tell me in your own subtle and colourful style the colours you require to surround you in this part. I still remember your gestures when you spoke to me about the clothes for *Rosmersholm*. It was autumn, and you pointed to the russet yellow trees in the Tuileries gardens—resplendent in all the shades of autumnal red and purple. And you will remember that your costumes were carried out in the same wine-red and russet-brown tints.'

He is tenderly considerate about her health, for he adds: If you are obliged to wear a dress of thin material you can put on a pink silk tricot underneath and thus avoid catching cold.'

Three days later Duse cabled: 'Was certain of your good will. Reflect that dress for first act must be worn in bright sunlight. Great simplicity but a little gold in the sleeves. The second must harmonize with the night that gradually descends upon the characters under the great starry sky of the backdrop.'

Worth replied the same day: 'I have received the photographs of *La città morta* and they gave me great pleasure. Your figure seems to stand in front of me, accompanying my thoughts as I read the play. The impression has remained so strong and clear that if I saw the play now I should feel as though I had seen it before, so strongly do your evocative powers work on my receptive mind.

'Your costumes (in the picture) still have great allure and are very impressive. In the new version I shall remove the broad sleeves, however effective they may look in the picture. Since nine-tenths of the public is incapable, during the play, of overlooking something which has to do with fashion, it will undoubtedly prefer a rejuvenated line.

'For the new Silhouette I have been looking for a very straight line, very slender and Greek. I want this purely symbolic and introspective figure to remain in a totally indefinable atmosphere as to the period in which this unusual tragedy takes place. I do not want people to say later: "Those were the models for the 1922 performance of *La città morta.*"

'Ever since you have done me the honour of choosing me to supplement your acting with my humble contribution I have always taken every opportunity in all your stage costumes of avoiding anything which could be described as couture, thus following the general idea of the work as interpreted by you.'

In another passage he says: 'From your telegrams I take it that our views coincide, and that despite the great distance between us we understand each other—each one naturally in his own role, mine confined to the dress.'

Two days later 'the Duse' telegraphed: 'Agree to dispense with gold on cloak, and ask for light contrast between the two acts to be stressed; first quite bright, in the second one plunges into the shadow. Thank you for *Ghosts*, I ordered white plaits by mistake but meant grey with a lot of silver in them.'

Worth's letter on the same day: 'I am sending you a choice of two cloaks, one glittering silver and a second without the silver. But you will be playing on a dark stage with moonlight illumination, and if I do not add a little trimming, some touch of silver, you risk being unseen. Please try them out on the stage with the actual stage lighting.'

Some days later the Duse replied with a single phrase: 'Only you know how to be helpful.'

Worth on the following day: 'The green dress remains green, and it will be dark; but I will endow it with a breath of moon and starlight.

'Thank you for your telegrams, so full of confidence. In contact with you I feel alive again, full of new and fresh ideas. Almost a thing of the past, for today, in my sad profession, I no longer receive excitement and inspiration from my clients. . . .'

Worth did not confine his attention to dress and finery—he did for Duse what should actually be the task of any sensitive couturier, he saw to her coiffure and make-up, for he realized that hair and complexion had to harmonize with the costume. Thus he helped her to choose the shade of colour of the hair according to each part. For *La città morta* he suggested a reddish wig and was only hesitant because it would be the first time that she had worn one of this colour.

'I remember that your head is about the same size as mine (your hair naturally included) for one day you tried on my hats and they suited you very well. I will send you a wig which can easily be secured with the aid of an indiarubber band. That is far better than if I were to send you individual switches and ringlets. And the black veil hanging down behind you will hide any little blemishes, should there happen to be any.'

The cabled reply came. 'Agree with you about wig, but please avoid red, which I have always loathed. Please choose my old brown colour.'

But Worth did not want her to appear too young, to reappear suddenly with dark hair, so with his usual tender discretion he suggested: 'a little powder on your hair so that the transition will be softer to the face. The heroine of *La città morta* is a young woman and yet already at an age when she can start to turn grey. In Paris there are many beautiful women between twenty and twenty-five who are already slightly grey and yet are considered beauties. The elegant ladies of the eighteenth century understood that so well.'

Once Duse had grown accustomed to the idea of a wig she would also wear one as Frau Alving. '*Alea jacta est*,' wrote Worth. 'I have been to the coiffeur and have ordered a grey wig. . . .'

And then came the delicate subject of make-up. On her return to the stage in 1921 after a long break, she appeared entirely without make-up. This aroused some distaste in her public. Worth handled the matter with exquisite tact.

'You are far too intelligent not to understand that fifteen years of a lifetime do not make anyone younger, and not to know that all of us are subject to a not particularly gratifying natural law.

'Obviously in *Ghosts* you do not need very much alteration, and yet let me remind you that the stage and footlights make even the freshest and youngest face look old. You must therefore have the courage to dampen down the disadvantageous effect of the footlights. Even in *Ghosts* you should seek for a harmony between your face and your hair. In the eighteenth century, paint was not only indispensable on account of the white wigs but almost a rule of etiquette, I might almost say of good manners. A woman who appeared without make-up at the Court of Louis XV would have been given a severe reprimand; so you too, even in *Ghosts*, must dab your complexion with a yellowish white.

'As far as *La città morta* is concerned, remember the advice I gave you when you played in Paris. Above all, never omit to put rouge below the eyes, which is the best way of banishing those dark rings which time or ill-health have left on all of us. I will send you a special rouge, which is rather more pink than the one you once used. Put on lightly it will remove the traces of weariness, from which we all suffer at certain periods of our lives.

'I am also making the costumes for Marie Marquet. She is a personification of the Venus de Milo, beautiful and young. Yet any dress she wears enhances her natural beauty on the stage.'

Only when one realizes how important cloaks were for the Duse, how she swathed herself in them as though in an endeavour to flee from all bitterness and care, can one understand her deep disappointment when one of them was not as successful as she had wished. 'The cloak will not follow the dress,' she complains in a letter to Worth. 'There is no unity and it makes "two". I do not know how to console myself, for as usual we have worked together with love and for the best. If you do not help me the magic leaves my roles, unfortunately. . . .

'And to make my misery complete I have no idea when I can come to Paris. Everything at the moment is at a standstill and shrouded in the unknown. We must await events. Forgive me my anxiety. . . .'

Almost at the same time comes another eight-page letter which Eleonora strews with *Hélas* like a doleful plaint. . . .

'If you could only come to Paris,' pleads Worth, 'we should get more done in a single day than in a month of correspondence and lengthy telegrams.'

Duse's telegraphic reply: 'Just received your enchanting and very plausible letter. Should like to leave immediately but at the moment things very complicated.'

On the following day Worth replied: 'Come, come, come.'

Two days later three telegrams from the Duse: 'Am almost certain to leave.' 'Happy to come, happy.' 'Shall be in Paris 25th. Patience. Thanks.'

Before her last tour in America, Eleonora came once more to Paris. To his great sorrow Eduard Schneider noticed the thin, frail body, how she shivered and drew her shawl close about her: 'And how many new wrinkles there were on the beloved face, how pinched her cheeks and how transparent her hands!'

She visited Worth for the last time, and he was very distressed to see how she had aged. When a few months later he heard the news of her death—she died in Pittsburg during the night of the 20th–21st April 1924—he was deeply moved, and yet relieved that her unhappy life had ended.

*VII*

# HAUTE COUTURE DURING 'LA BELLE EPOQUE'

## LA BELLE EPOQUE

PARIS 1900. The nineteenth century was dead and buried. War and defeats were forgotten; forgotten, too, the turbulent Commune. Wealth triumphant, an easy life, pleasures, political crises, social unrest, the Dreyfus Affair, the Panama scandal, the battle cries of the anti-clericals—this was the grey-black background against which 'gay Paris', the international pleasure city, stood out in sharp contrast.

The Eiffel Tower rose, frail and slender, from the silver mist. Crowds from five continents streamed to the Exhibition of 1900. A confusion of languages, ideas and political parties. . . . But peaceful, jovial harmony in the places where amusement was to be found, on the boulevards, at the Moulin Rouge, in the fashionable restaurants and Chez Maxim.

A time of triumph for woman, for the Parisienne! Her aura imbued colours, shapes and lines; the Grands Couturiers worked for her, furniture and fabrics were designed with a view to her charms, loveliness and seductive arts; lampshades to dim the light and colours to enhance her complexion.

It was an age of gallantry. Men were gallant, had gallant

rendezvous or adventures. The popular attractions at the theatre were not Ibsen or Strindberg tragedies but plays where the boudoir was the essential property, where the husband coveted his neighbour's wife and the wife her best friend's husband. An age of the *dessous*, of veiled glances and provocative scents.

In architecture and interior decoration contrasting principles opposed each other; the masculine, deriving its strength from the functional designs of the factory and the machine, from which springs an entirely new style—simplified forms, a new architecture searching for a new beauty in practical utility and the logical use of materials. And on the other hand, the feminine, symbolical of the accelerated rhythm of life: everything was in movement—forms and lines, house façades and furniture. Ornaments of naked female bodies and creepers, poppies and lilies spiralled and twined convulsively on cupboards, bookbindings and dress fabrics. The colours were light, transparent, with a gleam of mother-of-pearl and iridescent white. That was the new art, known alternately according to the country of its origin as *l'art nouveau*, Modern Style or *Jugendstil.*

The *Cul-de-Paris*, the draped and gathered dresses, disappeared from fashion. In harmony with the new development in building and decoration, the architecture of the dress was simplified, while at the same time trimmings became more complicated. In the 'nineties the wasp waist had still been de rigueur, so tightly laced that women could hardly breathe. The hips had been narrow, but from the knee downwards the skirt had spread out in the shape of a bell, which moved like waves and ended in a train. Beneath these had rustled the silk petticoat, the seductive melody of the frou-frou.

Just before the turn of the century sleeves were high, wide and puffed; then the breadth moved lower down and they became baggy on the forearm. 1900: the lines grew more simple, the waist less pronounced; the materials flowed round the body; they were sea-green, lilac, pastel-blue or grey, with arabesques of lilies or bead embroidery on brocaded silk.

Women had no breasts but a bust, tight laced, arched and adorned with glittering sequins, lace flounces and muslin frills, which cascaded from a bolero.

Feather boas round neck and shoulders, the quivering flowered hats secured by veils, twisted pendants and ear-rings, the high hairstyle with aigrettes, feather fans and leather gloves reaching to the elbow for evening wear—all these were the 'modern style'.

The train was indispensable—even by day. Not until a fashion paper of 1901 does one read that skirts were to become ever shorter and that the train would soon disappear from street clothes. A bold fashion-writer even prophesied for the year 1920 skirts so short that one would be able to admire the shapely charm of foot and ankle.

The corset remained a breastplate, shaped and rounded to give a fashionable line to the body. After 1900 it left the waist freer but pressed in the stomach, raising it high up towards the bosom. Hardly had the girl left her childhood than she was taken to the staymaker. The corset was a symbol of modesty for the respectable woman, and in the case of a cocotte a citadel to be stormed and captured.

On the one side virtue, on the other vice—that, too, is the Belle Epoque. After dinner the women retired to the drawing-room and the men to their smoking-room, but after midnight the smart men of the world and the financiers went to supper at Maxim's, the cocotte's paradise, a gay family gathering. Hugo, the *maître d'hotel*, who later published his memoirs, knew them all. He knew Boni de Castellane, the last of the dandies, who arrived in his carriage with liveried lackeys on the box;

Jacques Doucet, the couturier and collector; the good and bad payers and the demi-mondaines who set the tone and fashion: Emilienne d'Alençon, Liane de Pougy and La Belle Otéro.

Despite 'modern style' and arabesques, the mode was banal and over-sugared, almost on a par with the unbearable fashion reports of the day, which constantly talk of Dame Fashion and call her a goddess, a capricious woman, the idolized strumpet forgotten overnight, the great coquette. . . .

The couturiers were not at all pleased when artists began to interfere with fashion and to impose their new styles. They would brook no rivals, and since they themselves were completely barren of ideas they wallowed in flounces, trains, pleats and fancy buttons, seeking their new inspiration more than ever in old engravings. The reporter of a fashion show even queried whether the thefts of old fashion plates which had suddenly become so frequent might not be ascribed to this frantic search for something new from the past.

Nevertheless, the Parisian Haute Couture had no competitors. Julius Meyer-Graefe, the German art historian, writes in his report on the fashion section of the Paris exhibition of 1900: 'No foreign house dared to compete seriously with the Paris firms.'

The figures speak for the enormous boom in Haute Couture. The most important houses were grouped round the rue de la Paix and the Place Vendôme. The few large ones alone had a yearly turnover of thirty million francs, among them Worth and Doucet with more than five million each. In 1872 there had been in Paris seven hundred *ateliers* for made-to-measure work; by 1902 their number had risen almost threefold. But only the six or seven Grands Couturiers employed from four to nine hundred workers. The other tailors and dressmakers had work for fifty people at the most. One sees the difference, which developed even more strongly, between Haute Couture and the other made-to-measure firms.

Since the Franco-Prussian War the manufacture of export models had constantly risen. Foreign buyers purchased 65 per cent of the models while Paris and the provinces accounted for the remaining 35 per cent.

The difference in wages was so great that while a *première* often received a princely salary—she could earn as much as fifteen hundred francs a month—the small employees had to exist on starvation wages, although at the height of the season they worked as much as nineteen hours a day. In February 1901 the first strike broke out in Haute Couture. It was quickly suppressed; the women strikers were dismissed and replaced by others. Order was soon restored for nothing must be allowed to disturb the gay, happy Belle Epoque.

All the really smart couturiers showed their creations at the 1900 Exhibition—Doucet, Paquin, Callot Sœurs, Redfern, Rouff, Félix and Charles Frederick Worth's two sons, Jean Philippe and Gaston.

The Worth brothers conceived an idea, completely new for those days: the dresses were to be shown on wax figures and to portray certain scenes as, for example, ladies at Longchamps races, with a suitable autumnal background, or a summer scene with a backcloth showing the sea. Their colleagues, however, found this innovation too bizarre and unworthy of their distinguished corporation. Jean Philippe, therefore, on his own account leased a corner of a pavilion which he transformed into a Louis XVI salon. The wax figures displayed all variations in material and fashion from cloth to brocade, from a simple lady's maid's dress to the most expensive Court robe. There was a lady of the Court presenting her young sister to the Queen, a second, dressed in a white

Réjane, the great actress,
dressed by Jacques Doucet,
in 1905

Réjane at her couturier's

French fashions in London, 1910: 'the newest French tea-gown at Woolland Brothers'

Hats by the famous milliner Caroline Reboux

coat and skirt, being handed her cloak by a maid, while a third lady in a wonderful tea-gown was being offered tea by a young girl. 'This display aroused so much interest,' Jean Philippe reports, 'that eventually the police had to be called in to deal with the crowds, which never diminished during the next six months. Our colleagues very much regretted that they had not followed our original plan.'

Madame Paquin, too, had a theatrical success here. She had ordered a figure of herself in wax and thus the crowd could see her in a beautiful dress, sitting at her own silver toilette table. 'She possessed to an astonishing degree the chic we admire so much in the Parisienne,' says Meyer-Graefe.

Madame Paquin was the first woman to achieve any importance in Haute Couture. In an age which was so hostile to female emancipation she even became President of the fashion section of the Exhibition. Together with her banker husband, who was mainly concerned with the business side, she had opened her dress salon in the rue de la Paix nine years earlier. Soon she had become able to attract the smartest clients—the Queens of Belgium, Portugal and Spain, the mistresses of the then Prince of Wales and two of the most beautiful cocottes, Liane de Pougy and La Belle Otero.

The elegant Madame Paquin appeared at the races in her latest creations, had a villa at Trouville and a house at St Cloud, which was frequented by many artists. In addition to perfect taste she must have had great professional knowledge. Famous were her blue serge costume, relieved with braid and gold buttons, and her voluminous gold and silver lamé evening gowns whose excess of trimmings Poiret attributed to her Levantine origin.

As an organizer she was unique. She founded the first foreign branch of a Parisian Haute Couture concern. In 1912 the London branch opened, followed by others in Buenos Aires and Madrid. She sent ten mannequins dressed in the same model to the races and her fashion displays were a sensation. At the end of the show a score of young girls appeared in white dresses and performed a kind of ballet.

Worth and Paquin! What has remained of these great names, without which no description of the Belle Epoque, with its elegance and pleasures, would be complete?

For nearly a century the Worth dynasty had been able to maintain its tradition: the impeccable aristocratic administration of the house, dresses with the special Worth hall-mark, a note of discreet elegance. This continued until, as a result of a family quarrel, it was split into two branches, neither of which could continue to exist.

Only the names of Worth and Paquin were retained when their houses were bought by an English firm in 1954 and now even these have gone from the house in the Faubourg Saint-Honoré.

Next in line came a woman, or rather three women—Callot Soeurs. The firm was founded in 1895 by three sisters, daughters of an antique dealer. The eldest and most talented, Mme Gerber, later ran the business on her own. She had in common with Doucet a love for old lace, her knowledge of which she undoubtedly inherited from her father. Lace blouses, and silver or gold lamé as material for evening dresses, first became the fashion through her. To supply her orders the firm of Coudurier-Fructus was producing the most magnificent lamés long before the turn of the century. Mme Gerber loved the fashions of bygone ages and had dress materials with Renaissance patterns and rococo flowers embroidered in her workshops. The age demanded it, but she dominated the taste of the age and the fashion industry with her strong personality. In 1916, when her house in the rue Taitbout became too small, she bought a block of small buildings in the Avenue Matignon.

Among the original women leaders of Haute Couture must

also be numbered the beautiful Madame Chéruit, who ran the well-known fashion house of Raudnitz (founded in 1873) and later took it over herself. She installed herself in a beautiful seventeenth-century palace in the Place Vendôme, and was the first woman to have the courage to launch simple, almost severe models which were in contrast to the fussy, over-laden fashions of the day.

On the Place Vendôme from 1900 onwards also ruled Doeuillet, who started his career with Callot Soeurs. His house inaugurated the mannequin parade at the beginning of each season. In 1928 he went into partnership with Doucet. A business for quality ready-made goods, Doeuillet-Doucet, still exists today. Then we must not forget Rouff, Félix, Pinguat, Redfern and Drécoll.

In those days smart toilettes were unthinkable without hats. Three generations wore the creations of the famous modiste, Caroline Reboux. She died in 1927 at the age of almost ninety, and was already getting on in years at the time of the Belle Epoque. Caroline was the daughter of a journalist; she had sewn hats in an attic and sold them to wholesalers for three francs. The Princess Metternich, with her keen scent for fashion, discovered her just as she discovered Worth. Someone must have told her about this little workgirl who knew how to make such enchanting hats, for one day—it must have been in 1865—with the Comtesse Pourtalès she climbed the six storeys of the old house in the rue de Choiseul to the pathetic room of the young modiste.

In 1870 Caroline Reboux installed herself in the rue de la Paix and during the Belle Epoque there was no smart woman, whether it were Réjane or Cécile Sorel, who did not wear a hat from Caroline Reboux with their dresses from Worth, Doucet or Paquin. Only the cocottes were barred from her salon. This was part of her principles.

The most beautiful fur coats, trimmings, insertions and capes were made in those days by the House of Révillon which remains to this day one of the leading furriers.

These then were the kings of fashion at the turn of the century. The beauties dressed by them look out at us from faded photographs—mysterious glances from beneath flimsy, feathered and flowered hats, ruffles, flounces, glittering sequins, fur trimmings, a plethora of lace, feather boas and gentle colours, the sex appeal of 1900, a last pale vestige of an artificial romanticism, a melancholy vernal playfulness in the autumn of a dying fashion.

# VIII

# THE MAN WHO DRESSED ELEGANT WOMEN

## PRELUDE

AT recurring periods the Far East dominates art and fashion with its brilliance, turns black to blue, white to sunny gold, makes the light shimmer, plucks the colours from nature and spreads them over pictures, walls, carpets and fabrics.

This is no mere coincidence. No style, no fashion can be conjured out of nothing through outside influences or through a single genius if the soil is not ready to receive the seed of the new. Behind the façade of the Belle Epoque enhanced glittering under artificial spotlights, there fermented and pulsated new discoveries; new machines with their accelerated tempo brought new social problems, carriages gave place to cars, photography to films, railways to aircraft. . . .

In art, forms were dissolved, torn asunder and reassembled in cubes. The stage was set for an invasion of Eastern colours and barbaric shapes. Negro sculpture, the primitive art of the South Sea Islanders and colourful peasant art were discovered.

1903: Isadora Duncan dances at the Théâtre Sarah Bernhardt. No heavy draperies hamper her limbs. The peplum she affects heralds the dresses which will give freedom of movement.

1905: The first exhibition of 'Les Fauves'—the wild beasts.

Pure, gleaming colours. . . . Matisse changes flowers, trees, men and objects into decorative patterns like those on an Oriental carpet.

1906: Sergei Diaghilev, the creator of the Ballets Russes, organizes an exhibition of Russian Art at the Salon d'Automne. The *fin de siècle* is dead and buried. In the grey-white atmosphere there dances a glitter of colour, an Oriental world invested with the gentle melancholy of the Slavs.

1909: The first performance of Diaghilev's Russian ballet *Cleopatra*. The décor: an orange setting, lapis-lazuli blue stage floor with a massive pale-blue backdrop, the costumes of the dancers, Pavlova and Ida Rubinstein, brightly coloured, golden and encrusted with stars. The range of art has broadened, the glowing colours of Russian ikons have become part of the living present. Léon Bakst, the Russian artist, had designed the décor and costumes and his colours soon conquered the new art, interior decoration and artistic fabrics. Within a few weeks Paris had gone Oriental.

And what of Haute Couture? It ignored this new orgy of colour. No spark from it fired the creations of Worth, Doucet or the other great houses. They continued to provide distinction and seductiveness, but only according to the established pattern of rococo painting.

A young fashion designer who worked in the House of Worth produced a new straight-lined model. 'Do you call that a dress?' Jean Philippe Worth cried in a rage. 'That's a bug!'

The name of the young designer was Paul Poiret.

## ALLEGRO MA NON TROPPO

'The drab confines of my surroundings drove me into a land of dreams,' writes Paul Poiret. Thus he himself answers the question as to how a man who had been brought up in such a narrow Philistine milieu could at an early age show such a clearly defined instinct for extravagant luxury and artistic capacity.

His father was a cloth dealer, whose house was frequented by civil servants, wholesale provision merchants and big buyers from the *Halles*. His grandmother took snuff from a tortoiseshell box; his girl cousins wore ringlets, hair-slides and long, dark, woollen dresses, which occasionally allowed a glimpse of the crochet insertion of a white linen petticoat. The decoration in his father's house was like the interiors of all well-to-do French bourgeois houses in the last third of the nineteenth century: a Louis XVI drawing-room with chandeliers and bronzes, a dining-room with dark Renaissance furniture.

When Paul went with his mother to Mass, he would often run away to buy a bunch of violets from a flower girl and present it to an elegant lady. 'A precocious sign of noble generosity,' he notes.

The daily scenes between the grown-ups were also part of the atmosphere of the outwardly peaceful middle-class home, the boy fled to his room and drew pictures of the elegant women he had seen on the street. We find this urge to sketch smart dresses as a child in the biographies of most of the Grands Couturiers.

It is characteristic of Poiret's personality that he was greatly impressed by Jarry's *Ubu Roi*, a play which is an extravagant and grotesque caricature of the narrow-minded bourgeois attitude. Here he found what had always stirred in his subconscious. Like Jarry, young Poiret was a vagabond by nature. He had formed a trio—he played the violin, another boy the guitar, while a third sang. They went into courtyards and made music. The windows opened and small coins wrapped up in paper were thrown down to them. The three youngsters often earned as much as twenty francs, of which the concierges took their percentage. Naturally his parents must not hear of this. They only learned that Paul had bought himself a top-hat, and from M. Gibus, the inventor of the opera hat at that. The bill was sent home and his father was so disgusted that he destroyed this very expensive collapsible headgear.

Young Poiret had successfully passed his baccalaureate and he could have studied or become an artist. His father, however, was determined to clip his wings. 'If one wants to achieve anything in life, one must begin at the bottom of the ladder,' he said. So he found him a position with a walking-stick and umbrella dealer and was content to see his son wash the shop windows and sweep the floor. But Paul also delivered the goods and on these occasions he never forgot to take his sketch-book and pencil with him. On his errands he rapidly sketched the passing ladies, and on his arrival home made dresses for a doll, sixteen inches high, which his sisters had given him. Then again he sketched the doll he had dressed and a host of other beautiful costumes, in fact anything that came into his head.

Poiret showed these drawings to Grands Couturiers like Doucet, Worth and Chéruit. Jacques Doucet bought some from him and finally engaged him in 1896 at a monthly salary of five hundred francs. Young Poiret was very impressed by the atmosphere of refined elegance in Doucet's house—the Rococo salons, pink muslin curtains, spangled silk gowns with their lace, pink ribbons and frills and the beautiful cocottes who bought their clothes there. He was so impressed by Doucet's personal elegance, his silky white beard, patent leather shoes and dark-blue suits, that he found out the address of his tailor in order to be just as smart. Poiret was a success at Doucet's from the very start. His first model immediately sold four hundred copies.

Young Paul Poiret loved women and that is why he wanted to make them attractive. But he was already self-willed and autocratic, fanciful and generous; he spent money as quickly as it came in; he was an artist and an epicure. His beautiful girl friend had a weakness for clothes; nothing more natural than that he should design some beautiful dresses for her which she had made-up by a small dressmaker. And in these creations, accompanied by Poiret looking as smart as paint, they appeared on the parade. But Doucet, too, was an autocrat and tolerated no poaching on his preserves; least of all any action he considered a breach of confidence. He showed his young designer the door.

Military service spared Poiret the trouble of looking round for a new job, but as soon as he returned he was taken on by Worth, who already knew him as a designer. On being engaged he was told: 'You are here as in a restaurant where they make delicious *omelettes aux truffes*, but we have engaged you to produce ordinary roast potatoes.' But in spite of this Poiret made *omelettes aux truffes*, in his own particular style. His models were original, bold, and pleased the ladies. Gaston Worth, who had an eye to business, protected him, while the sensitive Jean Philippe took exception to his strident colours and simplified silhouettes.

Poiret held him in high esteem: 'The dresses he designed were masterpieces of artistic beauty and purity.' But he also knew that these dresses, for which the inspiration was always sought in the eighteenth century, belonged to the past and that he, the progressive, was not in his right place in a house so fettered by tradition.

In 1904 he opened his own small shop with eight employees and a capital of fifty thousand francs in the rue Auber, near the Opera.

Everything here was original, even the window displays.

On a dark purple ground rested Chinese embroideries, autumn leaves, spring blossoms. Here was a fragrance of the new, the foreign and the exotic. The whole of Paris rushed to admire this sensation.

### ALLEGRO CON BRIO

Clients came to his shop and were bold enough to allow Poiret to suggest dresses for them. It needed great courage to wear them. One could not simply order an afternoon dress from him and an evening dress from Worth or Doucet. Poiret meant a programme, a sect, a point of view. Any woman who bought in his shop sold him her soul.

The most sensational novelty of all: Poiret banned the corset. But how could one wear the dresses of other couturiers without this armour plating which forced the body into its own obstinate shape?

'I have freed the bust from its prison,' Poiret writes, 'but I have put chains on the legs.' For the more freedom and mobility women had now in their broad corsage, the looser the waist, the narrower became the skirt—so narrow in fact that finally they could hardly walk. And what was the reaction of these smart women? They did not shrink from tripping along in Poiret's long, narrow hobble skirts.

It would perhaps be interesting to psycho-analyse this innovation. Poiret wanted absolute mastery over women. At Doucet and at Worth he had got to know their whims, their hysterical irritation and their ruthlessness: 'What I saw there convinced me that one must dominate women unless one wishes to be delivered to them body and soul.' What repressions and desires lay behind Paul Poiret's determination to be so despotic with women that he invented this narrow skirt in which they could hardly walk?

Within a few years he was the King of Fashion. The women

danced to his tune even more readily since he knew all the secrets of seduction. Every woman believed that Poiret could make a Venus out of her, that it only depended upon *his* good will. But in order to obtain his good will, she had to win his favour.

He gave them more than they demanded—a joy in the exotic, the unexpected and the original; a taste for the original and personal. And he gave them colour. The anæmic tints of the eighteenth century were done away with. Red, green, violet, orange and lemon-yellow, the colours of the Fauves, were also Poiret's colours. It was perfectly true when he said: 'I have brought the dying shades back to health.'

Poiret searched for painters who, like himself, had drawn upon the new age for their colour. He found them: Paul Iribe and Georges Lepape. Poiret was delighted with Iribe's drawings and the artist was equally delighted with Poiret's creations and eagerly accepted his offer to 'tell the story' of his gowns in bright water-colours. In 1908 appeared the book: *Les robes de Paul Poiret, racontées par Paul Iribe.* The couturier sent this book with a personal dedication to all the Queens and Princesses of Europe. All of them acknowledged the gift with the exception of the Queen of England, who sent him a message through a lady-in-waiting that in future he must refrain from sending her things of this nature.

A young painter was introduced to him: Georges Lepape. Poiret hardly knew his pictures, but with his infallible instinct sensed that here was a kindred spirit. He had his mannequins paraded before Lepape in the latest models. The young artist sat deeply moved by these swaying marvels of colour and refined elegance. Then Poiret appeared: 'Good, now go home and set down your impressions on paper. It doesn't matter what comes out. Maybe only a picture of a rose in a vase, maybe a poem.' Lepape went home, drew and painted. The result was an album: *Les choses de Paul Poiret* (1911). In this album each dress was transformed into a miniature Parisian fairy-tale wonder. Lepape became famous overnight and contracts poured in. For decades he designed charming front pages for *Vogue*.

When Lepape came to Poiret for the first time, he brought a few sketches with him which he showed rather bashfully and hesitantly. They were fashion plates, and on one of them as a novelty he had drawn long trousers instead of a skirt. Poiret made a new model from this design. But perhaps the rumour of this astonishing novelty had leaked out or, as so often happens, several couturiers had thought of the same idea at the same time. The fact remains that the first harem skirt was seen on a mannequin whom Drécoll sent to the races in 1910.

Lepape and Iribe, who also designed modern and original jewellery, Bernard Naudin, Marty, Martin, Boutet de Monvel and Bakst, who designed models for Mme Paquin, were among the artists who worked round and for Poiret and with him set the seal upon the new fashion.

The long years during which Charles Frederick Worth was the dictator of fashion have been called 'the Age of Worth'. Poiret, with his artistic style, left his mark on his age infinitely more powerfully than did Worth and, with far more justification, the decade before the First World War can be called 'the Age of Poiret'. He made fashion so much a branch of art that the leading art magazines of the period, such as *Art et Décoration*, published articles on the art of fashion and fashion as an art. The enchanting journal *La gazette du bon ton* (1912–13) drew its wit and charm entirely from the '*Epoque Poiret*'.

Poiret also turned his attention to the artistic production of foreign countries; for this he made good use of his propaganda journeys. In Vienna he visited the *Wiener Werkstätte*, founded by Joseph Hoffmann. Here artists had re-entered the field of craftsmanship. For the first time the functional beauty of objects of daily use was discovered and enhanced by design.

Poiret returned to Paris greatly impressed. In 1912 he founded the Craft School which he called after his daughter Martine. Very young girls, almost children, were allowed to work here; he took them to the country and to flower shops. They had to sketch their impressions, sometimes even paint them large upon the wall. He often used these naïve and childish sketches for the materials which were made into dresses in his *atelier*. Artists also worked in the Martine School and were made to find inspiration in Oriental and folk-lore motifs, negro sculpture and South Sea Island painting. Poiret also gave Dufy a studio of his own. Dufy drew and painted his charming motifs, Poiret used them in his fabrics. The dividing line between fashion and design in arts and crafts became blurred: furnishing fabrics could be used for dresses and vice versa.

Another innovation: Poiret produced a scent which he called after his second daughter—Rosine. This was the first *parfum de couturier*. How many of his colleagues have since copied his idea and how many since then have recouped their losses by their brand of perfume.

Fashion as it developed between 1903 and 1914 is the typical 'Poiret style'. At first, women wore a sack-like, usually single coloured, straight skirt below a tunic, which at times fell down as a cloak as far as the hem of the skirt. The tunics or loose wraps for evening wear were of light material embroidered with Oriental gold and silver arabesques; the belt contrasted in colour with the dress and was often made of cord twisted into artistic arabesques. The materials were either plain or in brightly-coloured batik and decorated with wide borders of geometrical coloured patterns or Persian embroidery. One saw fur-trimmed evening cloaks of gold and silver material, loose Japanese kimonos, all in gleaming colours.

In 1906 the waist moved almost as high up as in the Directoire and the Empire. At first the stomach was pressed in, and then it was 'worn' once more, until it was almost emphasized in walking. Next came the hobble skirt gathered up to a high waist, so narrow and split at the sides that logically it developed into the much ridiculed harem skirt.

The hats, at first gigantic in size, grew ever smaller. While in London, Poiret had admired the Oriental headgear in the Victoria and Albert Museum and telegraphed for his *première*. She spent a week in the museum copying, and a few weeks later Poiret launched the turban in Paris.

1913–14: the years the world was in the grip of tango fever. Young and old alike, even ladies in conservative London, danced the tango. The tight, caught-up dresses, split in front, seemed ideally suited to the new dance.

Hair and turban mounted with an aigrette pulled down to the eyebrows, a narrow draped dress and a loose bright-coloured kimono blouse; eyes painted with black pencil, a hand on the hip, swaying slowly and languorously in a *corte*; this was the attire of the fashionable woman—the 'vamp' type—who, dressed by the Sultan of Fashion, danced her way gaily towards the world catastrophe.

## MAJESTOSO

And if the truth were to be told, he was a sultan in the harem of his employees and customers, an Assyrian king with his pot belly and a broad face surrounded by a black beard.

He did everything quite differently from his professional colleagues. He was the first not to settle in the rue de la Paix or its vicinity. In 1912 he bought a palace in the Faubourg

Saint-Honoré with a magnificent garden which he modelled on the pattern of the park of Versailles, and next to it a second house as a private residence.

Above the door of his house stood the words:

ATTENTION! DANGER!
AVANT D'ENTRER REFLECHISSEZ TROIS FOIS,
S'IL EST ABSOLUMENT NÉCESSAIRE DE LE DÉRANGER!

That is how a reputation is made. One is original, an outsider, a freak—in short, a genius. And one has countless enemies. . . . No couturier has ever had so many enemies, and at the same time so many fanatical supporters, as Poiret. In this respect he can be compared with Picasso—Picasso whom he hated, against whose 'intellectual speculations' he spat venom and gall. The man whom he considered responsible for the 'aberrations of art'.

Poiret brooked no competition from anyone, not even from his own sister, Nicole Groult who married an interior decorator. At an early age she had shown a talent for tailoring and had designed imaginative clothes for her husband's clients. They were so beautiful that Poiret wanted to engage her. She refused. What was his reply? He simply forbade the manufacturers to deliver materials to his sister. 'It's either she or I,' he said to them. Nicole, however, established herself successfully and soon employed over a hundred workers. On one occasion their cars were in collision in the Champs Elysées. The damage was slight. Poiret drove on and said, quite casually, to his friends: 'That lady was once my sister.'

Enemies and competitors, disciples and proselytes created around him. Poiret, however, was an intelligent man and saw himself with astonishing clarity as the questionable hero of his own legend. A man before whose shrine incense was constantly burnt, who was honoured like a prince; 'How could such a man,' he once said, 'not have quite the wrong idea of himself? He moves about in artificial surroundings, breathing the fragrance of luxury and living in a phantasmagoria . . . and so in a trice he turns into a clown who is fooled by his own reputation!'

His journeys abroad were the best propaganda for his fashion creations. With two cars, a secretary and nine mannequins he visited all the capitals of Europe, showing his very latest models and giving lectures. His nine mannequins wore a blue serge dress almost like a uniform, a beige-coloured cloth coat, and an oilcloth hat embroidered with a big P. In those days mannequins were not the haggard, slant-eyed boyish creatures of today; they were young, beautiful, plump women whose virtue Poiret guarded strictly. This was no light task. According to him, the young men, particularly in St Petersburg, were so aggressive and generous with flowers and bonbons that he had to keep his protégées under lock and key.

He took only one mannequin with him to the United States, to give the Americans lessons in Parisian taste. The mannequin stood beside him on the platform and Poiret improvised: in full view of the public he cut out material, draped it round the mannequin, pinned it up and the dress was ready. The girl had to wear modest underwear, and yet a film showing a display of his collection in his Paris *atelier* was banned because the Americans took exception to the skirts that allowed the feet to be seen!

Poiret has described the life of a couturier as 'an uninterrupted film of infinite variety'. And in fact his life was a film, a breathless sequence of masquerades, from his production of fashions to his sensational costume balls.

The first of these balls had an Oriental flavour. 'The Arabian Nights' was the device. No one was admitted unless he wore

Paul Poiret

Dress by Poiret, 1912, from a watercolour by Lepape

an authentic costume. His house had been transformed into an Oriental fairy palace. An actor sat on a mountain of cushions and told Eastern fairy tales. Ibises strutted in the park, apes and parrots frolicked in the trees. There was a real soothsayer's booth and a potter made vases to amuse the guests. Ballerinas in Oriental attire danced on the lawn. Twenty negroes and negresses burnt frankincense and myrrh throughout the night. The sweet music of flutes and zithers echoed from the bushes; fakirs displayed their arts and Indian cooks prepared extravagant specialities.

At the back of the garden was enthroned the Sultan of Fashion surrounded by his concubines. The three hundred guests had to make their obeisances before him.

He became even more extravagant and fantastic: in a wood not far from Paris Poiret bought the 'Butard'—Louis XV's hunting-lodge—and appointed it with period furniture, carpets, tapestries and chandeliers.

People still talk in Paris today of the famous *Kermesse* which he gave there in the summer of 1912. This time his ambitions were transferred to the wondrous world of mythology. His three hundred guests had to appear as gods, heroes or dryads. On their arrival they were received by nymphs in white veils who accompanied them with torches through the dark wood to the all-powerful: Poiret, dressed as Zeus, in high buskins, ivory-coloured drapery, a gold beard and golden curls. This Olympian fête soon developed into a bacchanal. Wine was drunk in horns which could be replenished from amphoræ. During the night the three hundred guests drank nine hundred litres of champagne. As the sun's first rays burst through the wood, supper was served—three hundred lobsters, three hundred pâtés de foie gras, three hundred melons and three hundred portions of ice-cream.

Poiret led this life of riotous enjoyment, even after the

First World War, when his financial position was threatened. The parties continued in his palace on the Rond Point des Champs Elysées, to where he had moved in 1924. He called the garden his oasis, and for one of his parties had it covered with an indiarubber roof to protect the guests from the rain.

The International Arts and Crafts Exhibition of 1925 provided him with a last opportunity to display his fantastic extravagance. Three ships, *Amours, Délices* and *Orgues* lay at anchor in the Seine, decked with flags and bunting. In the *Orgues* he had built a colour organ; a virtuoso struck the keys and a variety of coloured harmonies appeared on the screen.

### FINALE

That was what the film of Poiret's life was like. Taken all in all, the difference between his creations and the costumes for his fancy-dress balls was not very great. A fancy-dress costume was for Poiret a heightened form of fashion, the fulfilment of a wishful dream. But at last these dreams came to an end. His star was on the wane and the number of his creditors in the ascendant. In 1924 his business was turned into a limited company. His new creations were less and less successful and he believed himself to be cheated and surrounded by enemies.

In fashion as in art, who does not progress with the times and accept the future will be left behind. What was revolutionary yesterday becomes old-fashioned today. A couturier who did not understand the sober reality of modern life, the deep incision which the First World War had made in the fabric of society, and the beginnings of women's entry into the battle for their daily bread, was like a gardener who, in the artificial atmosphere of the conservatory, wants to breed flowers which are doomed to perish in natural surroundings.

Although Poiret was already old-fashioned, he still believed that he was ahead of the mode. He considered the functionalism of modern art reactionary, and found house façades without relief or adornment and bridges without statues lacking in taste. He railed at the age, the artists, his faithless customers, the simple tailor-mades which women wore from morning to evening and the couturiers who created fashions for an average clientele. 'It has profited them considerably,' he wrote in his book *En habillant l'Epoque* which appeared in 1931, 'but at the same time they have forfeited the title of couturier and fashion creator.'

This was Poiret's tragedy. He refused to accept that his new creations were simply unfashionable; that women no longer wanted to wear Oriental robes and garish colours because the post-war style was against it. While everything tended towards simplicity he thought out new toilettes adorned with gold embroidery and Persian motifs which were gayer than ever.

That Poiret made fashion design an important branch of the arts and crafts and thus an art, discovered new artists and encouraged them to give new beauties and life to fashion, was a stroke of genius. Why could he not adapt himself to the times? Simply because he looked upon fashion as art for art's sake—something which moves in a closed circle.

Poiret overlooked the fact that the popularization of fashion was the new trend. His dislike of the modern age was a tilt against windmills, a storm in a teacup. But he stood on the stage to the bitter end and gave the public the tragic performance of a king whose realm has been torn from him by bitter enemies, of a beggar with the ambitions of a ruler, waiting for the time when someone will help him to recover his throne.

The reports of those who were close to him during his last years are contradictory. (He died after a long illness in 1943.)

His sisters supported him with vast sums of money until the end. But no sooner had he a little money in his pocket, than he would invite sisters and friends to dinner in the most expensive restaurants. Others insist that he went on the dole and that he had been seen standing in a queue at a soup-kitchen. Cecil Beaton in his amusing *The Glass of Fashion* relates that during the war, in the South of France, Poiret wore a suit made out of a bath robe and that, completely impoverished and hungry, he waited outside restaurants for the proprietor to offer him a meal.

But perhaps Poiret was a prophet nevertheless when he wrote of standardized fashion: 'They have let the lights go out and they will never be relit.'

# IX

# BETWEEN TWO WORLD WARS

## A SHORT PROLOGUE (IN THE FORM OF A LETTER)

*Paris, January* 1916

MY DEAR JACQUES,
Today the first snow fell here and has turned Paris, as usual, into a morass. It is cold, we are freezing and thinking anxiously of you men at the Front.

You seem to be worried about the future of our daughters and you are displeased that both of them are preparing for serious occupations. And in addition you call them suffragettes. If you only knew how they laugh at such things! They declare that the suffragette movement and the struggle for equal rights are all part and parcel of the pre-war junk and they need no propaganda for a constructive existence. They say that they took up work because they had to, but now their active life has given them a self-assurance which they never possessed before. And so that you may not be over-surprised when you come home on leave, I will tell you something. In spite of the war they dress in a charming feminine manner. They have powder puffs and lipstick, wear pretty clothes, silk stockings and fine linen such as I myself never possessed. Think how terrible it was before the War. What hideous things, what wretched materials and unattractive prudish dresses were reserved for young girls. Hygiene, lipstick, powder, everything that makes a woman seductive was forbidden them. No wonder the young men left them languishing like wallflowers at dances.

So our photograph, which I sent you, reminds you of a Winterhalter picture! You call it 'Empress Eugénie with two young ladies in waiting'. Yes, you are right. The present fashion with the tailored jacket and wide skirt is really very Second Empire except that skirts are shorter and allow high laced boots to be seen. The caprices of fashion *are* crazy! Now when there is an ever-greater shortage of material and prices are rising, the skirts become wider and wider. Here we call these bell-like skirts 'war-time crinolines'. Most women dress in black and the braid and buttons on the jacket give them a slightly military appearance. The hats, on the contrary, are very unmilitary and with their high decoration are almost provoking in these gloomy days.

Our Marie visited us a few days ago (don't worry, we get on very well with only one maid); she does not seem to regret having given up her work as a cook. She appeared in her tram-ticket collector's garb—straight jacket and straight skirt. Today one sees many women in work clothes which are particularly chic when they have been made by our Grands Couturiers. The other day I saw the uniforms of dark grey gaberdine with four very practical pockets that Redfern made for the American Red Cross. I wonder whether these dresses will not eventually influence the fashion.

And now about myself. Why the many reproaches in your last letter? When you came home on leave last year, you were fully in agreement that I should carry on the business. It was going downhill and as soon as I took over everything was in order again and you were proud of me. Then the difficulties began to increase, it was much harder to obtain materials and yet I managed. In my last letter, I was stupid enough to tell you that I have to work from morning to night, and even on Sundays. And now you are against it and say that you have spoiled me for years on end and kept me away from all the hardships of life, and it upsets you that I have to cope with all these worries.

My dear Jacques, what a misunderstanding! Did you ever realize how unhappy I was in those days? How futile my existence was? The home which was to have been my world had nothing more to offer. Crocheting, knitting, making tapestry, those were the occupations of our grandmothers. As the world grew ever-more exciting we women grew lonelier. How did I spend my days? In trivialities. Running round the stores, looking for bargains and gossiping with other women in the afternoon. When you went to your work I saw you as a man plunging into a world full of grim conflicts. Now I myself am in this same world, engaged in the hard struggle for existence. The magic has vanished from your world and you are no longer a hero. But you are a human being just as I am and I am your comrade. My new view of things has made me poorer in illusions but made my human relationship with you much richer.

When you came home you were often met by an irritable, weeping woman. I felt so remote, so shut out from your interests. I thought that you did not understand me and I very nearly took refuge in the complex of 'the misunderstood wife. . . .'

Were you to see me today you would hardly recognize me. . . .

## THE NEW LOOK V. HAUTE COUTURE

1919 to 1920: The returning soldier and even more so the men who returned home from prison camps could hardly believe their eyes. Were these the same women?

The deep and painful incursion of four years of war into the old ways of life, the accelerated mechanization of working methods, the penetration of women into men's sphere of action had come so swiftly and in such a revolutionary manner. The fashion picture told the tale: women suddenly wanted to resemble men, in their outward appearance as well.

In the 'twenties the waist disappeared, the bust was banned, hair was shingled, masculine and brilliantined. Curls and soft waves were frowned upon. Even the bodies underwent a transformation. Like fashion, the æsthetic of the female form has its history.

The proportions of Aphrodite follow a prescribed canon as do the spiritualized slimness of a mediæval Eve or the noble proportions of a Cinquecento beauty. The voluptuous curves so beloved by Rubens were permitted to the beauties of 1900. By 1925 the female type had changed as radically as the clothes. Where natural curves refused to obey the fashion, starvation diets, massage and exercise were called in. In place of the corset one wore a light girdle. The brassière was now designed to flatten the breasts.

The ideal of the dainty little foot was played out. Long, slim, well-proportioned legs were the order of the day, for skirts grew ever shorter until they did not even reach to the knees. These were the days when men went to a music hall to look at legs.

The slim boyish woman in a skirt, which left the knees free, or in a mannish coat and skirt, a cloche hat pulled close over her head at an angle so that only one eye was visible, was known as the 'garçonne' type. Women in Vienna, Paris, Berlin and London all looked the same. . . .

But after the war did one go still to Paris expressly to see the latest recipes of Haute Couture on smartly dressed women? No, in those days one went to Paris to enjoy the sensations of

Bohemian life in Montparnasse; to see Kiki, the model of the Japanese painter Fujita, in the bar of the Dome; to hear scraps of some mighty debate on modern art at a café table. Or one went to the *Le Bœuf sur le Toit* cabaret to hear American songs, to the apache *bals* in the rue de Lappe or to the negro ball in the rue Blomet.

Overnight Haute Couture had lost its grip. Fashion styles are styles of life and now the style of life demanded houses made of glass and steel, living rooms that looked like laboratories, women whose radically transformed existence manifested itself in their equally radically transformed clothes. The mannishness of woman was at first artificial and exaggerated. Women lived more than ever in the present, yet they had not quite discovered the path to reality. Never had they made such a cult of their lack of inhibitions, their spleen and their psychoses.

Anything connected with the past was ridiculed. Everything had to be new. The behaviour of women was as revolutionary as the pictures of Picasso and Leger—for art, too, had broken with tradition.

The fashion designers had lost their sense of direction. The couturiers fought against the garçonne type: The fashion journals between 1920 and 1928 are a true reflection of opposition, compromise and counter-attack.

In 1921 Haute Couture declared war on short hair—without success. In 1922 it fought against short dresses, and in fact skirts suddenly became long again but with the waist very much lowered. The winter collections were very colourful in an attempt to banish the black preferred by women. It was a failure; in the spring collections, everything was black once again. The couturiers gave up the struggle and a fashion reporter sighed: '*Le couturier propose, la femme dispose.*'

In 1923 skirts became slightly shorter again and the following year they were half-length. The waist was so deep set that the dresses seemed to be bound below the knees. The couturiers could not enforce their suggestions for wide skirts, curves, gathers and finery. And suddenly they began to preach simplicity.

In 1925 they declared the pyjama, which women had already been wearing for three years, to be indispensable. Shapes were geometrical, angular and flat. It seemed as though cubism had penetrated fashion. One couturier showed his collection on the slimmest American mannequins in order to stress the tendency even more strongly. In June, skirts reached their peak in shortness and evening gowns were up to the knees. Nevertheless, at the beginning of each season it was stated: 'Skirts are now longer and waists higher.' The struggle against short hair was abandoned and in 1925 the famous coiffeur hairdresser Antoine's latest creation was the brilliantined 'Eton crop'.

Women worked, struggled to earn a living, had the same professional interests as their husbands and lived in the rhythm of the new age. They went in for sport, wore sports clothes and laughed at the pre-war 'motoring outfits' with their huge hats and thick veils. They danced not only at parties but in cafés and bars; they no longer took a tiny sip from a wine-glass, they drank, smoked and drove their own cars. And they had as many love affairs as they pleased. There were no longer any matrons, and elderly ladies were only to be met with in the provinces. Youth was de rigueur and youthful dress the fashion even for ladies of a certain age.

Women had found their uniform in the garçonne, but they all sought their own individual style beyond it. The Dolly Sisters with their round smooth heads and fringed, chemise-like dresses. Greta Garbo with her page-boy bob and broad-brimmed floppy hats did more for the formation of certain feminine types than did the couturiers. *Vogue* published photos of actresses and film-stars showing 'before and after'—this meant before and after they had succumbed to 'Greta Garboism'.

In 1928 skirts began to grow longer—but at first only with an irregular hemline. In 1929 they reached the knee in front and were much longer at the back. In October 1929 the waist was once more in its correct place. In November the long evening dress suddenly reappeared and the whole world sang the famous Berlin number: '*Wenn die Elisabeth, nicht so schöne Beine hätt . . .*' which tells the story of Elisabeth who had such lovely legs that she could not really enjoy the beautiful long dresses.

The revolutionary phase was over; women had won the day; the Parisienne was victorious in the struggle between the new masculine ideal and her own femininity. Fashion and Haute Couture were at one again. From this ten-year struggle only those couturiers who had understood how to create a fashion from women's new way of life emerged successful.

### 'COCO' CHANEL

Wherein lies the secret of successful fashion design?

Secret No. 1: When a fashion artist—and this is pure chance—starts off from where a revolution is impending in culture, art and fashion. Secret No. 2: His flair for this coming revolution—and this is no matter of chance. Secret Nos. 3, 4 and 5: His talent in finding the formula for this revolution, his individuality which allows him capriciously and resolutely to stand above the fashion, and his intelligence not to let the means with which he sets the fashion slip from his grasp.

This holds good for Poiret as well as for Chanel. For fifteen years their names stood peaceably next to each other in all the fashion papers. And yet on the stage of fashion they were antagonists to a degree that it would be hard to imagine. From Poiret to Chanel lies a giant's stride, far wider than the fifteen years that lie between their dates of birth.

A reporter wrote of Chanel's display in 1920, that he felt he was seeing clothes which an amazingly artistic and talented woman had had made for her own use alone, by a dressmaker who worked solely for her. Costumes of jersey wool with short accordion-pleated skirts, pullovers, simple jackets with fur-trimmed pockets for use and not merely as adornment, real buttons, straight-lined evening dresses and crêpe-de-Chine capes. Everything in simple lines and mostly dark in colour. During the next few years Chanel hardly altered the lines and in this lay her great strength. One might object that any little dressmaker could have carried out, or at least easily copied, such simple uncomplicated models. But Chanel's simple lines were far harder to copy than Poiret's fantastic creations, for she understood how to give them an incomparable chic. The renunciation of anything superfluous was the peak of elegance. Balzac's 'luxury through simplicity' had been realized.

A straight-lined, simple woollen dress from her house cost as much as a gold and silver adorned Poiret model. Chanel should have written a book called '*The art of dressing simply and paying a great deal of money for the pleasure*'.

All celebrities have a more or less romantic life-story, and naturally Chanel is no exception. The margin between truth and fiction is difficult to determine. She never answered interviewers' questions; she merely told them what she pleased and usually to each of them a different story.

Gabrielle Chanel is said to have been born in a station waiting-room. As a child she cut up the curtains in the house of the old aunts who brought her up to make dresses for her dolls. She was a dancer in a Pau night club where—naturally—she met a young Englishman who took her to Paris and set her up in her own shop at no. 23 rue Cambon. She was a modiste. In a fashion journal of 1912 there is a picture of the actress, Gabrielle Dorziat, in a spring model and below it the caption: 'Hat by Gabrielle Chanel.'

The war took her to Deauville where she worked in a Red Cross dressing station. A new *ami* provided her with a small elegant shop there. Her first stroke of genius; she discovered that, for the women who had replaced the men now at the Front, the straight jersey jacket, such as the Marines wore, or men's woollen pullovers, were far more suitable than the war-time crinolines which she hated. She bought sailors' jackets and men's pullovers; slightly adapted with a little trimming and a brooch, she wore them on the Promenade at Deauville. They were an unheard-of success. Orders poured in and she had jackets and pullovers knitted for her customers.

Then she returned to Paris, this time to no. 31 rue Cambon. The new Prince Charming duly appeared, an exceedingly wealthy English nobleman, and owner of a most beautiful yacht. 'Coco' (everyone now called her this, and that too has a story) went for long trips in this yacht, got sunburnt and descended upon Cannes in 1922. A sunburnt skin became the fashion overnight.

The fairy prince, who was already married, wanted to divorce his wife and marry Gabrielle provided she closed her Paris shop and lived a life according to her station. She made a heroic renunciation: the idyll was at an end. She continued to run her fashion house which had now become one of the most important. Each collection was a triumph; the smartest women let her dress them, ordering grey, black and beige jumpers with wide sleeves, short pleated skirts and stockingette dresses. At first Chanel used only one floor for her workrooms, but new storeys were soon added and finally the neighbouring houses on both sides. Her models were bought by American buyers and her style was greatly appreciated in America. Her summons to Hollywood did much to win the films over to the garçonne fashion.

In 1928 she was the first to launch fancy jewellery of coloured glass and crystal, just as she had been the first to replace trimmings and embroidery by jewellery. So with the simple black jumpers women now wore expensive many-stringed pearl necklaces and huge cabochon stones, as they are still worn today. Legend has it that one day her necklace broke. Coco was too impatient to restring the pearls in their proper order. The big ones were mixed with the small and a new type of necklace was born.

Another story. She was going to the Opera to see Cocteau's *Antigone* for which Honegger had written the music, Picasso designed the sets and she herself made the costumes. A fire broke out in her bathroom and the flames singed a handful of her hair. She took a pair of scissors and cut off the rest of her hair. She went like this to the Opera and the 'bob' was born. The truth of course is quite different. Women had already worn bobbed hair for years.

She launched a scent which bore her own name—Chanel No. 5. Five was her lucky number; she came into the world on the 5th August, she showed her summer models on the 5th February and her winter models on the 5th August.

Jumpers with false or real jewellery, the accordion-pleated skirt, all this was new and has not gone out of fashion to this day. Perhaps one day they *will* become unfashionable and take their place in the limbo of fashion history. What does that matter? As Chanel said to Michel de Brunhoff, the brilliant director of French *Vogue:* 'A happy find is only there to be lost again.'

## SCHIAPARELLI

'The Italian artist who makes dresses,' Chanel once called her competitor 'Schiap', as she is known in Paris.

Chanel and Elsa Schiaparelli were antagonists, just as she and Poiret had been, except that the latter pair had orchestrated the style of their age symphonically, whereas 'Schiap' entered the stage with jazz music. But after all, the saxophone, too, is a musical instrument.

The eight years which divided Schiap's first fashion displays from those of Chanel were decisive. The fact that she began in 1928 was one of the reasons for her success.

People were tired of the garçonne type—just as they suddenly got tired of living in a room full of laboratory furniture.

One wanted a return to a little more daintiness and colour, Baroque additions in decoration and spangles in fashion—something new whether it were beautiful or hideous. How far off were the days when the bourgeois had raised his walking-stick threateningly against the pictures of the Impressionists and the public bombarded *avant garde* plays with rotten apples!

To accept everything, and originality at all costs! The more eccentric, stubborn and hectic a life one led the more eagerly one was acknowledged. Anyone who liked perversions of taste ranked as an original. Art dealers searched for new trends in art, and publishers for literary sensation. The 'misunderstood' artist was as much a thing of the past as the 'misunderstood' woman.

It seems quite comprehensible that Baroque ornament should have been introduced into fashion by an Italian. An innate love of the theatrical, a fiery temperament less hide-bound than its French counterpart, still shows itself today in Italian arts and crafts, which range from the tasteless to the artistically perfect.

Nothing seemed to predestine Schiaparelli to her ultimate profession. But when, after an unhappy marriage, she was left with a child and had to fend for herself, she conceived the brilliant idea of letting women from the Armenian colony in Paris knit jumpers to her own design. In these jumpers she introduced motifs from Negro art, tattooists' designs and skeletons—Cubist and Surrealist patterns she knew so well. Their success was sensational. In 1935 she moved to one of the sumptuous houses in the Place Vendôme; she bought it from Mme Chéruit.

The jumpers were followed by knitted hats, shawls, trousered skirts and dresses. In her materials she developed Picasso's discovery of collage from newspaper cut-outs. Blouses, scarves, silk or woollen beach costumes had newspaper cuttings for patterns.

From each journey she brought back new ideas; peasant ornaments from the Tyrol, thick roomy sweaters from her ski-ing holidays, burnouses from North Africa, embroideries from Peru and Russia.

Cocteau and Bérard designed dresses for her. She adopted Bérard's colour-schemes and made a fashionable colour from his purple-pink, which she called 'shocking'.

Nothing escaped her. Hessian as material for dresses, American cloth with clip-fasteners for evening gowns. Her buttons were no longer in the shape of buttons, they were animals, masks, chains, padlocks and miniature guitars. 'Schiap' also adopted for ornaments the bright porcelain work with which Russian émigrés earned their living between the two world wars.

Schiaparelli invented handbags which were illuminated inside or played melodies like a musical-box when they were opened; phosphorescent brooches which lit up at night; all these experiments transformed themselves into dollars for her.

In the ten years before the war her clientele consisted of film-stars and smart society women. When ordering her dresses, Mae West sent her a plaster cast of her famous *devanture*.

More and more accessories, finery and ornaments. All this was characteristic of the pre-war period; the history of fashion shows that the years preceding great catastrophes invariably reveal a tendency towards the eccentric. The explanation of Schiaparelli's success can be found in the general loss of style in an age constantly in search of new sensations.

The fashion which began before the war and ended with the 1947 New Look was not, as Schiaparelli maintains, invented by her, nor did she invent the broad padded shoulders and the ever higher hairstyles. Fashion plates and magazines of the time show how this new silhouette appeared quite gradually and almost simultaneously in all the Haute Couture collections.

Schiaparelli once wrote that 70 per cent of all women live on illusions and that the remainder suffer from an inferiority complex. Schiaparelli catered for women with illusions, and when she was no longer able to offer them any more illusions her success was at an end.

## MADELEINE VIONNET

Madeleine Vionnet, an unobtrusive simple woman, was queen of Haute Couture for twenty years until she retired from her profession in 1939 without having had recourse to slogans, sensations or the blare of advertising.

She had started from the bottom and had worked herself up entirely by the force of her ability and without any outside help.

At the age of thirteen she was apprenticed in a small dress-maker's shop in the suburbs; five years later she went to England to learn English and soon found employment in a London fashion house. Then she returned to Paris.

This was before the First World War, when women still had well-stocked wardrobes and travelled with huge trunks, when Callot Sœurs were making voluminous Renaissance dresses for them in gold and embroidery. In these workrooms, under the eagle eye of Mme Gerber, one of the three sisters, the quiet little Madeleine sat as seamstress and learned her trade.

Five years later she went to Doucet, who was no longer at the peak of his fame, but who expected her to bring new life into his business. He allowed her to make her own models.

An expert in her profession, down to the last detail, refined by contact with a world of elegance and luxury, and full of her own creative ideas, she entered the House of Doucet at the age of thirty.

Small and round 'as a country *curé*' (disappointments or successes always ended, she confessed, in a good restaurant), as aggressive as a Protestant fanatic, she stood alone in her conflict against the *grand seigneur* of the eighteenth century and his blindly obedient minions.

The whole personnel of the House of Doucet boycotted the reforms of the new designer. The restraint of her models shocked, and their severity infuriated them. A few of the clients, however, particularly the smart demi-mondaines, sensed something new and gave her orders. Madeleine soon built up her own clientele and was able to win her independence. That was two years before the outbreak of war; then came the moratorium, unpaid bills and the closing of her shop in the rue de Rivoli.

In 1919 she reopened, and four years later was able to buy a smart house in the Avenue Montaigne. Her staff rose to over a thousand. In 1939 she retired. That is the story of her career.

Madeleine Vionnet has always been called 'the architect among dressmakers' because her creations always began with a clear idea of the construction of a dress. She herself admits that if this simplicity was transformed into elegance it was entirely thanks to Mme Gerber. 'Today I make Rolls-Royces,' she said, 'but without Mme Gerber I should probably only have made Fords.'

'To compare Mme Gerber with Doucet is to compare magnificent pomp with a pretty little trifle,' for Doucet's creations never started from a complete conception. When the dress was ready, he always added his finery and spangles to make the wearer appear more seductive—just like the milliners of the Rococo. 'Taken all in all,' says Mme Vionnet, 'the eighteenth century was an artificial age of flounces and fiddle-faddle.'

The season's models, she maintained, are only suited to very few women, and since the overwhelming majority look ridiculous in them, they must be dressed individually to suit their personal style, just as an interior decorator must suit his furnishing and trappings to the style of life of the occupant.

Individualism above all must determine the choice of material. A certain material suits a certain woman, and the two must enhance each other.

The ideal dress is the one that brings the body and its movements into harmony. Such a harmony is only possible when one obeys the rhythm peculiar to the material, whether its weave is straight or on the cross, and when one cuts it accordingly.

Jacques Worth maintained that Mme Vionnet was the greatest technician of modern Haute Couture. All professionals agree that she was the one to introduce a new technique of cutting. Her first step was to make the weavers increase the width of the material by two yards so that it could be made to suit a woman's figure. She modelled the shape by laying it on the cross, by quilting and braiding.

'One must examine the anatomy of every customer,' she declared. 'The dress must not hang on the body but follow its lines. It must accompany its wearer and when a woman smiles the dress must smile with her.

'The direction of the material, the weave and the cross lines on the one hand; precision, cut, proportion and balance on the other—that is what I oppose to the term fashion, which is an empty word and completely meaningless to a real dressmaker.'

In a letter she once wrote: 'I have discovered a system of cutting, and have ended up by becoming the slave of my own system.'

Even her trimmings were so much at one with the architecture of the dress that their patterns also followed the line of the weave as though 'welded into the material'.

The rigid discipline of her cut made her models far more difficult to copy than those of the other great houses. Copies in fact were only possible when her dresses were pulled to pieces and the different sections laid flat.

She first tried out her new ideas on the miniature wooden mannequin which stood on her table. People who watched spoke enthusiastically of the exciting moment when, like a sculptor, she modelled and draped, constantly in search of new harmonies. The draped classical gowns launched by other couturiers between the two world wars (contemporary with Picasso's classicist canvases) would have been quite impossible without Vionnet's technique of the cross-cut.

Her harmonies were never a static element but changed with each new trend of fashion. She had no special preference for this or that fashion. 'With each new alteration of the feminine ideal of beauty,' she said, 'I strive to find new harmonic variations on a given theme.' To the end of her activity she remained true to this theme with variations.

A spark of her genius seems to have passed to Mad Carpentier, the young pupil to whom Madeleine Vionnet presented her mannequin doll and who, since 1939, has run her own dress house with talent and unfailing taste.

## JEANNE LANVIN

When Jeanne Lanvin died in 1946, her fashion house was in full bloom and, a curious exception in Haute Couture, it had existed for almost half a century under the same leadership.

Already before the First World War she was world famous as a Grand Couturier. She reached the peak of her glory, or rather of her own particular style, between the two world wars.

Like Madeleine Vionnet, she started at the bottom of her profession as an apprentice at the age of thirteen. Jeanne, the eldest of ten children, came from a poor home and had to earn her living at a very early age. At first she specialized as a modiste. From the very start she made intriguing hats with an entirely personal note, which proved exceedingly popular.

In addition to this she made her little daughter's dresses. In those days, at the turn of the century, children's dresses were extremely shapeless, in reaction against the fashion of the two previous decades, in which little girls in stiff corsets, with tightly-laced waists, high collars and coy, long sleeves, had been made to look like little ladies. Now they were dressed once more as children, but the loose sailor blouses with their big collars, black stockings and black laced boots were utterly lacking in grace.

Jeanne Lanvin's little daughter, on the other hand, wore dresses which were at the same time smart and attractive, dainty and childish, in delicious combinations of colours and harmonious contrasts.

Strange women spoke to Jeanne Lanvin (she was divorced and had reverted to her maiden name) when she went for a walk with the little girl, and asked for the name of her dress-maker. Orders for children's dresses poured in from all sides. She soon amassed a little capital and was able to enlarge her premises in the same house in the Faubourg Saint-Honoré which today, with all its storeys, is the fashion house of Jeanne Lanvin. The children's clothes were followed by dresses for young girls, and then wedding dresses and complete trous-seaux. Within a few years she was one of the six or seven Grands Couturiers and her creations were displayed at every international exhibition.

For the Paris Arts and Crafts Exhibition of 1925 she was entrusted with the organization of the *Pavillon de l'Elégançe*, for at that time her creations had become synonymous with elegance. Through the years, Lanvin's style and her Lanvin clothes were talked of in all the fashion papers. Among them could be found period dresses with patterns which she had taken from the old masters. Yet her style always remained original—the style of Lanvin, the artist, who left her own mark on each change of fashion. Woman, dress and hat merged into a complete unit, a real composition. Even at the height of the tango fashion she remained true to her own style. Each of her models was completely original, and this is the reason for her unbroken success.

Jeanne Lanvin's first mannequin, the little daughter who was so charmingly dressed, is today the still beautiful Com-tesse de Polignac. She relates that it was not always pleasant as a child to be dressed and undressed four times a day and to be admired by all the ladies; but she speaks affectionately of her mother's profound and serious artistry. Jeanne Lanvin, the calm, taciturn woman, revelled in the colours and shapes of nature. Meadows in spring, fruit gleaming from the trellises, the contrasting shades in a flower-bed were the sources of her inspiration.

She was always in search of new beauties and new poetry. Jeanne Lanvin transposed into the realm of fashion Botticelli's lyrical and ethereal charm, and the gentle pastel tones of Renoir. She adored the work of these two painters. She conceived the famous *bleu Lanvin* which constantly reappeared in her models from the mediæval blue of church windows.

From the East she procured costly silks and brocades, silver and gold materials, and made them into the most beautiful gowns. Glittering bright-coloured scraps of material still lie in the show cases of her study, and her library is filled with the rare books on costume she collected for many years.

Hers was the first fashion house to have its own department for small girls. Childhood and youth were always her motto. During the First World War she opened branches in Nice, Cannes and Biarritz. It is impossible to give a list of all her famous well-dressed customers—the Princesse de Faucigny-Lucinge, known as 'the lady with the 365 toilettes', the smart Mme Henri de Rothschild, the novelist Louise de Vilmorin, the four actresses to whom Sacha Guitry has been married in succession. When Yvonne Printemps, his second wife, went to America she took with her eighty dresses from the House of Lanvin. The great poetess, Anna de Noailles, was so enamoured of Lanvin's genius that in her will she expressed the wish to be buried in one of her dresses. Eve Lavallière, the beautiful actress, was one of her best customers, until in 1914 she suddenly renounced the world.

Jeanne Lanvin has designed costumes for countless actresses and film-stars: for Arletty and Maria Casarès in *Les Enfants du Paradis*, the mermaid dresses for frail Madeleine Ozeray in

Giraudoux' *Ondine*. One of her mannequins looked so like Marlene Dietrich that when the great film-star came, accompanied by Jean Gabin, to order dresses *chez* Lanvin, the gowns were displayed by the mannequin Marlene; Jean Gabin fell in love with the younger edition of the film-star and married her.

These are little stories from the great House of Lanvin. The life of this great fashion artist herself was so simple and direct that her fame needs no romantic tales or legends to embellish it.

## THUMBNAIL SKETCHES OF GRANDS COUTURIERS

JEAN PATOU was already a name before the First World War when, in 1914, an American bought his whole collection from the fashion house, where he worked as a designer, and he was able to set up on his own. After the war he opened his salon in the rue Saint-Florentin and swiftly rose to fame. In 1924 his turnover had increased twenty-four times. He was the first of the couturiers to inaugurate a dress rehearsal for the home and foreign Press on the eve of his display.

Patou also fought against the garçonne fashion, against Chanel, the masculine style of 1925 and the ubiquitous black. He could afford a luxury which today no couturier can afford—to have his cloths and colours especially woven for him.

Patou's individuality lay in improvisation, and many people maintained that he was more of a conjurer than a couturier. In 1929 the long evening dress was shown for the first time in his collections.

His best customers were the Queen of Roumania, the Queen of Spain, Mary Pickford, Pola Negri and Gaby Morlay.

LUCIEN LELONG founded his business in 1919 and retired in 1948. He learned his trade in his parents' fashion house before the 1914 war. In 1924, as one of the first, he moved from the Place de la Madeleine to the Avenue Matignon, the coming centre of Haute Couture. Lelong rose to fame almost as quickly as Patou. He was soon obliged to build a seven-storey annexe in his garden, and by 1926 he was employing twelve hundred workers.

His style embodied his aim as a couturier: femininity and the embellishment of woman.

In 1934, in advance of his professional colleagues, he founded an 'Editions' department, in order that by duplicating certain models women of lesser means should have a chance of dressing smartly. This was an innovation which, like all novelties, was much criticized and opposed. Today there is hardly a great fashion house that does not possess a similar department for cheaper dresses. His talent for commerce and organization had ample scope since for many years he was president of the *Chambre syndicale de la couture.*

When asked one day for the names of his clients he replied: 'Well . . . the Duchess of Windsor, Ingrid Bergman, Marlene Dietrich, Jacqueline Delubac . . . Hmm, who have I not dressed?'

EDWARD MOLYNEUX, always known as Captain Molyneux, is an Irishman of Huguenot origin on his father's side. He wanted to be painter like his grandfather, but a sketch for an evening dress which he drew as a seventeen-year-old boy and which won him first prize in a competition staged by the London fashion house Lucile proved decisive for his future career.

After the First World War, in which he reached the rank of Captain in the British Army and won several decorations, he founded an Haute Couture business in Paris. With Chanel he had in common the fateful number 5. His house was no. 5 rue Royale, and his most successful perfume was Molyneux No. Cinq.

He was launched by Lord Northcliffe, the newspaper

magnate whom he never met personally; after each new collection the *Daily Mail* featured Captain Molyneux all over the front page. His style was distinction and the costliest possible ladylike simplicity.

MAGGY ROUFF, the daughter of the Belgian couple Besançon de Wagner, who ran the House of Drécoll, seemed predestined to play a part in the realm of fashion. This elderly but still beautiful and worldly woman, however, sees her career with other eyes. She always speaks of her profession as of an enchanting fantasy, the caprice of a Grande Dame. She wanted to become a surgeon, but after the Armistice of 1918 she decided to devote her life to Haute Couture under the pseudonym Maggy Rouff. She went from success to success. Her house became synonymous with refined and very feminine elegance. In order to put her imaginative ideas into practice she learned the ABC of the profession—cutting and sewing.

'My wife was the last great fashion creator,' said her husband, 'and please note, she was not in trade, she is an artist.'

'I was ahead of the fashion,' added Maggy Rouff. 'I took risks and used materials which had never before been used in Haute Couture; for historical plays I never used period costumes but merely stylized the epoch symbolically, thus creating a particularly modern style of costume design.'

Maggy Rouff also maintains that she fought against the garçonne mode and Chanel's muted tones. But what couturier today does not say this? Which of the designers of 1925 does not claim that he introduced colour into a colourless age?

For twenty-five years Maggy Rouff was among the leaders, and was then intelligent enough to retire at the right time from Haute Couture.

She likes to hold forth on elegance and fashion and has written a book: *La Philosophie de l'Elégance*. She is still considered today as an *arbiter elegantiarum*.

Whenever one asks for a judgment on the Grand Couturier ROBERT PIGUET one hears variations on the same theme: supersensitivity, delicacy, æstheticism, aristocratic elegance and graceful charm.

This most Parisian of all fashion artists, a prince in the Cocteau-Jean Marais-Christian Bérard circle, was the son of a Swiss banker and Federal Councillor; he came to Paris at the age of seventeen to become a couturier. ('At your age,' his father once said to him, 'I should have preferred to undress women rather than to dress them.')

As a designer he went through a good school—Redfern and Poiret. In 1933 he started his own house on the Rond Point des Champs Elysées which he had to close in 1951 on account of illness. He died in 1953.

He had the salons of his fashion house decorated like the halls of Italian Palaces with pillars, gigantic drapes and clouds of gauze for the ceiling. His style as a designer was in direct contrast to this: the refined simplicity of black and white dresses, tailor-mades with waistcoats and astrakhan-trimmed coats.

When MLLE ALIX showed her fashion drawings to Michel de Brunhoff, the editor of *Vogue*, he advised her most urgently to stop playing about with such things, for her sketches seemed to him utterly hopeless.

Shortly after this, one of his acquaintances asked him to look at her latest discoveries: they were gowns made by Alix, so smart and original that de Brunhoff devoted two pages with photographs in *Vogue* (1932) to these chefs-d'œuvre. Two years later Alix already had a large fashion salon in the Faubourg Saint-Honoré; in 1942 she became Mme Grès and moved to the rue de la Paix.

Style and working methods are one with her. In other words, her technique is dependent upon her style, and hei style upon her ideal of feminine beauty—the draped Greek statue.

Mme Grès has won her place in Haute Couture with this highly personal style. She cuts the material directly without pattern or drawing. She has never used reinforcements, shoulder padding or quilting, and the material alone has to obey her will. Women dressed by her wear neither brassière nor corset; she models a slip of stiff organdie ('I do whatever I please with the breasts,' she says), and prefers to drape with clinging silk jerseys which Rodier has made to her design since 1935. At that time Rodier also made materials for her of unusual width so that she could launch her seamless cloak.

Although one can date the draped gowns which take twenty yards of material and a month's work, they stand outside the fashion of the day and never become unfashionable. A 1955 newspaper reported that Marlene Dietrich's daughter wore a dress which Alix had made twenty years before for her mother.

Mme Grès has never really been able to impart the technique of her craftsmanship to anyone. Admittedly she trains a few girls, but never more than five. Their apprenticeship lasts two years, but she alone is responsible for the three hundred and fifty models which are shown each year in her *atelier*.

The fame of MARCEL ROCHAS began with a burlesque tragedy. In 1930, at a smart party, eight women suddenly noticed they were wearing the identical black silk gown with the same necklace of artificial flowers. There were hysterical tears, two torn dresses, necklaces stamped underfoot—and Rochas was made.

In the same year he opened in the Avenue Matignon. He was soon involved in a dispute with Schiaparelli, whom he accused of plagiarism.

Rochas was full of the most fantastic ideas. He launched

materials with flower and bird patterns, puffed sleeves, gay combinations of as many as ten different colours, boldly draped evening gowns. He loved lace, ribbon and tulle. The most important trait in his biography also holds good for his style in fashion: he loved women and was married three times.

Rochas' tendency towards a more feminine line already showed itself during the war, and consequently before the New Look, when he introduced models with rounded shoulders, lengthened skirts and more slender waists. His feminine '*silhouette amphore*' was a reaction against the then rustic outline of the Fath models.

In 1947 he invented a new corset, the *guêpière*, a solid girdle to narrow the waist, which finally set the seal upon the New Look.

Films were his passion and he designed many costumes for the great film-stars. In Jacques Becker's film *Falbalas* he even played the part of Bluebeard, who hung in a shop-window all the women he had loved in the dresses he had made for them.

Some years before the war, Rochas went to Hollywood, and Mae West's gowns, with their mass of black lace and trains, were not without influence on his models. Death took him suddenly in 1953 in the middle of an active, gay, hectic and fantastic life.

JACQUES HEIM'S parents were furriers. Shortly after the First World War his mother had the idea that one might use not only expensive furs in Haute Couture but rabbit skins as well. She suggested this to Gabrielle Chanel, who was one of her customers. A new fashion was born.

The young Jacques Heim showed his flair for the future when he designed bathing and beach costumes under the influence of the exotic native dresses from Tahiti, with their striking balik patterns, which were displayed at the Paris Colonial Exhibition.

Not only the exotic patterns but the material itself, the cotton fabric which is still in fashion, was used by him for the first time in Haute Couture.

Another innovation was his department for young girls, followed after the war by 'Heim-Actualité', where dresses are sold far more cheaply and, unlike similar departments in present-day Haute Couture, are designed on the premises and carried out with rigid working discipline.

Before the war Heim already owned a magnificent newspaper, the *Revue Heim*, which was born as a house magazine. It was edited by the well-known art critic Marcel Zahar, who set the pattern for modern fashion papers with his new and original ideas.

Some of the Grands Couturiers closed their workshops for good at the beginning of the war, among them Augusta Bernard, a Provençal who proved her talent as a copyist (particularly of Chanel models) before starting on her own in 1919, and Mainbocher, an American who established himself in 1929 and returned to America at the outbreak of war.

Others, like Mme Bruyère, whose collections are a highlight of Paris elegance, the Italian Nina Ricci (her biography, too, begins with the words, 'As a child she made dresses for her dolls'), the Greek Jean Dessès, who has worked in Paris since 1937, and Madeleine de Rauch, active since 1930, have been carrying on after the war with great success.

When hats were still a more important item of fashion than they are today, there were modistes who were just as famous as the couturiers. The Parisienne was well known for her love of hats and preferred whenever possible to possess a number of them to wear with the same dress.

Rose Valois, who started with the famous Caroline Reboux and founded her own house in 1927, Suzanne Talbot, Maria

Guy, Agnès, all were highly individual modistes and as such made a great contribution to Parisian chic.

One must not forget to mention, when we speak of chic, the beautiful well-fitting sports clothes from Hermès, the gloves from Perrin or Alexandrine, or the supple corsets from Charmis.

## THREATENING CLOUDS

Seven years after the end of the First World War France's position in the world market was still excellent and her trade figures reached new records in the international statistics. Within the framework of French exports the sum total of fashion articles—dresses, lingerie, furs and accessories—stood in second place. Ten years later it had fallen to twenty-seventh place.

At the outset it was a crisis in Haute Couture, caused by the social changes of the time and in no way due to economic factors: an anonymous crowd of women had taken the place of the smart society ladies of a bygone age and were no longer prepared to submit to the dictates of the Grands Couturiers. Clothes had ceased to be one of women's main preoccupations and hosts of working women took refuge in standardized fashion and bought ready-made garments, which saved them time and needless expense of thought.

In those days a new type of snobbery was born: people were afraid of being numbered among the nouveaux riches or war profiteers and indulged in over-simple, almost shabby clothes. This meant a further loss to Haute Couture.

Then, like a tornado, came the great international slump, which spread all over the world at the end of the 'twenties. Even American prosperity turned out to be without solid foundations.

The great Wall Street crash had a fatal effect upon French

fashion production. The American buyers of Haute Couture cancelled orders which had already been carried out and not a single one attended the dress shows for the mid-season in December.

French fashion exports fell by 70 per cent and the slide could no longer be stopped. In 1935 the losses of the French dress industry reached a figure of nearly 2 milliard francs. While in 1925 there had been no unemployment in the French fashion industry, in the year of the crash ten thousand workers were unemployed in Paris alone.

It was not only in America that millions became beggars overnight. Incomes in France and other countries fell alarmingly.

Nothing superfluous was now bought and there was hardly a woman who did not put the brake on her dress expenditure. It is a strange paradox: from 1929 the long evening gown came back into fashion, and since then, when purchasing power had virtually sunk to nothing, the new feminine line once more showed finery, jewellery and embroidery.

Economic crises are always followed by world-wide nationalistic movements; chauvinistic attitudes in economic propaganda find a fertile soil. Buy American! Buy British! Buy only German goods! These slogans became laws in international trade. Tariffs on imports were increased and, what was worse, some countries inaugurated the quota system. So effective was this national propaganda that even fashion articles, which could freely be imported, were boycotted, particularly in England.

The sharp decline in tourist travel, another result of the slump, also did immense damage to the French fashion trade. In 1934 the number of tourists who visited France from the United States fell by a quarter. Apart from that, there were currency restrictions in many countries, which prevented

'Coco' Chanel

Jean Patou

The Twenties: a fashionable dress at Ascot in 1925

tourists to France from making any substantial purchases in France.

Haute Couture has never really recovered from these blows. Its present-day difficulties are deeply rooted in those upheavals which began between the two world wars. For after the Wall Street crash, in view of the reduced purchasing power of the American fashion houses, the American buyers adopted a new tactic. While hitherto many of them had bought about ten models from each collection, they now joined forces to buy a single model. They lent each other the model, copied the cut, or, once they returned home, leased it to the ready-made houses for unlimited reproduction. As the models were finally returned to France, this practice freed the American fashion houses of all import duty.

In the last few years before the Second World War the dominance of Parisian fashion began to shift into a different sphere. With the falling off of private customers, the couturier's interest was mainly concentrated on producing models for export. They were no less beautiful and represented no less the concept of Parisian chic and elegance, but the unique individual model designed for a single customer disappeared. Woman appeared to have been banished from fashion creation as the human figure was from abstract art.

Twilight had fallen upon the world of Parisian Haute Couture.

# X

# THE INTERNATIONAL STAGE OF HAUTE COUTURE

## IDEAS (IN THE FORM OF AN INTERVIEW)

INTERVIEWER: Where do you get the inspirations for so many new ideas? Two hundred models for the winter season, two hundred models for the summer season, between-season models. Ideas and more ideas . . .?

COUTURIER: A brief question! But it would take a book to answer it. I take them from everywhere. Women I meet in the street, women I see on the films; a line, a movement, a colour—they are all pictures in the imagination which gradually take on shape and form.

Q: And from fashion plates and old works of art?

A: From those too. Even if I cannot give you any precise details they are exciting, whether you take the enchanting drapery of Tanagra figures, the clinging garments in Persian miniatures, or the strangely modern bathing costumes on Roman mosaics. My imagination often dries up, and then a glance at some old costume plates is enough to spur it on or to find a hint for some new form of trimming.

Q: Could such fashion plates actually influence a style of fashion?

A: No. Only when they accord with the taste of the times, when they find an echo in present-day lines.

Q: Are there not couturiers whose style still clings to the past, and thus becomes ageless?

A: Pure imagination. Of pictures of Grecian costumes by Vionner or period clothes by Lanvin, the future fashion historian will be able to say immediately: that is 1925, 1930 or 1940.

Q: Is fashion today really more short-lived than in the past, as nearly all the critics maintain?

A: It only appears so because we are not sufficiently far removed from our own time. If you look through the earliest fashion journals, beginning at the end of the eighteenth century, you find just as rapid a change. You can read from one month to the next: today this and that is worn. . . . There is always something new, and the hunt for fashion sensations was no less marked in the old days than it is today. Perhaps historians of costume in a hundred years' time will be able to notice a greater stability of style in our age than we at present are aware of.

Fashion is always composed of two elements—the comparatively stable general style, which only alters slowly, and the countless mobile features which change from one season to the next. To find a balance between these two is our task, and the solution of this problem is one of the many secrets of our success. A novelty is only acceptable if it is in harmony with the style of the age. Everything follows a strict logic.

INTERVIEWER: You talk like a philosopher. . . .

COUTURIER: And I act like an artist, for I interpret these laws in my own way.

Q: Do you then invariably recognize an empirical law in the change of fashion style?

A: Yes, the same law that applies in the constant change of society, justified by its ever new needs.

Q: Then you should in fact be able to forecast the new fashion?

A: No. We cannot foresee what tomorrow will bring by way of new art, new furniture shapes or new fashion. We have to sense the psychological moment when a line and a colour have outlived their day or will shortly do so.

Q: Can you give me an example?

A: Logically speaking, grey and its shades should be followed by beige and brown and their complementary colours. The same thing holds good also for the line. That is precisely the exciting and risky aspect of our profession: a model designed for the coming season may conflict with the mysterious development of style. In that case women will instinctively reject it.

Q: But can it be ahead of the fashion?

A: Certainly. Then it eventually comes into its own. But sometimes only two or three years later.

Q: Can you forecast which of your models will eventually justify themselves?

A: That is difficult to say. When a certain model is too eccentric and arouses hostility or little appreciation from women, I withdraw it from the collection and alter it slightly for the next season. The models, on the other hand, which have a great and often surprising success I accentuate for the next collection. I see that I have struck the right note and merely emphasize it.

Q: You spoke of the craving to shine in society. But are not erotic impulses even more determining?

A: Far less than many æsthetes and interpreters of fashion would like to think. The urge to shine, to gain social prestige, is very pronounced among women. Just watch the ladies in the restaurants, where they display their latest toilettes. It would seem that women only dress for other women. Erotic impulses are only decisive when a woman dresses for a certain man, or men; she will make herself as seductive as possible, but according to her own ideas.

Q: Then cannot a beautiful woman, whose couturier dresses her to suit her personality, influence the fashion?

A: Oh, that is quite a thing of the past. It was possible in the days of Marie Antoinette, Mme Tallien, Pauline Metternich and Réjane. In those days the couturier worked in close collaboration with the customer and had long conferences with her. Their joint imaginations created an individual dress. It was seen at receptions, balls and on the stage. It was sketched and copied. Today the couturier creates the model and thus influences the fashion.

Q: And where does this influence begin?

A: Already with the textile manufacturers. In the old days they were far more dependent on the caprices of fashion than they are today. If ample dresses were being worn, silk materials were most suitable and thus a great impulse was given to silk production. When the fashion for puffed sleeves replaced the wide skirts with the Restoration in 1818, there was a great crisis in the wool industry.

Q: So fashion actually begins with the material?

A: Even earlier than that. The fashion begins with the thread. Fashion already starts with the dyeing of the wool, skeins of cotton, silk and substitute threads such as artificial silk, nylon, orlon, etc.

Q: Does that require a very long preparation?

A: Of course. Two years before the chef-d'œuvre appears threads must be woven and dyed, and the patterns worked out on small looms. One has to have a great deal of foresight and optimism. Within two years the capriciousness of fashion might have led to such radical changes that all the preparations might prove to have been in vain.

Q: So the collaboration between textile manufacturer and couturier determines the new fashion?

A: The textile manufacturer must at least sense the ensuing fashion. For the winter fashions to be displayed in August he gives the couturier the patterns of his materials as early as May, and for the January dress shows the summer materials must be ready by the end of November. The production of the approximately hundred different patterns required takes a whole year, and although the manufacturer may think that he has recognized a preference for a certain colour on the part of the public, and bases his materials on this colour, it can in the end turn out to be unpopular. Moreover, the colours ordered by the couturier remain exclusive to him six months after the dress show. The cloth merchant, too, as a middleman between textile production and Haute Couture, today plays an ever greater part—he carries the fashion suggestions from one to another. He may be convinced that with a certain couturier certain colours will be pre-eminent and may suggest these to the cloth manufacturer.

Q: The material has its weaving effects and its design, so here too, I suppose, inspiration originates both in the sketches and in the twine?

A: Agreed. And the designer draws his material from contemporary events in the art world. The Russian ballet, cubism, the great exhibition of Mexican art in Paris, the fantastic success of the Chinese opera—all these were reflected in the designs. And the colours, too, follow the palettes of the great artists who happen to be in vogue—Goya, Gauguin or the Impressionists.

Q: And how is a new colour suddenly launched, as so often happens?

A: That, too, is quite different from the old days. For propaganda purposes a Lyons manufacturer gave the famous actress

Mlle Mars, Napoleon's protégée, a piece of canary-yellow velvet rep, from which, after some hesitation, she had a stage costume made. She finally appeared in it on the stage, because the great Talma had remarked that it was admirably suited to her black hair and sparkling eyes. The success was so great that orders poured in to the manufacturer. In a short time he had to enlarge his business and he became a very rich man.

Q: Does that no longer happen today?

A: Yes, but in quite a different way. Do you remember the vogue for the cognac colour of 1954? Well, the distillers in the Cognac region entrusted the advertising campaign of their brandy to an American agency. The agents visited all the big textile manufacturers, chose a certain yellowish-brown colour from their collections and called it cognac. Then the agency persuaded certain couturiers to create models in this shade and announced in the press: 'Cognac is the colour this season.'

And the grey cotton dresses in the summer of 1952 appeared because Boussac had a pile of grey cotton material left in his warehouses.

Q: But does the couturier ever use new or lesser known materials in Haute Couture?

A: Yes. And he suggests them to the makers. In 1919 Rodier produced for Chanel the Jersey wool which she made fashionable, and a few years later silk Jersey for Alix for her classical draperies. But ordering whole bales of material from the manufacturer, as Patou used to do, is today a great risk.

Q: Have there ever been couturiers who, in their quest for novelty, have invented new material themselves?

A: Yes. For example the dressmaker Georgette, who in 1909 gave a manufacturer the idea of a light, non-transparent weave, a kind of mixture between crêpe-de-Chine and muslin, which had the advantage of not losing its shape; this was the origin of crêpe Georgette.

Q: What have the manufacturers and fashion houses in mind when they launch completely new textiles?

A: The first impetus was given by a need for cheap imitations of expensive materials. Artificial silk, for example, has made it possible for nearly all classes of women to wear pretty dresses. And finally, the fashion industry has found new beauties in materials such as nylon or orlon, and thus aroused enthusiasm for their creations. Discovery and technical progress increase production and at the same time cheapen and popularize the fashion.

Q: We have deviated slightly from our original question. So the idea has taken a specific form in your imagination; well, what then?

A: Then I put it down on paper and the actual work of creation begins.

## PYGMALION

Fashion is a constant variation of a single theme: woman.

The fashion artist does his work with a mixture of playful arbitrariness and clear logic. He gives a flash of beauty to the transitory and lends grace and nobility to the lifeless material.

He is Pygmalion, breathing life into dead matter.

Hundreds of sketches lie spread out before him—sketches of tailor-mades, coats, simple woollen dresses, cocktail dresses and magnificent evening gowns. Like a Renaissance artist he is surrounded by acolytes—his designers, modellists and *premières d'atelier*. Modellists and *premières* choose the sketches with him, the former curb the imagination of the designers and transform the sketches into wearable forms, and the *premières* cut them out in white linen.

The wooden dummy stands before the fashion artist. The

strips of cotton material are laid round it, folded, draped, pinned, bound, taken to pieces again, changed and re-sewn. The beauty of the design arises primarily from the harmony between certain specific proportions; from this is formed the artistic element—the style.

The assembled strips, the *toile*, are made to retain their sculptural perfection by ironing. The *toiles* are then tried on the mannequins, but never indiscriminately. Here the *petite*, well-proportioned Madelon may have the right figure for a tailor-made; the smart Martine will give allure to the evening gown and the frail Arlette gay mobility to the dark puritanical woollen dress.

Pygmalion is inspired. He can already envisage the materials and colours, some to give the dress its architectural form, others to bring rhythm to the line. Now he makes his selection from the many samples which lie in front of him. An Oriental silk inspires him to produce a variation of a ceremonial robe, a certain colour will brighten the line of a dress and that stiff weave will best emphasize the new outline.

In his workrooms the *toile* has become a dress. With a small fold, a slight curve, Pygmalion brings out the grace; with a little quilting he accentuates his idea of the new line, which is to be the theme of the whole collection. He will go on modelling, building and altering, adding and subtracting, until the smallest discordant note has been removed, until mannequin, material and colour form one harmonious unit.

The *premières d'atelier* give professional advice on the direction of the weave and the cross-cuts, the technical exploitation of the material used. The designers suggest the accessories: hats, scarves, embroideries, bags, buckles, buttons, brooches and necklaces. The couturier and his acolytes must not only find new cuts but new trimmings and new colours, for a new picture of woman must be produced for the coming months.

## BEHIND THE SCENES

The new collection is being prepared. Two hundred models have to be created and tried on the mannequins, who can hardly stand on their feet from weariness.

Never-ending activity with scenes, excitement, quarrels and jubilation.

The collection must be ready within a few weeks. Excitement in the house is at fever pitch and night is turned into day.

The wheels of this delicate, well-oiled machinery turn ever faster, and at a more breath-taking speed with ever fewer breaks. Will the collection really be ready in time?

Never have the little apprentices so well earned their nickname: *lapins de couloir*. They are chivvied from workroom to workroom, from the storeroom back to the workroom and to the mannequins' dressing-rooms. They take it all in their stride, for an unpredictable future lies ahead of them. If they are talented and industrious they can climb all the steps of the hierarchy: *petite main*, *seconde main*, *première main*, *seconde d'atelier*, *première d'atelier*. . . .

One day, as *première d'atelier*, they will collaborate with the great chief, who will follow their advice, and they will rule the workrooms with an iron hand. Their names will be a byword in the Paris fashion world—Mme Marguerite, Mme Madeleine, Mme Yvonne.

Do all the midinettes really dream of a career in the fashion house where they are employed? Once upon a time they did. Anyone who today maintains that every seamstress, even if she works for a fashion king, is devoted to her chief, to the house where she works and to the dress she sews, has never been allowed a glimpse behind the scenes. Just as there are no longer any faithful butlers who serve their debt-ridden masters without wages until they die, no more maids who identify their fate with that of their employers, the faithful seamstresses who grow old in a fashion house are a dying race.

The enchanting little midinette of a bygone age, with the rakish hat (she seldom wears a hat today), with her dress skilfully conjured out of nothing, her gay gossip and irrepressible gaiety, the midinette who was the theme of a thousand songs, who once haunted the rue de la Paix, for whom gentlemen with monocles, walking-sticks and white spats haunted the boulevards when the workshops closed, has vanished for ever.

Seductive in their apparently carefree youth, they were still a feature of the Paris streets before the Second World War. Since then things have changed considerably. Paris chic still consists of that indefinable and inimitable *je ne sais quoi*; craftsmanship to which dressmaking belongs still exists as it has for centuries; it remains a typically French, highly skilled form of work. And even today optimism is a characteristic of the Parisian midinette.

But her work is hard and promotion is slow. At the age of fourteen, when she leaves school, her problems already begin: which is she to choose, technical school or apprenticeship? If her family is poor she is forced to start her career as an apprentice in a fashion house. But is it really an apprenticeship? The *lapins de couloir* are mostly used to fetch and carry, to hold pins and materials. Even at the end of their apprenticeship, when they have attended the compulsory one-hour courses five times a week (where apart from sewing they are also taught elementary subjects), they can often hardly sew a stitch. If they pass their exam successfully, for years they are hardly better paid than a charwoman. The three French trades unions (the Christian, Socialist and Communist) which press their claims for higher wages, holidays with pay (holiday money is only paid on their return from holidays, which compels many seamstresses to remain in the city), and better pension schemes, come up against the resistance of the employers. And it remains, of course, a fact not to be overlooked, that, despite the fantastically high prices of their dresses, most of the great fashion houses cannot exist without a subsidy.

But the unions also often report indifference on the part of the midinettes, who prefer to live for the day rather than fight for a better existence and a more secure future. The girls in the workrooms are hardly aware of the colossal prices of the dresses and the collections (one of their claims is to be allowed to see them), and scarcely come in contact with the smart customers. They live in the antechambers of a forbidden paradise.

Old-age insurance is one of the burning problems. Anything rather than grow old in this profession, rather than feel oneself unable to keep up the pace in this exciting hard work and to be dismissed for being unfit for it! Before it is too late the employees often choose to do outside work and go on sewing for Haute Couture at home—this, however, is considered as blacklegging and thus they forfeit their claims for sick pay and the protection of their union.

Many of them are married, but most of the marriages are childless. How could they find time to bring up children? Mme Lanvin, without taking advice and merely obeying her social sympathy—she was once a seamstress herself—had a crèche built for her employees' children; it was charmingly appointed, with plenty of beds, cradles and playrooms. When everything was ready it transpired that there were so few families among the hundreds of married employees that it could never be opened.

There is only one day in these fashion houses when, as in the old days, a spirit of relaxation and riotous gaiety reign—

the 25th November, St Catherine's Day. The employees save money all the year round in order to invite friends and relations to the dance given by the firm. There are amateur theatricals, often very original, on subjects connected with the history of fashion.

These are sunnier episodes in an existence that is often overshadowed by dark care.

In the storeroom lie the materials for the dresses—wools from the north of France, printed cottons with gay patterns, silks and velvets. The silks, the finest and most charming discovery of weaving, mostly come from Lyons, where for hundreds of years the home weavers have lovingly served their looms; where in the eighteenth century Philippe de Lasalle and Jean Pillemont produced their enchantingly beautiful designs. For centuries, moreover, since the Parisian fashion monopoly spread to silk patterns and the great Lyons manufacturers opened their depositories in Paris, the designs have often been created in Paris under the influence and often with the collaboration of famous painters.

The head of the storeroom must naturally know all the suppliers of materials and accessories, and all the sources for tasteful, quality goods.

The workrooms are the heart and pulse of Haute Couture. Without the tireless hands of the workgirls, their industry and gaiety, even the most brilliant couturier would not be able to realize his enchantments, which seems like a last fairy-tale in our drab world.

The variety of specialized work which takes place in the workrooms can hardly be summed up. Here woollen tailor-mades are made up and there fur capes and coats. Workrooms for afternoon and evening dresses of dainty silks and light summery materials, draped, gathered up and cut on the cross—*le flou*, which in the international world of fashion is considered the quintessence of Parisian chic.

Here are the *ateliers* where the models are repeated and altered individually for private customers, over there the *ateliers de créations* where the models designed by the chief and his modellist are realized, other rooms where hats are made to go with the dresses, and yet others for the designers.

Work in this domain is organized down to the last detail. Each *première* is given her instructions by the couturier, according to her own special capabilities. Some specialize in coats and skirts and others in afternoon or evening gowns. The *seconde* is given the cutting details by the *première*, explanations as to which way the stuff must be cut and the trimmings designed for it. The *seconde* then distributes the work among her *premières mains* and supervises the making of the models.

The *vendeuses* form an almost entirely separate unit in a fashion house. Like the modellists and mannequins they are incomparably better paid than the workgirls, and in addition receive a percentage on their sales.

The more Haute Couture produces seasonal models in preference to catering mainly for individual clients, the more the saleswoman takes over the function of the couturier. Her duties are many; she must help the customer to choose, supervise the fitting, and be careful that any alteration to the model required does not contradict the style of the man who created it; she must also know the foreign buyers and their agents.

A *vendeuse* not only receives a higher wage but often gifts and, in addition to this, Stock Exchange tips which allow her to look forward to a comfortable old age. One of the Worth saleswomen was able to give her daughter a princely dowry; constantly in contact with important clients, she was given such good financial advice that she was able to invest her savings in very profitable shares.

The *vendeuse* also often has a psychological duty to perform. The fitting-room is a confessional, or rather, since absolution will not be given there, a psychiatrist's consulting-room. While the *vendeuse* and the fitters are trying on her dress the customer talks about her private affairs, 'gets things off her chest', and feels far better for it.

Many a saleswoman could write a series of novels about her customers. There are the beautiful and frivolous, who preen themselves in front of the mirror obviously enjoying the fitting; then there are the ideal customers who look well in the boldest models; the severe women, who cast a professional eye on the smallest pleat, and the ill-tempered ones who are delighted when they can find faults or a mistake.

Behind the scenes sits a very important man of whom the public knows nothing. He is the chief accountant, surrounded by a host of employees, a bureaucrat and yet a focal point of this artistic high-speed business. Everything passes through his hands. All that the couturier designs and the hundreds of workgirls complete, the materials that are bought, the trimmings, embroideries, braid, jewellery, lie on his desk and are transformed into figures and tables. He checks, compares and calculates what a dress costs: wages, insurance, taxes, materials, canteen contributions, the entire turnover, the revenue and the subsidies. Without his calculations and his breakneck evolutions on the dangerous tightrope between debit and credit, the undertaking could never exist.

## MANNEQUINS

French encyclopedias define a mannequin as a wooden or cardboard doll in human form, upon which tailors, dressmakers and clothes' dealers fit and display their clothes.

Fashion dummies have existed for centuries. The Marquise de Pompadour possessed one of plaited straw on which her tailor used to try her dresses. At the beginning of the nineteenth century the 'mannequins' were of wire and fifty years later of cardboard. The tailoring busts filled with wool or sawdust and covered with linen have been a familiar sight in dressmakers' shops since the turn of the century.

One day these mannequins came to life. They were not as yet those beautiful girls around which so many romantic legends have been woven—girls who are carried off by Maharajahs or marry oil kings; or cinderellas who live in wretched garrets and for a few hours are transformed into elegant ladies in the fashion salons. Nor were they yet the tall fitter's girls with the beautiful figures, whose slimness made all the customers imagine that they would look just as slim and beautiful in the dress she displayed.

Live mannequins were used for the first time in the age when the impeccable and distinguished dandy, in whom Balzac saw the embodiment of elegance, ruled the fashion world and the great tailors put even the most able women dressmakers in the shade.

These men's tailors discovered a new form of advertising: young men appeared on the promenade in their latest creations, like those sent out by the famous Humann, who dressed the fastidious Balzac; they wore on their backs a tiny shield with the name and the address of the tailor. 'They are known as mannequins,' writes Huart, in his *Physiologie de tailleur*, which appeared in 1840. They were the first of their name.

Dress show at the House of Jacques Fath

Evening dress by Christian Dior

Christian Dior

The great Worth who founded Haute Couture was the first to have his dresses displayed by young beautiful women, and he accurately assessed the snobbery of his customers. Even if these *essayeuses* came from a Paris slum or some back-alley, his 'sense of theatre' transformed them into English girls with names like Miss Lizzie, Miss Kitty and Miss Mary.

We can easily see (particularly from a fashion article written in 1867) that models in those days were designed for each client individually. One girl was fat and the other thin. Worth chose them to correspond with the figures of his great clients. As a result of this they were also called *sosies*, or doubles. A *sosie* was not allowed to put on or take off weight before she received her orders, but then she had to hurry or else she risked losing her job.

A few years later the fashion journalist of the *Vie Parisienne* gave them the name which they still bear today: 'The couturier gives Mlle Mannequin a sign. That well-proportioned blonde, you know, whom everyone wants to display the new dresses. . . . Mannequin has understood; she disappears, changes, and soon returns in the new model.'

With the sale of models for industrial purposes at the turn of the century, the role of the mannequin became much more important. The couturier now displayed his creations not for his customers alone. Twice a year he showed his season's collection to the buyers from the provinces and abroad.

It was possibly this extended function and the industrial objective which, in the course of the next decades, gradually seemed to extinguish the mobility and personality of the mannequin. As far as possible they had to be alike in figure and movement.

The mannequin parade at a big fashion show is like a mechanical ballet of marionettes. Everything is thought out and studied: the light, discreet, dancing step with which she enters, advances and retreats, steps forward again; the opening of the coat to show the lining, the removal of the wrap which she then trails behind her, her cool glances at the public until she catches the eyes of a prospective client. Glances, steps and movements have become internationalized. The mannequins of San Francisco, Rio de Janeiro and Chicago all trip alike.

To become adepts they train in special schools where they learn how to use their feet and eyes. They have their clubs, statutes, rates of pay and they need no side income. And naturally they have their diets and their hunger cures.

The social position of the mannequins has also changed. Before the First World War the profession was a trifle disreputable. With the Russian emigration, however, when Princesses and Grand Duchesses, who had never learned to do anything practical, seized upon it as a golden opportunity, the profession also changed. With the entrance of mannequins into middle-class society, the romance which once surrounded them disappeared.

They are of the utmost importance as collaborators in the creation of the models. A discontented glance at a *toile* or a dress during a fitting is often enough to call the attention of the chief or *première* to a mistake.

The mannequin's job is moreover far harder than the public would imagine when, beneath the arc-lights, with an impassive face and stereotyped smile, she flits down the steps and through the hall. No one realizes what difficult weeks lie behind her. How irritating and tiresome the lightning changes in the dressing-rooms can be. A woman—the *chef de cabine*—supervises the proceedings—and the *habilleuses* give their aid. For each dress a hat, bag, sunshade and other accessories lie to hand. The whole drill of changing is worked out with split-second precision, for the smallest error would be enough to destroy the harmony of the ensemble.

The prelude to the fashion show is just like a dress rehearsal in the theatre. The mannequins file past the couturier and his general staff remain standing in front of him while he, like the producer in the theatre, makes some little alteration here and there. There are last doubts and last searching looks. . . .

On the following day begins the first performance, reserved for the fashion press. The setting is neutral. The carpeted salons, chandeliers, candelabra, silk upholstered chairs, fragile gilt stools, muslin curtains and velvet drapes—the whole décor is closer to the eighteenth century than to our sober age, and as a result has become ageless. Nothing in these lofty rooms with their discreet colours and cunningly thought-out lighting is allowed to distract the spectators from what they have come to see.

And while the *directrice* amidst whispers and great excitement calls out the names or numbers of the models in English and French, the mannequins appear in sports clothes, tailor-mades, fur coats, evening gowns and wedding dresses—heralds of fashions to come.

## FASHION JOURNALISM

On the stairs and in the salons sit the fashion reporters—women in the overwhelming majority—columnists of big and small fashion journals from five continents, watching and taking notes.

They, too, have their history: with the founding of the first French fashion journal, the *Cabinet des modes*, a few years before the Revolution, a new profession was born—fashion reporting. The fashion reporter had to furnish a society élite with a picture of its own worldly existence, to write in a graceful and lyrical form on fashion and finery, sometimes with a touch of moralizing and sometimes with a keen sense of business: for it was his task to play the role of middleman between the fashion needs of society and the textile industry.

Until late in the nineteenth century, fashion articles were written by men. In the 1830's, Delphine Gay, the wife of the newspaper proprietor Emile de Girardin, wrote her enchanting articles—real mines of information for the society of her age under the pseudonym Vicomte de Launay. Gradually, however, with the levelling of male costume, when all fashion interest concentrated on women's clothes, more and more fashion papers were run and written by women. Now one was inclined to smile at men who bothered their heads too much about such fripperies. The Vicomtesse de Renneville, the first great fashion reporter, in her *Gazette rose* (1857) ridiculed her male colleagues who signed their work with female names as 'the Marquises in stiff collars'.

The poet Mallarmé apologized in a letter that lack of money had forced him to write for fashion papers. And yet the articles he wrote in 1874 for the journal *La dernière mode* under the pen names 'Marguerite de Ponty' and 'Miss Satin' are very graceful and readable. His embarrassment reminds one of Balzac, whose constant lack of money forced him to write such articles, and who obstinately denied his authorship of the *Physiologie de la Cravate*.

From the earliest days, the illustrations were an essential part of fashion reporting. Since time immemorial, beautiful women's dresses have inspired the greatest artists to sketch costumes. The more a frivolous way of life and capricious freedom of choice superseded a rigid etiquette of manners and clothes, the more important became the role of the artist who specialized in sketching for fashion papers. He was, no less than the journalist, a reporter of the latest modes. In this sense, Constantin Guys was the first of the modern fashion reporters.

There have always been artists and painters who have had

some influence on fashion, such as Poiret's protégés and, more recently, Christian Bérard.

Today, fashion photography outdoes the fashion draughtsman with its new sensations. Mannequins are often sent for a day by air to some distant place to give picturesque effects to the couturiers' latest creations; they are photographed against a flowery background on the Riviera, in the dark streets of a Spanish village or in a sunlit African oasis.

Before the pictures of the latest French models can be published in the papers, a whole month must elapse in order to prevent plagiarism. The fashion-hungry women of five continents try to guess the new tendencies of the Grands Couturiers merely from the journalist's reports. On the day of the first dress show, reports are cabled and telephoned, articles despatched by air all over the world to inform people who are waiting eagerly to learn the latest line. And then, photos and sketches are released for publication; when the great journals like *Vogue* or *Harper's Bazaar* bring out their special numbers on the spring or autumn collections, the selection of the pictures which they publish will set the season's fashion.

## BUYERS AND COMMISSION AGENTS

At the fashion equinoxes in February and August the buyers flock to Paris. After the great evening function, the show is repeated on the following day for the buyers. They come from Rome, Berlin, Hollywood, New York or Rio, from the whole wide world.

The foreign buyers often know each other: they are mostly representatives of the large American stores, departmental heads or directors, the 'general staff' of the American ready-made trade which today has only one object in mind: to buy as quickly as possible certain prescribed and carefully selected models even before the private customers have seen and ordered them.

Their choice is not a matter of personal taste. It is purely a matter of business. What is bought depends upon their customers, their budget and upon the town where their shops are situated. Boston society women who aspire to British distinction dress quite differently from Hollywood film stars, and busy, capable, New York career-women quite differently from smart hostesses in Buenos Aires.

Things are not made easy for the foreign buyers: they have to pay a deposit of about a thousand dollars with the biggest couturiers before they are even allowed to see the collection. The couturier looks upon this as a small compensation for the losses he will suffer from the 'viewing'. Several houses as a further guarantee insist that at least one model or *toile* must be bought. While a model often costs double the price a private customer pays, a *toile*, or pattern, may cost far less. Furthermore, to the *toile* are attached samples of materials and trimmings with the addresses of the houses who supply them. Naturally the reproduction of the pattern as such is strictly forbidden.

The import duties on models are fabulously high. They are based on the trimmings of the dress, the costliness of the embroidery or lace, and may on occasions amount to as much as 90 per cent of the purchase price.

The profit must, therefore, be made solely out of the number of models reproduced. Here the consummate skill of the American ready-made outfitters shows itself. The great American fashion houses are real masters of the art of reproduction. In the most skilful way they understand how to choose materials and trimmings so that they resemble those of the model, while being in fact far cheaper. And finally their brilliantly organized working methods enable them to reproduce the Paris models quite superbly for sale at a far cheaper price.

In order to circumvent the high duties a particular method of import has been devised. Occasionally models are only loaned and must be returned to France between three to six months after importation. This is severely controlled by the American Customs officers, who have lists of all objects imported into the United States. The returned models will be sold in Paris as bargains. They are already six months old, but the purchaser will proudly be able to show her friends the Grand Couturier's label.

Naturally the copies are given the necessary 'American look' in the United States. But not too much of it. Many clothes manufacturers take the greatest care to see that the alterations do not go too far.

Seventh Avenue is the centre of the New York fashion industry. Today, between Thirty-third and Forty-first Streets there are several thousand ready-made houses. Here, too, reports and rumours are picked up from fashion reporters and representatives of these houses long before the first Paris shows. New York ready-made houses, luxury shops, fashion advisers and designers are sensitive to the slightest suggestion from Paris and skilfully exploit every rumour and report for the preparation of the American collections.

The first step taken by a foreign buyer in Paris is to get in touch with his agent. In this gigantic business the commission agent is a very important man and plays an almost invisible role. He is adviser, middle-man, banker and organizer. In fact, he is everything rolled into one. Upon his advice depends the choice of the model; upon his efficiency and foresight the smooth course of the purchase.

The agent is usually a salaried member of a big foreign store who lives in Paris. Long before the collections appear he orders material for his firm, learns from the textile manufacturers' agents what fabrics this or that couturier has ordered, what colours predominate, and keeps himself informed about the details of hats, gloves, trimmings and jewellery. Throughout the year he has sent samples and patterns of materials to his firm.

In addition to this he must also have a flair for the coming fashions and alterations in the line, and provide his chief with a constant stream of new ideas.

The agent accompanies the buyer to the dress show, arranges the purchases and knows how to discover among the wealth of models those upon which competitors have already cast a professional eye.

And while the buyer is on his way back to his own country the agent must look after the prompt delivery of the models, see that they are packed properly and pay the duties and insurance. The despatch of the models, however, must not take place until about three weeks after the purchase.

Haute Couture and its export is one of the most important factors in the French balance of trade. Countless industries depend upon its success and any loss it suffers is naturally a loss for the dependent industries. But before the French models are despatched abroad with permission to copy, before they are unpacked, even before the crates with the goods arrive, their content is already known.

What has happened?

A great dressmaker once said: 'When a model is successful, the sales develop first in normal fashion. But then quite suddenly they come to a stop: the pirated version has been thrown on the market.'

## PIRATES OF HAUTE COUTURE

An extremely smart Italian woman met a friend one day on the Piazza del Duomo in Milan. For a while the two ladies stared at each other. They were both wearing identical dresses. The friend, however, had paid 15,000 lire (about £10) in Rome for her dress, which bore the label of the house of Dior, while the lady in Paris, on the other hand, had paid ten times that price for the authentic model. Livid with rage, she phoned the Parisian couturier, who immediately notified the police.

The second act of this tragi-comedy was played in the summer of the same year, on the 9th August 1948. At Christian Dior's winter collection a reinforced supervisory system was put into force. An employee tried to leave the house. She was stopped, her brief-case was searched and the complete cut of the 'Auvergne' cape was discovered. The clues led to the Hotel Scribe, where under the mattresses and in the trunks of an Italian couturier and his accomplices (among them was an Italian countess) a host of prototypes and drawings were discovered, including models not yet shown from the houses of Dior, Jacques Fath, Balenciaga, etc.

This 'king of the plagiarists' managed to escape. An aircraft took him to Lyons and a taxi to Modane, where he bought a stick and a rucksack and hired a guide to take him over the mountains to Italy.

For several years investigations and trials followed each other while the Italian press went over to the counter-attack. Thefts in Haute Couture were a common occurrence, wrote the *Voce d'Italia*, but the French had become more careful than ever because the Italian fashion firms could now produce just as beautiful and far cheaper models which were attracting an international clientele.

The magazine *Oggi* even maintained that Dior's models would figure well in mediæval cavalry since one of them weighed forty pounds and women who tried to wear it fainted.

The Italian crooks were magnificently organized. Not only did they get hold of the prototypes, but smart women attended the dress shows accompanied by skilled draughtsmen. It also happened that one of these elegant and outwardly very *distinguée* women invited a mannequin to supper in an expensive restaurant. The mannequin appeared in one of the models of her house, completely unaware that fashion spies were sitting at the next table making their drawings. The documents of the case eventually consisted of seventy-five huge volumes weighing several pounds. One single expert's report filled five hundred pages.

The chief criminal, however, who could only be sentenced *in contumaciam* unleased a veritable campaign of publicity in Italy. In an interview, he brazenly extolled the skill and unbelievable memory of his artists who could reproduce all the models with the greatest precision. He finally declared that the high prices one had to pay for visiting the collection could only be considered as a licence to copy.

Fashion piracy is as old as the history of Haute Couture. The plagiarists began their work when Charles Frederick Worth inaugurated the first seasonal models. From then onwards a propaganda war has constantly been waged by the foreign press to try and persuade readers that the centre of fashion creation was no longer Paris, but had been transferred to this or that country. All kinds of tricks were used. The editor of a well-known Paris fashion journal had sold drawings to a Berlin house and the sketches of the finished models were shown six days before their appearance in Paris and praised as Berlin models. Such bait proved itself very profitable. Towards the turn of the century many American buyers went to Berlin to get cheap copies of the Paris models.

If one scans the minutes of the organization which protects the interests of the whole Parisian couture, the *Chambre syndicale de la couture*, one can follow the struggle against fashion piracy through the years and decades.

Already several years before the First World War a firm was discovered in Paris which sold the prototypes of great couturiers such as Callot Sœurs. In the year 1913 a lawyer was commissioned to keep a discreet eye on the production of a certain Berlin fashion house.

During the First World War the Americans circulated a rumour that the French fashion houses had stopped production. As a result, the propaganda for Haute Couture had to be strengthened after the war. In 1921 the *Chambre syndicale* organized a travelling display to Canada; it showed Paris fashions and fashion films in forty-two cities.

Something very similar happened during the Second World War. An International Fashion Council was founded in the Rockefeller Centre with the Mayor of New York, La Guardia, as President to boost the 'American look'.

In Paris, too, the houses which specialize in copying models have increased in number, particularly in those parts of the city which are adjacent to the Haute Couture centres. Special combines were founded; small *ateliers* amalgamated themselves into big concerns, powerful enough to buy the models *en gros*. Here the best workers are often employed—they have been weaned away from the great fashion houses by the lure of higher wages.

Many of these *ateliers* are specialized. There are some for dresses, some for hats, while others sell only patterns or sketches. It is a bad business for the State, for their revenue cannot be controlled and naturally they pay no taxes.

When one of these undertakings is discovered, the police have a difficult task. Before they ever get to the workrooms the grapevine has functioned and all compromising material—dresses, patterns, drawings and addresses—has vanished into clever hiding-places, double floors, secret cupboards or merely into the flat next door. The nest is empty and the police find only a few dresses of the most harmless kind.

For whoever stands behind these fashion plagiarists, they are organized like real gangs. They have their chiefs, their henchmen, their stool pigeons and their contacts.

The foreign pirates who only take patterns of the cut or sketches need no residence and no workroom. A simple hotel room is enough. Smart women come as customers to the shows, and with the excuse that they are shortly leaving the country have the models they have bought sent to their hotel. Then work goes on throughout the night. Sketches are made in minutest detail, photos are taken and patterns copied. A highly lucrative business. It triggers off a chain reaction: copies are made of the copies and more and more copies of these . . .

The professional copyists who sometimes attend the dress shows with forged press cards have worked out a most refined system. Some specialize in sleeves, others in skirts, coats or evening gowns—in fact there are probably more specialists among them than in the workrooms. Moreover, they all have the most important asset of all—the famous so-called photographic eye. Immediately after the parade they meet in a café, make their sketches and fit the details together like a jigsaw puzzle. And the whole collection lies there in a series of fashion plates.

Unfortunately they are all too rarely caught. The following incident took place in 1950 in the House of Dior. In the middle of the parade a curtain opened and Christian Dior, who normally never appears, strode through the salon, caught hold of a woman whom he had seen sketching in secret and flung her out. On searching her it was discovered that she had a fake press card and worked for a firm which sold sketches. Among her papers was a letter from this firm in which, among other things, were the words: 'So far you have done magnificent work but we must be even more careful.' Many of these fashion pirates have minute cameras which they stick in a buttonhole or in a handbag. Again it was in the House of Dior that a man was caught with one of these cameras. When the film was developed, it revealed that he had photographed almost the entire collection.

The big plagiarist concerns have so extensive a spy network that they already know details of the materials and the accessories before the first fashion shows. Many of them buy pieces of material which the charwomen have swept off the floor. In this way it is comparatively easy to copy the models down to the last detail and furnish them with fake labels. When raiding pirates' nests the police have found hundreds of prototypes and sketches to which patterns of the actual material were pinned.

Since the Second World War fashion piracy has assumed a scale which spells disaster to Parisian Haute Couture. To choose only a few cases from the wealth of documents at the *Chambre Syndicale's* headquarters: immediately after the war an American soldier announced that as soon as the Paris collections appeared he was in a position to sell all the models: 'A GI will step in where angels fear to tread.' In Beirut in 1952, a couturier gave a great display of models which were all copies from the House of Carven. In the autumn of 1955 a concern was discovered which exceeded in its ramifications anything that had gone before. Four times a year an American fashion pirate had delivered to his subscribers, five days' after the appearance of the seasonal and mid-season models, whole books full of sketches and accurate descriptions. If such a thing is possible, why should foreign buyers bother to come to Paris?

When can the copy, that most refined and insidious enemy of the fashion creator, even be termed a plagiarism? It assumes so many forms, calls itself inspiration, variation or 'in the manner of . . .' And where does plagiarism begin? With the small dressmaker who knows a *première* or a *seconde d'atelier* and gets hold of prototypes for her customers? With the customer who takes her dressmaker with her to the fashion show? With the woman who borrows a model from a rich friend and has it copied?

In former days the protection afforded against this piracy was very slight. There are two laws which give a certain amount of safeguard; the first dating from the year 1793—from the French Revolution—protects works of literature and art; the second, of 1909, extended copyright to the creations of fashion artists who, from then onwards had to register their models, by depositing drawings or photographs showing the model from three sides.

On closer inspection, the old statute from the time of the Revolution was the more effective because it gave the creator of a work of art the chance of informing the police and letting them confiscate the copies without the permission of higher authorities. By the law of 1909, on the other hand, the permission of a magistrate had to be obtained for each confiscation. The results are obvious. Before the permit was issued the pirates had vanished.

But even the Revolution statute was seldom applied to fashion during the nineteenth century. In 1860, a modiste who caused copies of her hats to be seized finally had to pay damages to the copyist. 'Hats are articles of fashion and cannot therefore demand special protection', was the ruling of the Paris Court.

The great fashion artist, Madeleine Vionnet, was the first who sounded the alarm and declared that fashion piracy must be done away with once and for all. In 1921, therefore, a union was formed for the safeguarding of creations in art and fashion. Even more effective was the PAIS, also founded on the initiative of Madeleine Vionnet in 1930. Since then buyers can no longer visit the fashion shows without official identity cards.

But not until 1952 were really effective measures introduced. Paul Caldagues, a tireless champion of reforms in Haute Couture, drafted a Bill which became law through being passed by the National Assembly.

The most important point of this law is that here, for the first time, there is mention of a production which lasts only for a season. No law had previously mentioned the short life of a fashion design. A sharp distinction is also made between the comparatively harmless bargain copies of the small dress-maker and the professionally organized plagiarists. And finally, this law not only lays down fines—a trifle for wholesale copyists—but heavy terms of imprisonment. And no bumble-dom—once the police have been informed by the couturier, they can swoop by day or night and impound the stocks before the gangsters can make a getaway.

As far as the United States are concerned, the struggle of the French couturier against illegal copying of his models is particularly difficult. The American concept of copyright is completely different from the European one. The old pioneer-ing spirit, the urge to seize what one conquers, is still alive over there. In many court decisions one finds the view that a buyer has the right to sell the copies of honestly acquired models as his own creation. And when, in 1929, through the intervention of the French Trade Attaché it came to a law suit against an American firm, the representative of this firm declared that he did not understand such procedure since copies were an open and obvious source of income for the American fashion houses.

How, then, can the creations of French Haute Couture be safeguarded? The very features which give it fame are their undoing—the short-lived brilliance which hardly lasts for a season, their originality which cannot remain a secret and becomes common property almost as soon as it is born.

# XI

# THE PRESENT

## FASHION TODAY

OUR age has been called dynamic. Chaplin's little tramp who cannot follow the movement of the conveyor-belt has become the symbol of twentieth-century man who has lost his place in the universe.

Science is the modern sorcerer's apprentice. It has overrun and taken control of its discoverer. There is no longer any escape from time; we rush after and beyond it, breaking through the sound barrier. Man and visible nature are no longer the main themes of art. We think that we are being constructive where destruction and disintegration are at work. In abstract art it might still be possible for the artist to enter into metaphysical and non-human spheres; it is left to the public to read human values into the picture, to discover a superior humanism in impersonal de-humanized art.

These are dangerous and destructive trends of thought which cannot be applied to fashion. Woman is and remains the object and the theme of fashion creation. If the couturier by-passes this theme, if the dress and the woman are no longer a single unit, this becomes abstract art applied to fashion and a solecism. Such a couturier would see the shape of the dress and not the woman, would produce a fashion which bears no relation to the female body.

Each fashion has followed the image of the erotic ideal of its age. The 'heavenly distortion of nature', as Baudelaire called fashion, was no more than the accentuation of the erotic. The muslin dress of the Directoire overstressed it; the crinoline created a pedestal for the bust; the disfiguring protuberance of the bustle betrayed the frustrated lubricity of a respectable age.

The erotic motifs which the couturier purposely underlined in the old days have disappeared today from Haute Couture. Worth, Doucet and Poiret lived with woman and conjured the alchemy of her charms from the pulse-beats of her universe. For forty years women like Mme Paquin, Mme Lanvin and Mme Vionnet transformed their period's ideal of feminine beauty into the fashions of the day.

Today Paris fashion creation lies in the hands of sensitive, neurotic aesthetes who seem to have emerged from Marcel Proust's peculiar world of sensibility. Like so many artists and poets of today, they are a product of our age. This must be stated. It explains the fascination of so many abstract models in modern Haute Couture.

On the body of modern woman so magnificently free, whose beauty, slimness and good proportions are the result of sport, dancing and an intelligent diet, they impose new shackles. They screw the breasts up high; let the material fall straight from the shoulders so that the waist disappears. Light fabrics are stiffened with canvas, giving harshness to the natural feminine curves. They create models which seem to be conceived for the stylized body of a Gothic Eve.

The couturiers conjure up an image of woman which does not really exist. They have intentionally produced an illusion —the mannequin. Are the mannequins of the leading couturiers, those incredibly slim, frail, hot-house flowers with their boyish bodies, mask-like features and slanting painted eyebrows still women? A deep gulf lies between these couturiers and women. One asks oneself for whom they produce their models.

Not for the masses. The 'masses', they are the working men and women of all classes of society. Today there are hardly any women who do not work and they certainly do not succumb to the slogans of the H-line and the Y-line. Utility rules life, and buildings, living-rooms and clothes are appropriate. The couturiers' slogans are followed by a society which believes that it sets the fashion: a handful of idle aristocrats grouped round dethroned monarchs. Certain papers fill their society columns with photographs and descriptions of fêtes given by these phantoms of a vanishing world. This society has not the virility to create a style. The snobbery it affects today has nothing to do with well-bred manners. So little appreciated is it, in fact, that the witty Parisians have invented its caricature, 'Marie Chantal', a comic figure, who obeys the laws of her caste and knows nothing of social problems—the snob par excellence, related perhaps to the cretinous Viennese aristocrat 'Count Bobby'. Marie Chantal's idiotic remarks are a daily feature in Paris; and ridicule kills, as they say in France.

But sex-appeal maintains its sway. Hollywood and Italy, each in their own fashion, produce a seductive feminine type which has far greater influence on today's international modes. The spectacular breasts and capricious curves of pin-up and cover girls frustrate and nullify the plans of Haute Couture.

So one might be inclined to think that the Grands Couturiers produce in a vacuum for an imaginary class of society. Far from it, although this sounds paradoxical. Despite the unwearability of their boldest models they bring life into fashion because they preach something new and original. Without them there would be no fruitful note of surprise.

From this very source of sensitive artistry, slowly, almost

imperceptibly, the coming fashion struggles into life. The inventor's caprice slowly turns into something that can be used. By way of the ready-made houses, after odysseys through other countries, the ideas of the couturiers become humanized. In a new form and yet embodying the same elements of style they finally reach the mass of women.

The fashion goes, as the French say, among the masses. It is tamed, moderated and accepted.

## KINGS AND CROWN PRINCES OF THE FOURTH REPUBLIC

When, as a young man, Christian Dior gave up his studies for the Diplomatic Service in order to become an art dealer, it is easy to see what went on in his mind: 'I should like to be an artist, but since I don't know whether I have enough talent, I've chosen a profession which brings me in contact with art.'

In 1928 he opened a gallery with two friends. The artists whose works he displayed must have had a certain affinity with his future profession. Salvador Dali and Eugène Berman painted dreams and fantasies. The visions of these surrealists are of palpable reality, of a clearly defined concrete lucidity. Christian Dior also sold drawings and water-colours by Jean Cocteau and Christian Bérard, both of them brilliant fashion stylists. Bérard, in particular, with his stage décors and water-colour fashion sketches produced a pot-pourri of surprising colour tones which, without him, few people would have ventured to use. It is certain that he opened young Christian Dior's eyes to piquant contrasts.

A few years later Dior had to retire from his art dealer's business on account of ill-health. A friend encouraged him to do some fashion drawings. In 1938 he went as a designer to

Piguet, of whom he said later: 'I have to thank him for being the first to open my eyes to simple elegance.'

In 1942 he was engaged by Lucien Lelong. This famous couturier had a magnificent team of women who initiated the young designer into the technique of the profession.

Christian Dior might perhaps have remained Lelong's designer for the rest of his life, but one day, as he was walking down the Champs Elysées, he met an old acquaintance—Marcel Boussac, the textile king.

Little piebald vans with the inscription '*Tissu garanti Boussac*' are a familiar sight in the streets of Paris. Marcel Boussac is a mythical figure in France. In the old days people used to say, 'as wealthy as Rothschild'. Today they say, 'rich and powerful as Boussac'. This big industrialist, hated by the little man, grudgingly admired by the great, is the 'eminence grise' of fashion.

Fashion and materials are interdependent, and whoever gives a new impetus to fashion also gives a helping hand to the textile trade. At the age of eighteen Marcel Boussac already had a remarkable flair for the understanding of this interdependence, although he lived far from the capital in the small town of Chateauroux, where his father owned an insignificant cloth factory.

While in the Paris of 1907 Poiret, the Russian ballet and a colour-loving élite ruled the fashion world, the provincial ladies dressed during the day in dark, colourless woollens and appeared at evening parties in black silk gowns.

Boussac came to the conclusion that some colours must be brought into this drab monotony. Cheap, bright, printed cottons could be just as attractive as expensive silks. He put his ideas into practice in his father's factory.

Soon the small town of Chateauroux offered him insufficient

scope and he joined his mother in Paris. She was a poetess, and by her second marriage was now the wife of the well-known writer, Catulle Mendès. Young Boussac already showed an astonishing business acumen. On making enquiries he learned that the cheapest materials came from the Vosges where a number of factories produced grey, brown and black cheap utility grades. He inundated them with orders (his father had given him a little capital) and persuaded them to go in for bright colours. He found a ready sale for his new wares, and incidentally was able to undercut his competitors. In a single month he sold nearly three-quarters of a million yards.

Now not only the smart Parisienne but the ordinary woman wore gay clothes. At a later date Boussac said: 'The face of France was completely changed.'

At the age of twenty-five he was a millionaire, acquired his first factory in the Vosges, a Rolls-Royce and his first race-horse.

Then came 1914 and the war. The Government commissioned Boussac to organize war production in the Vosges and in particular to produce fabrics to cover the wings of aeroplanes. The difficulties seemed insuperable. The raw materials were in British and Egyptian warehouses and communications with places abroad were interrupted. Boussac found the solution. He organized a pool with enormous financial resources, and chartered five Norwegian ships to bring the goods by sea. Communication with English and Egyptian harbours was ensured.

By the end of the war Boussac's fortune had increased by several millions. Once more he was faced with a new problem. In his Vosges factories lay thousands of bales of completely useless fabric for aircraft wings.

Boussac launched a new fashion. He bought up all the stocks, including the British, and from the light, untearable *écru*-coloured material made shirts, blouses, pyjamas, aprons and summer dresses.

Everyone warned him that this could only be a disastrous gamble, but he refused to be intimidated. He opened retail shops and created a new fashion with materials christened *à la toile d'avion*. Queues of men and women immediately gathered outside these shops, only too eager to buy these light blouses, shirts and dresses. His huge stocks were soon exhausted and he had to repeat the orders.

At the same time successful speculation on the Stock Exchange increased his fortune into the realms of the fabulous. During the economic crisis which engulfed the world at the end of the 'twenties he was able to buy for a song many of the textile factories in the Vosges, at Rouen, in Alsace, and two of the largest shirt manufacturers who were on the verge of bankruptcy. He reconstructed, modernized and equipped his acquisitions with the latest machinery.

Boussac knows—and this is one of the secrets of his great success—that a maximum in quality can be achieved through specialization. Each factory serves a single phase of production—from the preparation of the hemp to spinning, weaving, finishing, dyeing and printing. A regiment of designers is busy on new modern designs; new artificial fabrics are invented in giant research laboratories.

Boussac is a man of iron will and great ambition. In the summer of 1940 the German armies invaded France. For Boussac this posed a single question. Who would win the war? The Allies, for they ruled the seas. And who had won the Battle of France? The Germans. So Boussac came to a temporary agreement with the Occupation authorities. All his factories went on functioning, although production sank by 20 per cent and the Germans took another 6 per cent.

When the Allied divisions landed in the summer of 1944,

Boussac immediately switched to war supplies. American uniforms were produced in forty-five of his factories.

Boussac's domain extends over the whole of the present-day and former French colonies. He has branches in Dakar, on the Ivory Coast, in French Guinea, Senegal, the Cameroons and Indo-China. He furnishes the natives with specially woven, garish-coloured materials which are bartered for colonial products.

In 1951 his fortune was estimated at sixty milliard francs (about £60,000,000).

Horse-racing, which for most people is a luxury, has become a profitable business for Boussac. He has won countless prizes, including the Grand Prix and the Derby. From the sale of thoroughbred stallions—one of them brought him in four hundred thousand American dollars—he was able to buy his materials in the dollar area.

He is a wizard among market operators. Whether in war or peace, in boom or slump, with a racehorse or with the Haute Ecole of fashion, Haute Couture, Boussac is always a winner.

Boussac and Christian Dior—that is a combination of capital and art. While Dior prepared his first collection in the elegant house on the Avenue Montaigne, bought for him by Boussac, while dresses were being cut, fitted and sewn, a seven-storey building for the workrooms and offices rose in the courtyard.

From the outset Dior employed a staff of eighty-five. No couturier had ever started on such a large scale.

Bald, with blue eyes, rosy cheeks, a large but not disfiguring nose and a receding chin; gentle, polite and correct, he mastered the technique of sober reserve. By his outward appearance and behaviour one would have taken him for a senior civil servant from the Quai D'Orsay.

And yet he was an artist. The solid bases on which he built his work would have been fruitless without his creative intuition. Boussac had once more put his money on the right horse.

In February 1947 Christian Dior opened his fashion house and gave his spring dress show.

Many biographies maintain that Christian Dior obeyed Boussac's instructions to use a generous quantity of material and that this was the reason for the New Look.

But fashion is neither the discovery of a brilliant couturier nor the result of economic necessity. Wars have never caused a fashion which led to a saving of material, nor have textile magnates ever conjured a fashion rich in material out of the blue.

The New Look was the logical reaction to the Old Look. And the Old Look was the fashion which had started before the war: the short skirt, narrow or loose pleated at the knee; the broad, padded shoulders. The war years accentuated this style: skirts grew shorter and shoulders broader, hair styles higher and the wooden-soled shoes clattered ever more noisily. In short, it was a fashion which everyone could see must be coming to an end.

The New Look was born before it became the fashion. There was the American girl who boycotted the rather elderly looking narrow skirts and broad shoulders and wore shirt blouses and longer, wider dresses tight at the waist. There were also girls and women in France who, with close-cropped hair and billowing bell skirts rode their bicycles during the enemy occupation, carrying documents and secret coded messages. The New Look was synonymous with youth, freedom and the future.

The New Look also had its connection with a handful of people who called themselves Existentialists and proclaimed

Heidegger's 'feeling-that-one-exists' in their clothes: girls in short jeans, young men with untidy shirts hanging out of vivid jumpers, sandals and stringy hair, worthy descendants of the '*muscadins*' and the '*petits maîtres*'. This Saint Germain-des-Prés style of life found its echo in the bohemian circles of other big cities. A new style of youthful, free-and-easy dress had been born, elements of which found their echo in the creations of Haute Couture.

In the post-war years many couturiers sensed and hinted at the coming fashion. As early as the 1947 February collections a new silhouette appeared. Models by Dior, Fath, Balmain, Piguet, Dessès and Balenciaga showed a tendency to longer and wider skirts and less exaggerated shoulders. Marcel Rochas had already launched his '*guêpière*', a short corset which pinched the waist tight and emphasized the curve of the hips. The American *Vogue*, which by its remoteness from Paris often shows the tendency of the moment better than the Paris fashion journals, declared: 'The excitement over a new star on the Parisian fashion horizon might almost have made us forget that the other spring models, too, were novel and charming.'

What then justifies the general conclusion that Dior created the New Look? Firstly, because his flair for the coming style was several degrees stronger than the others. Secondly, he was backed by almost unlimited capital and in consequence had the advantage of a vast advertising campaign.

In the autumn collections of the same year the New Look had won on all counts. The models of nearly all the other couturiers showed the round, almost sloping shoulders, the long full skirts.

Photographs of well-known society women and film stars, however, prove that the New Look did not set in immediately among the smart public. Skirts were a trifle longer, but the shoulders were still on the broad side. Youth accepted it with delight and today it has almost become a uniform for the young girl.

While the broad, becoming skirts were adopted by the ready-made houses, the couturiers with Dior at their head were preparing a counter-attack. In 1949 dresses were caught up once more; horizontal waves and trains disrupted the vertical fall of the drapery. Hats, too, which had been small and insignificant with the wide bell skirts, once more became wide-brimmed and important. Each season from his first collection onwards, Dior found a new fashion line with a suitable slogan for his advertising campaign. That this sometimes went for four was not his fault.

In the summer of 1953 his publicity men proclaimed: 'Skirts are now no longer knee length; they must not be higher than twenty inches from the ground.' That was the famous 'Dior bomb'. The English called it the 'Shock Look' and reacted unfavourably. A Danish writer, on the other hand, waxed lyrical. In the short skirt he saw a return to optimism—the Armistice in Korea had just been signed.

The 'Dior bomb' was a failure. Abroad women shortened their skirts by six inches only to lengthen them again a few weeks later by four inches. In Paris the bomb turned out to be a dud.

Like all great couturiers, Dior created each collection round a stylistic leit-motif. In the autumn of 1954–55 emerged the H-line, which infuriated the male population. In the spring of 1955 the A-line, followed by the Y-line and in 1956 the F-line.

The colossal capital that stands behind the Maison Dior allow it great latitude. A few hundred yards of tulle can be used for a single dress or an evening gown trimmed with embroidery costing 400,000 francs (£400).

The concern in the Avenue Montaigne is a cross between a government department and a factory: twelve hundred employees, twenty-eight workrooms, his own police force with a superintendent and a filing system which contains the names of all suspicious characters and prevents spies from viewing the collections.

In the field of social welfare it is far more progressive than any of the other big couturiers. There is medical attention for the staff, a free bed in a hospital, convalescent homes for the employees and holiday camps for their children. Eight hundred workers eat in the canteens and eat remarkably well; the House of Dior has a first-class reputation in this respect.

The staff is on a percentage and profit-sharing basis. 'This acts like a raise in salary,' was Dior's reply whenever a journalist dared to criticize the low standard wage in Haute Couture.

His empire expanded from month to month and from year to year. In 1948 'Christian Dior-New York' was founded to supply North and South America. Next came the subsidiaries for scent, furs, hats and stocking manufacture; an export branch for gloves, bags, jewellery and neck-ties; the London branch which caters for some of the Commonwealth countries, branches and concessions in Venezuela, Chile, Mexico, Cuba, Syria and Morocco. Before a new branch is opened, a team from the Paris commercial and technical general staff appear in order to impart the business routine and practices of the House of Dior.

Twice a year the Dior American collection is shown in New York. He was aware that French taste here must not be too loud. And therefore he imparted it to American women in a gentle but firm whisper. The lines which are used in Dior's New York headquarters are worked out in the Avenue Montaigne. Twice a year the American mannequins come to Paris and the models are tried on them.

The fashion king's domain is controlled by Boussac's central office, the *Comptoir de l'Industrie Cotonnière* which owns the majority of the shares in the Dior companies. This control not only has financial effects: it gave Dior an incalculable advantage from the very start by taking all the cares of administration off his shoulders.

Boussac is wise to keep in the background. France loves its artists but not its millionaires. Alas, Christian Dior died, at the height of his fame. The future will decide whether the enthusiasm shown by Paris for his young successor, Yves Saint-Laurent, is justified.

The Boussac millions, the foundation stones of the House of Dior, radiated with energy. Their influence reached the other couturiers, electrifying customers and buyers.

Haute Couture, depressed by the crises of the pre-war years, cut off from abroad during the war, was galvanized into new life. And now once more a golden bridge leads from American prosperity to Paris, the centre of fashion creation.

Young JACQUES FATH profited greatly from the re-awakened greed of American women for Paris fashions. His big chance came in the shape of an offer from a big outfitter on Seventh Avenue, New York. An agreement was signed in 1948, and in the autumn of the same year Fath delivered an American spring collection which was reproduced in its thousands.

'Jacques Fath has given our women a maximum of French look,' reported the American magazines.

In the course of two years his turnover trebled; more than half of this can be attributed to his American business.

Fath embarked upon his profession without any of the usual background. He was to have become an insurance agent like his father, but art was in his blood. His grandfather, René

Fath, was a well-known landscape painter. His great-grandmother was a well-known designer of pretty fashion plates during the Second Empire.

Jacques Fath, the blond, graceful, hypersensitive Endymion, irresponsibly threw up his dull insurance job and plunged into couture. He started in 1939 with five workgirls and two mannequins in a three-storey house which soon began to look like the ship's cabin in the Marx Brothers' film. At his shows customers and mannequins had to go into the courtyard for the small rooms were filled to overflowing.

Fath showed his first wartime collection by the light of candles which one of his employees had bought in the church of St Genevieve. The wives of the new big industrialists flocked to him. 'I don't like them,' he used to say, 'but I want to succeed.' In 1944 he had made enough money to buy smart premises in the Avenue Pierre 1^er^ de Serbie.

At the age of thirty-three he was at the peak of his fame. An adept in accountancy, he was the only Grand Couturier who had no sleeping partners, no subsidy and no debts. 'Magnificent,' he used to cry at the end of each month, 'all the suppliers are paid.' He was a virtuoso, too, in the world of silks, tulle and lace. Standing in front of the mirror, he used to drape serges, velvets and brocades round his own body, turning round to examine the material from all angles. In this way ideas came to him. He would send for his *premières* and mannequins, electrifying everyone in the whirl of his own exuberance, in the thrill of artistic creation.

He had never learned how to sew or cut. He was an acrobat of Haute Couture. Creations were born from mistakes; a sleeve put in the wrong way, a skirt being pulled over the head and stuck over the chest, a cloak wrapped back to front. Everything inspired him.

How magnificent to see oneself also on the screen. Jacques

Fath played the couturier in the film *Scandale sur les Champs Elysées*.

His own sparkling gaiety was his best advertisement. Creation, fantasy, enjoyment; one cannot help thinking of Poiret. Like Poiret, Fath loved discovering recipes for new dishes; his name, too, was a byword in the world of fêtes and pleasures. With one difference, however; Poiret's bacchanalia took place at a time of general prosperity, while Fath's occurred during the post-war years of hardship. As a result, they were stopped, after a few years, by higher authority.

Women with famous names who appeared in his dresses at balls or cocktail parties and did not forget to say, 'It came from Fath', took care of his propaganda. The couturier never sent them any bills.

His best mannequin was his wife, fair-haired Geneviève, whom he had met when she was Chanel's secretary; she was very much photographed as a cover girl. Taking her on his first American trip in 1948 was regarded over there as his most brilliant advertising stunt.

With great courage the beautiful Geneviève Fath took over his business when death took this forty-two-year-old genius out of his gay whirl of creation; but the firm couldn't survive its creator for long and, alas, the Maison Fath is no more.

The atmosphere at BALENCIAGA'S is diametrically opposed to that at the Maison Fath. Impossible to get an interview with the chief. Impossible to learn anything about his origins.

It is as though the shadow of the Spanish Inquisition lay over the invisible maestro and, who knows, his mask-like mannequins might be the shades of its unhappy victims.

Balenciaga was born in a village on the Gulf of Biscay. His childhood memories are the rambling houses, the poor fishermen and his mother's sewing-room, where he learned to make clothes.

Not far from this fishing village stands a villa which belonged to the Marquesa de Casa-Torres. Each Sunday at Mass could be seen a beautifully dressed woman whose elegance fascinated young Balenciaga.

One day he plucked up courage, went up to the Marquesa and said: 'Who made you that wonderful dress? It could only have been a Parisian couturier!' The lady was taken aback. No villager had ever dared to address a word to her and now this small urchin appeared and wanted to know who had made her dress.

'What is your name?' she asked.

'Cristobal Balenciaga.'

'And how old are you?'

'Fourteen, but I can already sew and tailor, señora. Would you allow me to copy your dress?'

The Marquesa was interested. She sent for the boy and lent him the dress, which happened to be a Drecoll model. Delighted, he ran off with it to his mother and took a pattern. His patron gave him a length of material. He cut out the dress, tried it on the Marquesa two or three times and it was ready. Moreover, it was so pretty and chic that she bought it from him and wore it the next time she went to Mass.

A few years later Balenciaga opened a small dressmaking shop in San Sebastian. On the outbreak of the Spanish Civil War he was able to move to Paris with a considerable fortune; he took the smart premises where he still works today with his five hundred employees on the Avenue Georges V.

The atmosphere of mystery which surrounds this Spanish individualist, the icy coldness with which every journalist is received, whether intentional or not, are just as effective as the loud beating of advertising drums.

Dior designed, so do Fath and Balmain, but Balenciaga tailors. He is said to spend days on a single dress, pulling it apart again, recutting and altering until he is satisfied.

Today he is one of the greatest creators of fashion. It is even maintained in professional circles that his models with their daring severity and masterly choice of colour, in which Spanish local tints often dominate, have the most decisive influence on fashion.

PIERRE BALMAIN always likes to evoke his architectural education. For two years he attended the Ecole des Beaux Arts, and learned how to draw blue-prints, sections and plans. Couturiers are no different from artists, scholars or archæologists—an irresistible impulse drives them from earliest youth. Charles Frederick Worth tore himself away from his stool in a counting-house in order to copy costumes in a London Museum. Poiret, while delivering umbrellas, sketched smart ladies in his notebook. All of them decorated the margins of their school books, account books or stock-exchange reports with fashion drawings.

Balmain was no exception. He drew fashion sketches round the borders of his blue-prints—at first to while away the time. Captain Molyneux liked his drawings and engaged him. A few years later—in 1940—he joined the Maison Lelong as a designer and opened his own house shortly after the Liberation.

'I often think and act like an architect,' says Balmain. In his first autumn collection, in 1945, an architectural element undoubtedly predominated. Dresses, capes, cossack-like high-buttoned wraps, straight skirts with severe, fur-edged, tailored jackets fell in vertical lines.

But even though Balmain continued to hold forth on the relationship between architecture and tailoring, the static elements have long since disappeared from his creations. Like Dior, Fath, Piguet and Balenciaga, he was a prophet of the New Look, of the light, fluid, mobile line.

Balmain's ideas are not outré and blaze no trails. On the other hand, his models are smart, wearable and discreet in their colours. He has remained faithful to his characteristic line which has so aptly been called the 'Belle Madame' style.

In his philosophy Balmain came to the conclusion that 'Dressmaking is the architecture of movement'. His creations are adapted to the movement of the wearer. His old enthusiasm only comes to light in playful marginalia: today he borders his fashion designs with architectural sketches, ground plans and section drawings.

It would seem today that the pioneers of Haute Couture express themselves in a new language entirely incomprehensible to the layman. Woe to the fashion critic who no longer understands it. He will be blackballed by misunderstood artists and not invited to the next collection. The same applies today in Haute Couture as in modern art. An original attempt is considered an *a priori* winner and must be accepted unconditionally.

Among the bold innovators, mocked by some and applauded by others, must be numbered the Crown Prince of originality—HUBERT DE GIVENCHY. This fair-haired twenty-five-year-old youth opened his business in 1952. He has no financial worries, for the shares in his fashion house are held by one of the largest Parisian stores.

The audacity he displayed when designing his own collection has turned out to be exceedingly profitable. One of his boldest and most individualistic creations was the 'Bettina' blouse, made of shirt material which has become an international success. In each new collection there is evidence of his originality. His models are always new experiments and fit his androgynous mannequins to perfection.

The *Chambre syndicale de la couture* embraces sixty concerns, some twenty of which bear the title *Couture-Création*, thus ranking as Haute Couture. Today, however, only four or five couturiers blaze new trails with their original creations. The others do not, of course, lack the great art of elegance and cultured taste.

Jeanne Lanvin's House is directed by her daughter, the Comtesse de Polignac, while the new models are created by the Spaniard Canovas de Castillo, who has worked most successfully in New York as a dress designer for ladies of society as well as for films.

Jean Patou's House is run by his successor and brother-in-law, Raymond Barbas. The firm of Molyneux was taken over in 1951 by Jacques Griffe, a former Chanel designer.

Chanel reopened her fashion house in 1954, after a break of fifteen years. The famous pre-war couturiers, Heim, Dessès, Nina Ricci and Madeleine de Rauch have been joined by the Italian woman designer Carven, who caters for '*la petite femme*', and two young and very talented couturiers Pierre Cardin and Guy Laroche.

### HAUTE COUTURE OR MASS-PRODUCTION?

A hundred years have passed since Charles Frederick Worth founded his House in the rue de la Paix—a century of Haute Couture. If we follow its history we recognize that the seed of present-day troubles was already present in its beginnings.

The woman who created the fashion in collaboration with

her couturier, the aristocracy of title or wealth which fostered the propagation of original ideas, belongs to the past.

The huge fortunes have melted away and so have the great and small courts, with their numerous queens, princesses and grand duchesses who made a yearly pilgrimage to Paris. The ideal customer today is only a romantic legend. If one asks today for a list of the most important customers one will receive the same names from nearly all the great houses. This means that the woman who can afford the high prices asked by the couturiers places orders with all of them in turn.

Even before the First World War it was not exceptional for a client to spend 300,000 francs a year (at the former valuation) in one fashion house. Sometimes even entire workrooms were set aside to work for one single client. There are such cases in the annals of the House of Worth.

The turnover of the leading houses has also dropped considerably. In 1867 Worth had a turnover of between five and six million francs. Paquin, Doucet and the House of Worth, in 1896, each topped five million. At today's value of the franc this means that their turnover was five times as large as that of Dior—and Dior's turnover is twice as large as either Fath's or Balmain's.

With regard to the high prices of the creations, the layman imagines that the couturier must make enormous profits from the sale of a single model. This is a completely wrong assumption. After deduction of working costs, insurance, taxes, duties and short-term redemption, the couturier is left with a bare 10 per cent.

The very feature that gives Haute Couture its high reputation is at the same time its tragedy; nearly everything is sewn by hand, in accordance with an age-old tradition. Today, when new machinery is invented daily, these methods seem anachronistic. Hence the costs of producing a single collection is immense. Fifty million francs (£50,000) is not too high an estimate in the case of the leading houses.

Even export, which on an average represents not more than 25 per cent of revenue, has its limitations. Many couturiers have imposed import quotas on fashion articles and others have completely banned their imports. Restrictions are imposed and lifted constantly and their fluctuations are dependent on the changes of the political and economic situation.

It is not the couturier who profits by the reproduction of a model, but the ready-made houses and the copyists. Even if his model is copied a thousand times through the legal channels, he gets no royalty from the copies. His profit is a single outright payment.

These are the main difficulties with which the couturiers have to battle. The prestige that French fashion enjoys abroad has also encouraged rivals. A few years after the war the first attacks came from England, whose fashion houses made concerted efforts to place their goods on the Paris market. 'From now on,' said *Picture Post*, 'we must supply the Frenchwoman with the clothes that have become too expensive in her own country.' The three great American papers, *Life*, *Vogue* and *Harper's Bazaar* reacted in the same way.

Even louder thundered the barrage of the counter-attack from Italy, where serious efforts to achieve autonomy have been made for some years. The new Italy which has risen from the ashes of a political disaster has developed its own subsidized Haute Couture. Italian competition has proved not without danger for Paris. Wages and taxes are lower and the materials—particularly silk, with its very large range of colours—are far cheaper than in France. Beautiful and picturesque evening gowns are produced with very original trimmings. It is no wonder that German, Swiss and American buyers hurry to acquire models in Italy, especially since they are Paris inspired.

The troubles of Haute Couture affect far more people than the few thousands it employs. All its satellites—makers of hats, shoes, gloves, flowers, feathers, lace and bags—are always just as hard hit by any crisis in Haute Couture.

And since the textile industry lives from and for fashion, it is understandable that wool and cotton magnates should finance individual houses.

But fashion not only has its cradle in France; it is the French patrimony. This is why the State tries to encourage it by direct and indirect subsidies.

Patronage and subsidies are not enough to overcome the countless difficulties. Self-help is imperative.

The *parfum du couturier*, invented by Poiret, that great connoisseur of the feminine arts of seduction, has been a financial godsend to many couturiers. So much so, in fact, that many of them, particularly in the crucial period before the Second World War, gave up their couture business and invested their capital more and more in the profitable manufacture of scent.

At that time, too, the idea of the boutique was born: the department on the ground floor, where attractive accessories —bags, gloves, jewellery and scarves—catch the eye of the customer before she is taken up to the actual salons.

Since the war most of the couturiers have gone in for these boutiques, which have become far more than a mere side line. Special collections of dresses, considerably cheaper than the exclusive models, are shown in the boutiques. The materials are less expensive and the line is simplified. Moreover the client cannot indulge her caprices, for only two fittings are allowed.

In some firms ready-to-wear clothes designed by the couturier are made on the premises. This has the advantage that the workgirls are busy in the dead season and the firm's capital does not lie idle.

Other couturiers have the models made outside and also buy accessories such as shoes, stockings, gloves and lingerie from other sources. This is also advantageous as it reduces the burden of social insurance contributions.

But invariably, whether it is a question of dresses, lingerie, stockings or gloves, everything is selected by the couturier and his taste is the final yardstick.

The collections of ready-to-wear dresses are shown a few weeks before the big parade and are largely an echo of the previous season's best sellers. But the customers know that the couturier has incorporated some of his ideas which will be seen in the forthcoming collection. The genius of the fashion creator gives the firm's name, even when it is accompanied by the word *Boutique*, its particular value.

In practice, therefore, many wealthy women who are completely satisfied with the boutique models no longer need to go upstairs to the *Couture-Création* salons. As a result the couturier with his boutique has become his own competitor.

In individualistic France ready-made goods still have a slightly undesirable flavour of their own. The Frenchwoman still hates the idea of standardization.

It is here that a movement has started for a reform in mass-produced clothing. An association has been formed comprising over thirty members. But not everyone who is prepared to join it can do so. The Ministry of Trade and Industry organizes an annual competition and sends a representative to sit on a jury composed of the heads of fashion schools and well-known fashion journalists. Each ready-made house can display four models yearly. They are created by skilled designers, carried out in some cases in quality materials, and are later altered for the individual customer.

These collections appear two months before those of Haute Couture and are shown to the buyers and the press. This advanced date means in practice that the designers of the ready-made dresses must have a particularly keen scent for the coming fashions.

In 1955 the Association sent a commission to the United States in order to study American ready-made methods.

Thus all European prejudice has been buried. To their surprise, the members of the commission recognized that American dress is by no means as standardized as was believed in Europe. Across the Atlantic, too, eccentric models created in Paris can be worn without arousing the slightest comment. Coquetry is a virtue, and to appear young a duty. In America a woman is entitled to falsify her age by several years to her advantage in official documents.

Here we have the crux of the problem and at the same time its solution. With the progressive industrialization of women's dress, America has discovered the means whereby women, instead of becoming standardized, can be educated to the pleasure of dressing in the latest fashion. This could only have been done with the help of close co-operation between the textile industry, the clothes manufacturers, the retail trade, of the fashion press and advertising.

## EPILOGUE

Many fear that there is no place for a highly selective fashion in the world of mass production; that mass-produced clothes, which improve daily, that the tasteful ready-to-wear dress will deal a death blow to Haute Couture.

Those who cannot keep pace with economic development are doomed. Tradition in itself is not a constructive element. One must get used to seeing culture even where new tendencies are at work.

The working woman today represents the solid majority of customers. She would be only too pleased to accept great originals rather than banal clothes, for even though, as some people complain sadly, fashion went into exile with the disappearance of a society élite, it has returned; it has spread through the masses down to the smallest village. The interest in fashionable clothes, now that elegance has been popularized, is more widespread than ever.

The combination of mass-produced, ready-to-wear dresses and Haute Couture is only fatal where there is a lack of co-ordination. They must produce jointly and for mutual benefit.

The couturiers, too, should come out of the twilight atmosphere of their hot-houses into the bright daylight of modern economics. Only by amalgamation and co-ordination of all effort can Haute Couture be placed on a sound economic basis.

And this will only be the case, moreover, when the abstract, intellectual virtuosity of the present-day couturier makes way for New Accents, when the eternal theme of feminine grace once again provides the framework for the full scope of their ingenuity.

But to listen to the voice of defeatism would mean to doubt French genius. This vivacious, self-willed, talented race will once again, with its customary Cartesian clarity, transform all its discords into bright harmonies.

Once more French fashion will spread out its net to all the corners of the world and Paris will still produce its great couturiers, wherever they may have come from—England, Italy or Spain.

In the future, too, the secret of the supremacy of French fashion will consist in its wonderful orchestration: in the harmony of the couturier's bold improvisations, the sure, skilled hands of his *premières*, the skill of his *midinettes* and the incomparable chic of the Parisienne.

## ACKNOWLEDGMENTS

I should like to thank the following people, without whose help and encouragement this book might never have been written: M. Paul Caldaguès, Editor of *Edition du Jardin des Modes*; M. Michel de Brunhoff, Editor of French *Vogue*; M. François Boucher, the well-known costume historian, and his collaborator, Mlle Vannier; Madame Vionnet; Jeanne Lanvin's daughter, the Comtesse Polignac; Mlle Smaith of the *Chambre Syndicale de la Couture* and Mlle Lemarié who worked for many years at Worth.

In many dress houses I have met with kindness and understanding, but the late Jacques Fath and M. Jacques Heim, President of the *Chambre Syndicale de la Couture*, deserve my special thanks.

The illustrations in this book are reproduced by kind permission of the following: those facing pages 53 (upper), 116 (upper), 117 (lower) and 164 (upper), the Gernsheim Collection; 100 (upper), 101, 116 (lower), 180, 212, 213, 228 and 229, the Hulton Picture Library; 36, 37, 52, 53 (upper), 100 (lower), 117 (upper), 164 (lower) and 165, the Mansell Collection; and 117, Underwood.